Black Images

in American Literature

HAYDEN HUMANITIES SERIES

F. PARVIN SHARPLESS, *Series Editor*
Headmaster, The Park School of Baltimore

THE FEMININE IMAGE IN LITERATURE
Barbara Warren

THE MYTH OF THE FALL: LITERATURE OF INNOCENCE AND EXPERIENCE
F. Parvin Sharpless

SYMBOL AND MYTH IN MODERN LITERATURE
F. Parvin Sharpless

UTOPIAN AMERICA: DREAMS AND REALITIES
Ivan Doig

BLACK IMAGES IN AMERICAN LITERATURE
Joan Cannady

Black Images in American Literature

JOAN CANNADY

HAYDEN BOOK COMPANY, INC.
Rochelle Park, New Jersey

Library of Congress Cataloging in Publication Data

Main entry under title:

Black images in American literature.

(Hayden humanities series)
1. American literature. 2. Afro-Americans—
Literary collections. I. Cannady, Joan.
PS509.N4B5 810'.8'0896 77-2987
ISBN 0-8104-5795-4

Printed in the United States of America

1	2	3	4	5	6	7	8	9	PRINTING
77	78	79	80	81	82	83	84	85	YEAR

Preface

The Hayden Humanities Series uses the term "humanities" in both a narrower and broader sense than in many examples of current curriculum structuring. We see humanities texts neither as conglomerations of stuff from literature, art, music, history, and philosophy purporting to express the spirit of a given time or place, nor as collections of readings supposedly illuminating vaguely suggested themes or subjects. Rather, we see them as focusing on the abiding ideas and values that men have wrestled with and lived by, as reflected through literature (broadly defined) and as informed by a variety of related disciplines: psychology, sociology, anthropology, religion, philosophy, history.

The texts in this series deal with the significant human concerns upon which all human actions, great or small, social or individual, are based, whether we know it and admit it or not. These concerns are the stuff of all literature, yesterday and today; and they provide a background for recognizing, understanding, and defining the issues of the moment that claim our attention and wonder.

The approach in these texts is thematic, since such a structure has proved useful in traditional teaching units and in newer elective programs. But again there is a difference. The weakness of the thematic approach has been its tendency to yield units which are impossibly vague or impossibly broad, or both. What we have tried to do is declare and define an idea or issue thoughtfully and deeply so that others may test that declaration and definition through what they read and know, and find dealing with it a cumulative, organic experience, allowing growth and change.

In contrast to most thematically arranged anthologies, these texts do not pretend a faceless editor or the illusion of authorial objectivity or distance. The compilers have a voice and a point of view, and a conviction that they know what they are talking about. The introductory essays both introduce and interpret: they define an idea—in this case *Black Images in American Literature*—and then try to see it in the round by explaining its past, asserting its continuing vitality and viability, and suggesting some of the things that can be done with it.

This approach takes us far beyond the usual "knowing about" or "talking about" to which literature is too often reduced. We believe the themes have lasting value as organizing constructs for making sense out of our world and for comprehending how the literary artist makes sense out of it. The themes also have a coherence that such thematic structures as, say, "Man and Society" or "Man and the Environment" or "War and Peace" cannot possibly have. One import of both these observations is that the question of "modern" literature vs. "classical" or "traditional" makes little real sense. Literature, by our lights, is always new and renewable. Forever is now. The idiom and the cultural demands and expectations may be different, but the underlying human concerns that the artist is examining are timeless and universal—and that's what counts.

The reader is not expected to agree with everything in the introduction, but is urged to consider it carefully; a casual reading won't do. The argument needs to be understood, and then questions must be raised about validity, emphasis, application, ramification, relevance to experience, and ultimate usefulness in ordering ideas, feelings, beliefs, and values. The defining essay should be a point of departure and a point of return. Along with the headnotes and questions for each group of selections, it serves as a guide for analysis and discussion, not as a gospel to be ingested, remembered, and regurgitated.

There is no attempt in these texts at coverage of literary periods or schools of writing, but there is a variety of genres, modes, backgrounds, times, and writers. Certain long works have been excerpted; enough has been included from any work to feed the thematic demands and yet not misrepresent the total piece. The aim throughout has been to show how widely diffused in our literature the central concern of each text has been and still is.

Black Images in America Literature is divided into three parts, with suggestions for further reading listed at the end of each part. These include a variety of additional works, pieces too long for inclusion in a text this size and further material from books included in part.

The study questions at the end of each section are offered as stimulants to dialogue on issues raised in the selections. They are meant to highlight specific images that support the introductory essay and to aid in the synthesis of ideas gleaned from various works. They should serve as the focus of continuing discussion.

F. Parvin Sharpless
Series Editor

Contents

Black Images
in American Literature

Introduction

The nameless protagonist in Ralph Ellison's *Invisible Man* discovers on the journey from childhood to manhood that his blackness renders him invisible to most people.

> I am invisible, understand, simply because people refuse to see me. Like the bodiless heads you see sometimes in circus sideshows, it is as though I have been surrounded by mirrors of hard, distorting glass. When they approach me they see only my surroundings, themselves, or figments of their imagination—indeed, everything and anything except me.°

Invisibility is a recurrent theme in the literature of black people. It stands both as a symbol of the modern concern with identity and, more simply, as an ironic comment on the effect of the high visibility of black people in a society that is predominantly white. Black writers have said, in effect, "We may stand out because of our color, but in fact what you think you see is too often not what is really there." Indeed, skin color has proved to be a rich source of imagery for black American literature.

Nor should we assume that interest in skin color and racial identity is limited to black writers. America, throughout its history and often in its literature, is concerned with a search for identity, with understanding the meaning of its origins, with reconciling its practices with its ideals. Nowhere are these concerns more clearly illuminated than in the situation of black people in America. Perhaps this explains the force with which these themes are explored by our great 19th century novelists.°

Color, then, provides a metaphor through which American writers explore concerns that are central to their cultural experience. How has that metaphor been used? This collection of works by black and white American writers shows that out of the theme of invisibility three different, though related, images emerge: the shadow, the mask, and the lamp. Before describing each of these in detail, however, we should examine the differences between images and stereotypes. Are there black images in literature? Is a stereotype a proper literary image?

In a study of modern literature and philosophy, Maurice Friedman suggests that an "image of man . . . is an integral part of man's search for an authentic, personal existence." Though descriptive, for it tries to tell what man is and cannot ignore the truths of science or art, an image is also

°Ellison, Ralph, *Invisible Man* (New York: Random House, 1952) p. 3.
°For example, Herman Melville and Mark Twain

normative, for it suggests what man ought to be. One speaks of "exemplary images of man."° What can be said about the images of blacks which appear in American literature? Too often, of course, the black people that we find are not images at all. They are stereotypes, false characters that occasionally amuse and often annoy our sense not only of what black people are but also of what people, in general, might be. Sterling Brown, for example, in a study of black characters created by white writers lists as early stereotypes: (1) the contented slave, (2) the wretched freedman, (3) the comic Negro, (4) the brute Negro, (5) the tragic mulatto, (6) the local color Negro, and (7) the exotic primitive.°

More recently, black people have appeared as symbols of social problems and as prototypes of the human condition. Symbols and roles, though useful still, do not qualify as images in the sense that we require. What we need and what can be found in the best writing are precisely those exemplars that Friedman describes. Babo, for example, the leader of the slave revolt in *Benito Cereno* might be seen as the very contented slave that Brown includes in his list of stereotypes, but only through the eyes of Amasa Delano, the American captain. The reader, and Benito Cereno, the Spanish captain, find in Babo more qualities to admire and to fear than to mock. Phoenix Jackson, the old woman of Eudora Welty's "A Worn Path," may appear as an ancient granny to the white people she encounters, but the reader will find in her the highest form of human charity.

In Babo, Phoenix Walker, and other characters appearing in this collection, we find writers exploring the theme of invisibility, the question of what is seen and what is not seen in black people. In the first section, blacks are presented both as shadows and as those who cast the shadows that lie athwart the lives of Americans and Europeans. As figures who cast shadows, their presence confuses or beclouds reality. When seen as the shadow itself, a black person becomes an obstacle which must be surmounted. As shadows, black people often represent evil; they appear as sullen, clever, violent figures, dangerous persons one would hope to destroy lest one be destroyed by them. When a shadow figure acts—leads a revolt, commits a crime, or whatever—the evil may be destroyed, or it may be unmasked, revealed as a projection of the evil that was first perpetrated on blacks.

Often, the true nature of a black character is invisible because he hides it behind a mask. Babo appears as a masked figure throughout most of Melville's account of the revolt. He is not, in fact, as he seems, the faithful servant, the blend of sorrow and affection, the shepherd's dog attentive to his master's every whim. Rather, he deliberately uses this pose to further

---

°Friedman, Maurice, *To Deny Our Nothingness: Images of Modern Man* (New York: Delacorte Press, 1967).

°Brown, Sterling, "Negro Character as Seen by White Authors," *Journal of Negro Education II*, 1933.

his own ends, to gain freedom and safe return to Africa for himself and his fellow blacks. Masks can be used to disguise as well as to conceal and, as can be seen in the case of Babo, who almost succeeds, they are a powerful tool. Stereotypes, when they appear in black fiction, are often used as deliberate masquerades:

> Very often, however, the Negro's masking is motivated not so much by fear as by a profound rejection of the image created to usurp his identity. Sometimes it is for the sheer joy of the joke: sometimes to challenge those who presume to know his identity. Nonetheless, it is in the American grain. Benjamin Franklin, the practical scientist, skilled statesman and sophisticated lover, allowed the French to mistake him for Rousseau's natural man; Hemingway poses as a nonliterary sportsman, Faulkner as a farmer; Abe Lincoln allowed himself to be taken for a simple country lawyer—until the chips were down. Here the "darky act" makes brothers of us all. America is a land of masking jokers. We wear the mask for purposes of aggression as well as for defense; when we are projecting the future and preserving the past. In short, the motives hidden behind the mask are as numerous as the ambiguities the mask conceals.°

The third component of the black image, the lamp, while again not sufficient or complete in itself, still serves to enrich our understanding of the human condition. The light that is shed, particularly on the experience of blacks in America but also on the effects of that presence on all of us, serves to break down our isolation from each other, to dispel our illusions, to make real our experience.

> The time has come to realize that the interracial drama acted out on the American continent has not only created a new black man, it has created a new white man, too. No road whatever will lead Americans back to the simplicity of this European village where white men still have the luxury of looking on me as a stranger. I am not, really, a stranger any longer for any American alive. One of the things that distinguishes Americans from other people is that no other people has ever been so deeply involved in the lives of black men, and vice versa. This fact faced, with all its implications, it can be seen that the history of the American Negro problem is not merely shameful, it is also something of an achievement. For even when the worst has been said, it must also be added that the perpetual challenge posed by this problem was always, somehow, perpetually met. It is precisely this black-white experience which may prove of indispensable value to us

°Ellison, Ralph, "Change the Joke and Slip the Yoke," in *Shadow and Act* (New York: Random House, 1964) p. 55.

in the world we face today. This world is white no longer, and it will never be white again.°

A Note on the Color of the Writers

Anyone assembling an anthology on black images in literature must wrestle with a number of questions concerning the color of the writers whose works are to be included. Can white writers create black characters? Can black writers describe anything but "the black experience"? Who creates a black image?

Responses to these questions may explain something about the selections as well. I believe that "the black experience" as such exists solely because of the multiracial character of the society. If all Americans were black, we would speak not of the black experience but of the human experience. Black and white people define each other as white and black; they reflect each other's images and fix, refine, and alter the truths about those images. Therefore, the inclusion of black and white writers in this collection is both intentional and significant. Such a mix does raise questions of authenticity, however. How real, or unstereotypical, are the black characters of Faulkner or Melville? Are stereotypes ever useful? Students may want to compare the blacks of Eudora Welty and Alice Walker or of Claude McKay and Sherwood Anderson. My feeling is that we black and white Americans know each other well, indeed that good writing creates real images no matter what the color of the author. It is possible to misread *Huckleberry Finn*, but to do so is to miss the point, and the genuis of Mark Twain.

The last section of the book, the lamp, includes fewer white writers than black ones. This occurs, in part, because, as the lamp image suggests, so much of what was true about black people never appeared in our literature, and black writers are needed to shed light on their own experience.

°Baldwin, James, "Stranger in the Village," *Notes of a Native Son* (Boston: Beacon Press, 1955) pp. 148-9.

PART I

The Shadow

I remember well when the shadow swept across me.
—W.E.B. DuBois, from "The Souls of Black Folk"

Evil Without or Within

The image of the black person casting a shadow upon American life, or being the shadow which makes that life so difficult, is common to our literature and thought. Though the history of black people and the history of America are forever intertwined, the shadow image suggests that we have not always faced this fact. Rather we have tried to ignore the reality of our experience, the nature of the encounters between blacks and whites, indeed, often the very existence of blacks. The effect of living in a shadow is to experience reality in a dim, cloudy grayness, not unlike the atmosphere surrounding the *San Dominick* at the opening of *Benito Cereno*. Inside such a fog, truth is usually masked or hidden entirely from view.

Babo, the rebel slave in Melville's story, is one of the more extraordinary projections in American fiction. In his shadow Melville casts Don Benito, the European captain who has seen his childhood friend murdered and the skeleton used to replace the ship's figurehead, and Amasa Delano, the naive, trusting American. Melville does not presume to know the innermost mind of Babo, the slave-shadow. We see him only through the eyes of Delano and know him only by his acts. When these occur, however, as the revolt unfolds, Don Benito gains an understanding of the hidden aspects of his own personality. For Delano, the shadow remains a projection of evil, outside himself.

What is the source of this shadow? Where does it originate? Who, or what, casts us into darkness? Is it possible that the shadow, the dim atmosphere in which we move, really emanates from the evil within ourselves? Whatever the source, it is clear that until the shadow is lifted, the projections withdrawn, real relationships between blacks and whites, indeed any healthy personal encounters between people, cannot occur.

° ° °

Robert Hayden was born in Detroit in 1913 and received degrees from Wayne State and Michigan universities. Now a member of the faculty of Fisk University, he has published four collections of his poetry. "Tour Five" and "Middle Passage" appear in his *Selected Poems*, 1966. "Middle Passage" is based on the *Armistad* mutiny in 1839 which was led by Cinquez, an African slave who tried to return to Africa. The ship landed in the United States, where the mutineers were tried (defended by John Quincy Adams), freed, and allowed to return to Africa.

Herman Melville's *Benito Cereno* was included in *Piazza Tales*, published in 1856. It is based on a chapter in Captain Amasa Delano's *A Narrative of Voyages and Travels* (1817), though Melville made a number of changes, including the names of the ships, the characteristics of major figures in the story, and the date of the event (from 1805 to 1799). The issue of slave rebellion was of great concern in the 1850s. Debate still raged over legal questions arising from the mutiny aboard the *Armistad*.

° ° °

TOUR 5

Robert Hayden (1913-   )

The road winds down through autumn hills
in blazonry of farewell scarlet
and recessional gold,
past cedar groves, through static villages
whose names are all that's left
of Choctaw, Chickasaw.

We stop a moment in a town
watched over by Confederate sentinels,
buy gas and ask directions of a rawboned man
whose eyes revile us as the enemy.

Shrill gorgon silence breathes behind
his taut civility
and in the ever-tautening air,
dark for us despite its Indian summer glow.
We drive on, following the route
of highwaymen and phantoms,

Of slaves and armies.
Children, wordless and remote,
wave at us from kindling porches.
And now the land is flat for miles,
the landscape lush, metallic, flayed,
its brightness harsh as bloodstained swords.

MIDDLE PASSAGE

Robert Hayden

I

Jesús, Estrella, Esperanza, Mercy:°
Sails flashing to the wind like weapons,
sharks following the moans the fever and the dying;
horror the corposant° and compass rose.

Middle Passage:
voyage through death
to life upon these shores.

"10 April 1800—
Blacks rebellious. Crew uneasy. Our linguist says
their moaning is a prayer for death,
ours and their own. Some try to starve themselves.
Lost three this morning leaped with crazy laughter
to the waiting sharks, sang as they went under."

Desire, Adventure, Tartar, Ann:

Standing to America, bringing home
black gold, black ivory, black seed.

Deep in the festering hold thy father lies,
of his bones New England pews are made,
those are altar lights that were his eyes.

Jesus Saviour Pilot Me
Over Life's Tempestuous Sea

We pray that Thou wilt grant, O Lord,
safe passage to our vessel bringing
heathen souls unto Thy chastening

Jesus Saviour

°*Jesús, Estrella, Esperanza, Mercy:* names of slave ships; Jesus, Star, Hope, Mercy °*corposant:* St Elmo's Fire, a flaming phenomenon sometimes seen in stormy weather at prominent points on a ship

"8 bells. I cannot sleep, for I am sick
with fear, but writing eases fear a little
since still my eyes can see these words take shape
upon the page & so I write, as one
would turn to exorcism.° 4 days scudding,
but now the sea is calm again. Misfortune
follows in our wake like sharks (our grinning
tutelary° gods). Which one of us
has killed an albatross?° A plague among
our blacks—Ophthalmia:° blindness—& we
have jettisoned° the blind to no avail.
It spreads, the terrifying sickness spreads.
Its claws have scratched sight from the Capt.'s eyes
& there is blindness in the fo'c'sle
& we must sail 3 weeks before we come
to port."

What port awaits us, Davy Jones'
or home? I've heard of slavers drifting, drifting,
playthings of wind and storm and chance, their crews
gone blind, the jungle hatred
crawling up on deck.

Thou Who Walked On Galilee

"Deponent° further sayeth *The Bella J*
left the Guinea Coast
with cargo of five hundred blacks and odd
for the barracoons° of Florida:

"That there was hardly room 'tween-decks for half
the sweltering cattle stowed spoon-fashion there;
that some went mad of thirst and tore their flesh
and sucked the blood:

"That Crew and Captain lusted with the comeliest
of the savage girls kept naked in the cabins;
that there was one they called the Guinea Rose
and they cast lots and fought to lie with her:

°*exorcism:* a spell to get rid of evil spirits °*tutelary:* guardian °*albatross:* a seabird used in "The Rime of the Ancient Mariner" to symbolize an innocent animal killed without reason °*Opthalmia:* an eye disease that causes blindness °*jettisoned:* threw overboard °*deponent:* a person who gives evidence °*barracoons:* enclosure(s) in which slaves were kept

"That when the Bo's'n piped all hands, the flames
spreading from starboard already were beyond
control, the Negroes howling and their chains
entangled with the flames:

"That the burning blacks could not be reached,
that the Crew abandoned ship,
leaving their shrieking Negresses behind,
that the Captain perished drunken with the wenches:

"Further Deponent sayeth not."

Pilot Oh Pilot Me

2

Aye, lad, and I have seen those factories,°
Gambia, Rio Pongo, Calabar;°
have watched the artful mongos° baiting traps
of war wherein the victor and the vanquished

Were caught as prizes for our barracoons.
Have seen the nigger kings whose vanity
and greed turned wild black hides of Fellatah,
Mandingo, Ibo, Kru° to gold for us.

And there was one—King Anthracite we named him—
fetish face beneath French parasols
of brass and orange velvet, impudent mouth
whose cups were carven skulls of enemies:

He'd honor us with drum and feast and conjo
and palm-oil-glistening wenches deft in love,
and for tin crowns that shone with paste,
red calico and German-silver trinkets.

Would have the drums talk war and send
his warriors to burn the sleeping villages
and kill the sick and old and lead the young
in coffles° to our factories.

°*factories:* prison camps in Africa where slaves were kept before being sold to slave ships °*Gambia, Rio Pongo, Calabar:* African ports °*mongos:* a group of tribes of West Africa. Some tribes waged war to capture slaves to sell to the whites °*Fellatah, Mandingo, Ibo, Kru:* West African tribes °*coffles:* groups of slaves shackled together

Twenty years a trader, twenty years,
for there was wealth aplenty to be harvested
from those black fields, and I'd be trading still
but for the fevers melting down my bones.

3

Shuttles in the rocking loom of history,
the dark ships move, the dark ships move,
their bright ironical names
like jests of kindness on a murderer's mouth;
plough through thrashing glister toward
fata morgana's° lucent melting shore,
weave toward New World littorals° that are
mirage and myth and actual shore.

Voyage through death,
                    voyage whose chartings are unlove

A charnel stench, effuvium of living death
spreads outward from the hold,
where the living and the dead, the horribly dying,
lie interlocked, lie foul with blood and excrement.

Deep in the festering hold thy father lies,
the corpse of mercy rots with him,
rats eat love's rotten gelid° eyes.

But, oh, the living look at you
with human eyes whose suffering accuses you,
whose hatred reaches through the swill of dark
to strike you like a leper's claw.

You cannot stare that hatred down
or chain the fear that stalks the watches
and breathes on you its fetid scorching breath;
cannot kill the deep immortal human wish,
the timeless will.

"But for the storm that flung up barriers . . .
of wind and wave, *The Armistad*, señores,
would have reached the port of Príncipe in two,

°*fata morgana:* something illusory and unattainable; a mirage °*littorals:* coastal regions °*gelid:* icy

three days at most; but for the storm we should
have been prepared for what befell.
Swift as the puma's leap it came. There was
that interval of moonless calm filled only
with the water's and the rigging's usual sounds,
then sudden movement, blows and snarling cries
and they had fallen on us with machete
and marlinspike. It was as though the very
air, the night itself were striking us.
Exhausted by the rigors of the storm,
we were no match for them. Our men went down
before the murderous Africans. Our loyal
Celestino ran from below with gun
and lantern and I saw, before the cane-
snife's wounding flash, Cinquez,
that surly brute who calls himself a prince,
directing, urging on the ghastly work.
He hacked the poor mulatto down, and then
he turned on me. The decks were slippery
when daylight finally came. It sickens me
to think of what I saw, of how these apes
threw overboard the butchered bodies of
our men, true Christians all, like so much jetsam.
Enough, enough. The rest is quickly told:
Cinquez was forced to spare the two of us
you see to steer the ship to Africa,
and we like phantoms doomed to rove the sea
voyaged east by day and west by night,
deceiving them, hoping for rescue,
prisoners on our own vessel, till
at length we drifted to the shores of this
your land, America, where we were freed
from our unspeakable misery. Now we
demand, good sirs, the extradition of
Cinquez and his accomplices to La
Havana. And it distresses us to know
there are so many here who seem inclined
to justify the mutiny of these blacks.
We find it paradoxical indeed
that you whose wealth, whose tree of liberty
are rooted in the labor of your slaves
should suffer the august John Quincy Adams
to speak with so much passion of the right
of chattel slaves to kill their lawful masters

and with his Roman rhetoric weave a hero's
garland for Cinquez. I tell you that
we are determined to return to Cuba
with our slaves and there see justice done.
        Cinquez—
or let us say 'the Prince'—Cinquez shall die."

The deep immortal human wish,
the timeless will:

Cinquez its deathless primaveral° image,
life that transfigures many lives.

Voyage through death
                    to life upon these shores.

° ° °

BENITO CERENO

Herman Melville (1819-1891)

IN THE year 1799, Captain Amasa Delano, of Duxbury, in Massachusetts, commanding a large sealer and general trader, lay at anchor with a valuable cargo, in the harbor of Santa Maria—a small, desert, uninhabited island toward the southern extremity of the long coast of Chile. There he had touched for water.

On the second day, not long after dawn, while lying in his berth, his mate came below, informing him that a strange sail was coming into the bay. Ships were then not so plenty in those waters as now. He rose, dressed, and went on deck.

The morning was one peculiar to that coast. Everything was mute and calm; everything grey. The sea, though undulated into long roods° of swells, seemed fixed, and was sleeked at the surface like waved lead that has cooled and set in the smelter's mold. The sky seemed a grey surtout.° Flights of troubled grey fowl, kith and kin with flights of troubled grey vapors among which they were mixed, skimmed low and fitfully over the waters, as swallows over meadows before storms. Shadows present, foreshadowing deeper shadows to come.

To Captain Delano's surprise, the stranger, viewed through the glass, showed no colors; though to do so upon entering a haven, however uninhabited in its shores, where but a single other ship might be lying,

---

°*primaveral:* referring to earliest spring

°*roods:* a rood is about eight yards °*surtout:* overcoat

was the custom among peaceful seamen of all nations. Considering the lawlessness and loneliness of the spot, and the sort of stories, at that day, associated with those seas, Captain Delano's surprise might have deepened into some uneasiness had he not been a person of a singularly undistrustful good nature, not liable, except on extraordinary and repeated incentives, and hardly then, to indulge in personal alarms, any way involving the imputation of malign evil in man. Whether, in view of what humanity is capable, such a trait implies, along with a benevolent heart, more than ordinary quickness and accuracy of intellectual perception, may be left to the wise to determine.

But whatever misgivings might have obtruded on first seeing the stranger, would almost, in any seaman's mind, have been dissipated by observing, that the ship, in navigating into the harbor, was drawing too near the land; a sunken reef making out off her bow. This seemed to prove her a stranger, indeed, not only to the sealer, but the island; consequently, she could be no wonted freebooter on that ocean. With no small interest, Captain Delano continued to watch her—a proceeding not much facilitated by the vapors partly mantling the hull, through which the far matin light from her cabin streamed equivocally enough; much like the sun—by this time hemisphered on the rim of the horizon, and, apparently in company with the strange ship entering the harbor—which, wimpled by the same low, creeping clouds, showed not unlike a Lima intriguante's° one sinister eye peering across the Plaza from the Indian loop-hole of her dusk *saya-y-manto.*°

It might have been but a deception of the vapors, but, the longer the stranger was watched the more singular appeared her maneuvers. Ere long it seemed hard to decide whether she meant to come in or no—what she wanted, or what she was about. The wind, which had breezed up a little during the night, was now extremely light and baffling, which the more increased the apparent uncertainty of her movements.

Surmising, at last, that it might be a ship in distress, Captain Delano ordered his whale-boat to be dropped, and, much to the wary opposition of his mate, prepared to board her, and, at the least, pilot her in. On the night previous, a fishing party of the seamen had gone a long distance to some detached rocks out of sight from the sealer, and, an hour or two before daybreak, had returned, having met with no small success. Presuming that the stranger might have been long off soundings,° the good captain put several baskets of the fish, for presents, into his boat, and so pulled away. From her continuing too near the sunken reef, deeming her in danger, calling to his men, he made all haste to apprize those on board of their situation. But, some time ere the boat came up,

---

°***intriguante*** (Sp.): prostitute °*saya-y-manto* (Sp.): a long shawl commonly worn over the head °*soundings:* shallows; water near land

the wind, light though it was, having shifted, had headed the vessel off, as well as partly broken the vapors from about her.

Upon gaining a less remote view, the ship, when made signally visible on the verge of the leaden-hued swells, with the shreds of fog here and there raggedly furring her, appeared like a whitewashed monastery after a thunderstorm, seen perched upon some dun cliff among the Pyrenees. But it was no purely fanciful resemblance which now, for a moment, almost led Captain Delano to think that nothing less than a ship-load of monks was before him. Peering over the bulwarks were what really seemed, in the hazy distance, throngs of dark cowls; while, fitfully revealed through the open portholes, other dark moving figures were dimly descried, as of Black Friars pacing the cloisters.

Upon a still nigher approach, this appearance was modified, and the true character of the vessel was plain— a Spanish merchantman of the first class, carrying negro slaves, amongst other valuable freight, from one colonial port to another. A very large, and, in its time, a very fine vessel, such as in those days were at intervals encountered along that main; sometimes superseded Acapulco treasure-ships, or retired frigates of the Spanish king's navy, which, like superannuated Italian palaces, still, under a decline of masters, preserved signs of former state.

As the whale-boat drew more and more nigh, the cause of the peculiar pipe-clayed aspect of the stranger was seen in the slovenly neglect pervading her. The spars, ropes, and great part of the bulwarks, looked woolly, from long unacquaintance with the scraper, tar, and the brush. Her keel seemed laid, her ribs put together, and she launched, from Ezekiel's Valley of Dry Bones.°

In the present business in which she was engaged, the ship's general model and rig appeared to have undergone no material change from their original warlike and Froissart pattern.° However, no guns were seen.

The tops were large, and were railed about with what had once been octagonal net-work, all now in sad disrepair. These tops hung overhead like three ruinous aviaries, in one of which was seen perched, on a ratlin, a white noddy, a strange fowl, so called from its lethargic, somnambulistic character, being frequently caught by hand at sea. Battered and moldy, the castellated forecastle seemed some ancient turrent, long ago taken by assault, and then left to decay. Toward the stern, two high-raised quarter galleries—the balustrades here and there covered with dry, tindery sea-moss—opening out from the unoccupied state-cabin, whose dead-lights, for all the mild weather, were hermetically closed and calked —these tenantless balconies hung over the sea as if it were the grand Venetian canal. But the principal relic of faded grandeur was the ample

°*Ezekiel's Valley of Dry Bones:* Ezekiel 37:1-10 °*Froissart pattern:* Reference is to Jean Froissart (c. 1337-c. 1404), French poet whose work is dominated by a concern with romantic chivalry, aristocratic ritual, and martial pageantry.

oval of the shield-like sternpiece, intricately carved with the arms of Castile and Leon,° medallioned about by groups of mythological or symbolical devices; uppermost and central of which was a dark satyr° in a mask, holding his foot on the prostrate neck of a writhing figure, likewise masked.

Whether the ship had a figurehead, or only a plain beak, was not quite certain, owing to canvas wrapped about that part, either to protect it while undergoing a refurbishing, or else decently to hide its decay. Rudely painted or chalked, as in a sailor freak,° along the forward side of a sort of pedestal below the canvas was the sentence, "*Sequid vuestro jefe*" (follow your leader); while upon the tarnished headboards, nearby, appeared, in stately capitals, once gilt, the ship's name, "SAN DOMINICK," each letter streakingly corroded with tricklings of copper-spike rust; while, like mourning weeds, dark festoons of sea-grass slimily swept to and fro over the name, with every hearselike roll of the hull.

As, at last, the boat was hooked from the bow along toward the gangway amidship, its keel, while yet some inches separated from the hull, harshly grated as on a sunken coral reef. It proved a huge bunch of conglobated barnacles adhering below the water to the side like a wen° —a token of baffling airs and long calms passed somewhere in those seas.

Climbing the side, the visitor was at once surrounded by a clamorous throng of whites and blacks, but the latter outnumbering the former more than could have been expected, negro transportation-ship as the stranger in port was. But, in one language, and as with one voice, all poured out a common tale of suffering; in which the negresses, of whom there were not a few, exceeded the others in their dolorous vehemence. The scurvy, together with the fever, had swept off a great part of their number, more especially the Spaniards. Off Cape Horn° they had narrowly escaped shipwreck; then, for days together, they had lain tranced without wind; their provisions were low; their water next to none; their lips that moment were baked.

While Captain Delano was thus made the mark of all eager tongues, his one eager glance took in all faces, with every other object about him.

Always upon first boarding a large and populous ship at sea, especially a foreign one, with a nondescript crew such as Lascars or Manila men,° the impression varies in a peculiar way from that produced by first entering a strange house with strange inmates in a strange land. Both house and ship—the one by its walls and blinds, the other by its high

---

°*Castile and Leon:* the two royal houses whose union established the crown dynasty of Spain °*satyr:* a nature demigod found in Greek and Roman mythology; usually depicted as having horns and hooves; generally associated with wildness and freedom from civilized convention °*freak:* the kind of simple prank or "gag" that men long at sea might play to relieve monotony °*wen:* an encysted growth or tumor °*Cape Horn:* the southernmost tip of South America; famous for storms and shipwrecks °*Lascars or Manila men:* East Indian or Filipino sailors

ENDORSE CHECK HERE

X

DO NOT WRITE / SIGN / STAMP BELOW THIS LINE

DEPOSITORY BANK ENDORSEMENT

RAYOVAC®

P.O. BOX 8499
CLINTON, IA 52736

762

FIRST CLASS MAIL
U.S. Postage
PAID
Clinton, Iowa
Permit No. 59

PAY THIS AMOUNT

1304398

ONE AND------------ 50/100 Dollars

NOT GOOD OVER $10.00

$ **1.50*

VOID AFTER 2/25/93

TO THE ORDER OF

1A 1262900000146 M 616 M
R HOWARD
702 SPING ST
PEORIA IL
61603

AUTHORIZED SIGNATURE

PAYABLE THROUGH CLINTON NATIONAL BANK
CLINTON, IOWA

72-44
739

3⑆073900441⑆ 01 3042 7⑈

bulwarks like ramparts—hoard from view their interiors till the last moment; but in the case of the ship there is this addition: that the living spectacle it contains, upon its sudden and complete disclosure, has, in contrast with the blank ocean which zones it, something of the effect of enchantment. The ship seemes unreal; these strange costumes, gestures, and faces, but a shadowy tableau just emerged from the deep, which directly must receive back what it gave.

Perhaps it was some such influence, as above is attempted to be described, which, in Captain Delano's mind, heightened whatever, upon a staid scrutiny, might have seemed unusual; especially the conspicuous figures of four elderly grizzled negroes, their heads like black, doddered willow tops, who, in venerable contrast to the tumult below them, were couched, sphynxlike, one on the starboard cat-head,° another on the larboard, and the remaining pair face to face on the opposite bulwarks above the main-chains. They each had bits of unstranded old junk° in their hands, and, with a sort of stoical self-content, were picking the junk into oakum,° a small heap of which lay by their sides. They accompanied the task with a continuous, low, monotonous chant; droning and drooling away like so many grey-headed bagpipers playing a funeral march.

The quarter-deck rose into an ample elevated poop, upon the forward verge of which, lifted, like the oakum-pickers, some eight feet above the general throng, sat along in a row, separated by regular spaces, the cross-legged figures of six other blacks; each with a rusty hatchet in his hand, which, with a bit of brick and a rag, he was engaged like a scullion in scouring; while between each two was a small stack of hatchets, their rusted edges turned forward awaiting a like operation. Though occasionally the four oakum-pickers would briefly address some person or persons in the crowd below, yet the six hatchet-polishers neither spoke to others, nor breathed a whisper among themselves, but sat intent upon their task, except at intervals, when, with the peculiar love in negroes of uniting industry with pastime, two and two they sideways, clashed their hatchets together, like cymbals, with a barbarous din. All six, unlike the generality, had the raw aspect of unsophisticated Africans.

But that first comprehensive glance which took in those ten figures, with scores less conspicuous, rested but an instant upon them, as, impatient of the hubbub of voices, the visitor turned in quest of whomsoever it might be that commanded the ship.

But as if not unwilling to let nature make known her own case among his suffering charge, or else in despair of restraining it for the time, the Spanish captain, a gentlemanly, reserved-looking, and rather young man to a stranger's eye, dressed with singular richness, but bearing plain traces of recent sleepless cares and disquietudes, stood passively by, leaning

---

°*cat-head:* projection of timber on deck near the bow; used to secure the anchor °*junk:* strands and fragments of old cordage °*oakum:* calking material

against the main-mast, at one moment casting a dreary, spiritless look upon his excited people, at the next an unhappy glance toward his visitor. By his side stood a black of small stature, in whose rude face, as occasionally, like a shepherd's dog, he mutely turned it up into the Spaniard's, sorrow and affection were equally blended.

Struggling through the throng, the American advanced to the Spaniard, assuring him of his sympathies, and offering to render whatever assistance might be in his power. To which the Spaniard returned for the present but grave and ceremonious acknowledgments, his national formality dusked by the saturnine mood of ill health.

But losing no time in mere compliments, Captain Delano, returning to the gangway, had his baskets of fish brought up; and as the wind still continued light, so that some hours at least must elapse ere the ship could be brought to the anchorange, he bade his men return to the sealer, and fetch back as much water as the whale-boat could carry, with whatever soft bread the steward might have, all the remaining pumpkins on board, with a box of sugar, and a dozen of his private bottles of cider.

Not many minutes after the boat's pushing off, to the vexation of all, the wind entirely died away, and the tide turning, began drifting back the ship helplessly seaward. But trusting this would not long last, Captain Delano sought, with good hopes, to cheer up the strangers, feeling no small satisfaction that, with persons in their condition, he could—thanks to his frequent voyages along the Spanish main—converse with some freedom in their native tongue.

While left alone with them, he was not long in observing some things tending to heighten his first impressions; but surprise was lost in pity, both for the Spaniards and blacks, alike evidently reduced from scarcity of water and provisions; while long-continued suffering seemed to have brought out the less good-natured qualities of the negroes, besides, at the same time, impairing the Spaniard's authority over them. But, under the circumstances, precisely this condition of things was to have been anticipated. In armies, navies, cities, or families, in nature herself, nothing more relaxes good order than misery. Still, Captain Delano was not without the idea, that had Benito Cereno been a man of greater energy, misrule would hardly have come to the present pass. But the debility, constitutional or induced by hardships, bodily and mental, of the Spanish captain, was too obvious to be overlooked. A prey to settled dejection, as if long mocked with hope he would not now indulge it, even when it had ceased to be a mock, the prospect of that day, or evening at furthest, lying at anchor, with plenty of water for his people, and a brother captain to counsel and befriend, seemed in no perceptible degree to encourage him. His mind appeared unstrung, if not still more seriously affected. Shut up in these oaken walls, chained to one dull round of command, whose unconditionality cloyed him, like some hypochondriac abbot he moved slowly about, at times suddenly pausing, starting, or staring, biting his lip, biting his fingernail, flushing, paling, twitching his beard, with other symptoms of an absent or moody mind. This distempered spirit was lodged, as before hinted, in as distempered a frame. He was rather tall, but seemed never to have been robust, and now with nervous suffering was almost worn to a skeleton. A tendency to some pulmonary complaint appeared to have been lately confirmed. His voice was like that of one with lungs half gone—hoarsely suppressed, a husky whisper. No wonder that, as in this state he tottered about, his private servant apprehensively followed him. Sometimes the negro gave his master his arm, or took his handkerchief out of his pocket for him; performing these and similar offices with that affectionate zeal which transmutes into something filial or fraternal acts in themselves but menial; and which has gained for the negro the repute of making the most pleasing body-servant in the world; one, too, whom a master need be on no stiffly superior terms with, but may treat with familiar trust; less a servant than a devoted companion.

Marking the noisy indocility of the blacks in general, as well as what seemed the sullen inefficiency of the whites, it was not without humane satisfaction that Captain Delano witnessed the steady good conduct of Babo.

But the good conduct of Babo, hardly more than the ill behavior of others, seemed to withdraw the half-lunatic Don Benito from his cloudy languor. Not that such precisely was the impression made by the Spaniard on the mind of his visitor. The Spaniard's individual unrest was, for the present, but noted as a conspicuous feature in the ship's general affliction. Still, Captain Delano was not a little concerned at what he could not help taking for the time to be Don Benito's unfriendly indifference towards himself. The Spaniard's manner, too, conveyed a sort of sour and gloomy disdain, which he seemed at no pains to disguise. But this the American in charity ascribed to the harassing effects of sickness, since, in former instances, he had noted that there are peculiar natures on whom prolonged physical suffering seems to cancel every social instinct of kindness; as if, forced to black bread themselves, they deemed it but equity that each person coming nigh them should, indirectly, by some slight or affront, be made to partake of their fare.

But ere long Captain Delano bethought him that, indulgent as he was at the first, in judging the Spaniard, he might not, after all, have exercised charity enough. At bottom it was Don Benito's reserve which displeased him; but the same reserve was shown towards all but his faithful personal attendant. Even the formal reports which, according to sea-usage, were, at stated times, made to him by some petty underling, either a white, mulatto, or black, he hardly had patience enough to listen to, without betraying contemptuous aversion. His manner upon such occasions was, in its degree, not unlike that which might be supposed to have been his imperial countryman's, Charles V,° just previous to the anchoritish retirement of that monarch from the throne.

This splenetic disrelish of his place was evinced in almost every function pertaining to it. Proud as he was moody, he condescended to no personal mandate. Whatever special orders were necessary, their delivery was delegated to his body-servant, who in turn transferred them to their ultimate destination, through runners, alert Spanish boys or slave boys, like pages or pilotfish° within easy call continually hovering round Don Benito. So that to have beheld this undemonstrative invalid gliding about, apathetic and mute, no landsman could have dreamed that in him was lodged a dictatorship beyond which, while at sea, there was no earthly appeal.

Thus, the Spaniard, regarded in his reserve, seemed the involuntary victim of mental disorder. But, in fact, his reserve might, in some degree, have proceeded from design. If so, then in Don Benito was evinced the unhealthy climax of that icy though conscientious policy, more or less adopted by all commanders of large ships, which, except in signal emergencies, obliterates alike the manifestation of sway with every trace of sociality; transforming the man into a block, or rather into a loaded cannon, which, until there is call for thunder, has nothing to say.

Viewing him in this light, it seemed but a natural token of the perverse habit induced by a long course of such hard self-restraint, that, notwithstanding the present condition of his ship, the Spaniard should still persist in a demeanor, which however harmless, or, it may be, appropriate, in a well-appointed vessel, such as the *San Dominick* might have been at the outset of the voyage, was anything but judicious now. But the Spaniard, perhaps, thought that it was with captains as with gods: reserve, under all events, must still be their cue. But probably this appearance of slumbering dominion might have been but an attempted disguise to conscious imbecility—not deep policy, but shallow device. But be all this as it might, whether Don Benito's manner was designed or not, the more Captain Delano noted its pervading reserve, the less he felt uneasiness at any particular manifestation of that reserve towards himself.

Neither were his thoughts taken up by the captain alone. Wonted to the quiet orderliness of the sealer's comfortable family of a crew, the noisy confusion of the *San Dominick's* suffering host repeatedly challenged his eye. Some prominent breaches, not only of discipline but of decency. were observed. These Captain Delano could not but ascribe, in the main, to the absence of those subordinate deck-officers to whom, along with higher duties, is intrusted what may be styled the police department of a populous ship. True, the old oakum-pickers appeared at times to act

---

°*Charles* V (1550-1558): powerful king of Spain, who abdicated and retired to a monastery °*pilotfish:* small parasitical fish which commonly accompany sharks

the part of monitorial constables to their countrymen, the blacks; but though occasionally succeeding in allaying trifling outbreaks now and then between man and man, they could do little or nothing toward establishing general quiet. The *San Dominick* was in the condition of a transatlantic emigrant ship, among whose multitude of living freight are some individuals, doubtless, as little troublesome as crates and bales; but the friendly remonstrances of such with their ruder companions are of not so much avail as the unfriendly arm of the mate. What the *San Dominick* wanted was, what the emigrant ship has, stern superior officers. But on these decks not so much as a fourth-mate was to be seen.

The visitor's curiosity was roused to learn the particulars of those mishaps which had brought about such absenteeism, with its consequences; because, though deriving some inkling of the voyage from the wails which at the first moment had greeted him, yet of the details no clear understanding had been had. The best account would, doubtless, be given by the captain. Yet at first the visitor was loath to ask it, unwilling to provoke some distant rebuff. But plucking up courage, he at last accosted Don Benito, renewing the expression of his benevolent interest, adding, that did he (Captain Delano) but know the particulars of the ship's misfortunes, he would, perhaps, be better able in the end to relieve them. Would Don Benito favor him with the whole story?

Don Benito faltered; then, like some somnambulist suddenly interfered with, vacantly stared at his visitor, and ended by looking down on the deck. He maintained this posture so long, that Captain Delano, almost equally disconcerted, and involuntarily almost as rude, turned suddenly from him, walking forward to accost one of the Spanish seamen for the desired information. But he had hardly gone five paces, when, with a sort of eagerness, Don Benito invited him back, regretting his momentary absence of mind, and professing readiness to gratify him.

While most part of the story was being given, the two captains stood on the after part of the main-deck, a privileged spot, no one being near but the servant.

"It is now a hundred and ninety days," began the Spaniard, in his husky whisper, "that this ship, well officered and well manned, with several cabin passengers—some fifty Spaniards in all—sailed from Buenos Aires bound to Lima, with a general cargo, hardware, Paraguay tea and the like—and," pointing forward, "that parcel of negroes, now not more than a hundred and fifty, as you see, but then numbering over three hundred souls. Off Cape Horn we had heavy gales. In one moment, by night, three of my best officers, with fifteen sailors, were lost, with the main yard;° the spar snapping under them in the slings,° as they sought, with heavers,° to beat down the icy sail. To lighten the hull, the heavier

°*main yard:* horizontal spar supporting mainsail °*slings:* supports for yards °*heavers:* short levers for pulling and prying rigging and spars

sacks of maté° were thrown into the sea, with most of the water-pipes° lashed on deck at the time. And this last necessity it was, combined with the prolonged detentions afterwards experienced, which eventually brought about our chief causes of suffering. When——"

Here there was a sudden fainting attack of his cough, brought on, no doubt, by his mental distress. His servant sustained him, and drawing a cordial from his pocket placed it to his lips. He a little revived. But unwilling to leave him unsupported while yet imperfectly restored, the black with one arm still encircled his master, at the same time keeping his eye fixed on his face, as if to watch for the first sign of complete restoration, or relapse, as the event might prove.

The Spaniard proceeded, but brokenly and obscurely, as one in a dream.

—"Oh, my God! rather than pass through what I have, with joy I would have hailed the most terrible gales; but ——"

His cough returned and with increased violence; this subsiding, with reddened lips and closed eyes he fell heavily against his supporter.

"His mind wanders. He was thinking of the plague that followed the gales," plaintively sighed the servant; "my poor, poor master!" wringing one hand, and with the other wiping the mouth. "But be patient, Señor," again turning to Captain Delano, "these fits do not last long; master will soon be himself."

Don Benito reviving, went on; but as this portion of the story was very brokenly delivered, the substance only will here be set down.

It appeared that after the ship had been many days tossed in storms off the Cape, the scurvy broke out, carrying off numbers of the whites and blacks. When at last they had worked round into the Pacific, their spars and sails were so damaged, and so inadequately handled by the surviving mariners, most of whom were become invalids, that, unable to lay her northerly course by the wind, which was powerful, the unmanageable ship, for successive days and nights, was blown northwestward, where the breeze suddenly deserted her, in unknown waters, to sultry calms. The absence of the water-pipes now proved as fatal to life as before their presence had menaced it. Induced, or at least aggravated, by the more than scanty allowance of water, a malignant fever followed the scurvy; with the excessive heat of the lengthened calm, making such short work of it as to sweep away, as by billows, whole families of the Africans, and a yet larger number, proportionably, of the Spaniards, including, by a luckless fatality, every remaining officer on board. Consequently, in the smart west winds eventually following the calm, the already rent sails, having to be simply dropped, not furled, at need, had been gradually reduced to the beggar's rags they were now. To

---

°*maté:* a kind of South American tea °*water pipes:* tanks for drinking water

procure substitutes for his lost sailors, as well as supplies of water and sails, the captain, at the earliest opportunity, had made for Valdivia, the southernmost civilized port of Chile and South America; but upon nearing the coast the thick weather had prevented him from so much as sighting that harbor. Since which period, almost without a crew, and almost without canvas and almost without water, and, at intervals, giving its added dead to the sea, the *San Dominick* had been battledored° about by contrary winds, inveigled by currents, or grown weedy in calms. Like a man lost in woods, more than once she had doubled upon her own track.

"But throughout these calamities," huskily continued Don Benito, painfully turning in the half embrace of his servant, "I have to thank those negroes you see, who, though to your inexperienced eyes appearing unruly, have, indeed, conducted themselves with less of restlessness than even their owner could have thought possible under such circumstances."

Here he again fell faintly back. Again his mind wandered; but he rallied, and less obscurely proceeded.

"Yes, their owner was quite right in assuring me that no fetters would be needed with his blacks; so that while, as is wont in this transportation, those negroes have always remained upon deck—not thrust below, as in the Guineamen°—they have, also, from the beginning, been freely permitted to range within given bounds at their pleasure."

Once more the faintness returned—his mind roved—but, recovering, he resumed:

"But it is Babo here to whom, under God, I owe not only my own preservation, but likewise to him, chiefly, the merit is due, of pacifying his more ignorant brethren, when at intervals tempted to murmurings."

"Ah, master," sighed the black, bowing his face, "don't speak of me; Babo is nothing; what Babo has done was but duty."

"Faithful fellow!" cried Captain Delano. "Don Benito, I envy you such a friend; slave I cannot call him."

As master and man stood before him, the black upholding the white, Captain Delano could not but bethink him of the beauty of that relationship which could present such a spectacle of fidelity on the one hand and confidence on the other. The scene was heightened by the contrast in dress, denoting their relative positions. The Spaniard wore a loose Chile jacket of dark velvet, white small-clothes° and stockings, with silver buckles at the knee and instep; a high-crowned sombrero, of fine grass; a slender sword, silver mounted, hung from a knot in his sash—the last being an almost invariable adjunct, more for utility than ornament, of a South American gentleman's dress to this hour. Excepting when his occasional nervous

---

°***battledored:*** probably Melville's coinage. A battledore is a paddle used in the game of battledore and shuttlecock. Melville's verb here means "beaten to and fro." °***Guineamen:*** slave ships in the regular trade of bringing Negroes from Africa to the Americas °***small-clothes:*** breeches

contortions brought about disarray, there was a certain precision in his attire curiously at variance with the unsightly disorder around; especially in the belittered Ghetto, forward of the main-mast, wholly occupied by the blacks.

The servant wore nothing but wide trousers, apparently, from their coarseness and patches, made out of some old topsail; they were clean, and confined at the waist by a bit of unstranded rope, which, with his composed, deprecatory air at times, made him look something like a begging friar of St. Francis.

However unsuitable for the time and place, at least in the blunt-thinking American's eyes, and however strangely surviving in the midst of all his afflictions, the toilette of Don Benito might not, in fashion at least, have gone beyond the style of the day among South Americans of his class. Though on the present voyage sailing from Buenos Aires, he had avowed himself a native and resident of Chile, whose inhabitants had not so generally adopted the plain coat and once plebeian pantaloons; but, with a becoming modification, adhered to their provincial costume, picturesque as any in the world. Still, relatively to the pale history of the voyage, and his own pale face, there seemed something so incongruous in the Spaniard's apparel, as almost to suggest the image of an invalid courtier tottering about London streets in the time of the plague.

The portion of the narrative which, perhaps, most excited interest, as well as some surprise, considering the latitudes in question, was the long calms spoken of, and more particularly the ship's so long drifting about. Without communicating the opinion, of course, the American could not but impute at least part of the detentions both to clumsy seamanship and faulty navigation. Eyeing Don Benito's small, yellow hands, he easily inferred that the young captain had not got into command at the hawse-hole, but the cabin-window° and if so, why wonder at incompetence, in youth, sickness, and gentility united?

But drowning criticism in compassion, after a fresh repetition of his sympathies, Captain Delano, having heard out his story, not only engaged, as in the first place, to see Don Benito and his people supplied in their immediate bodily needs, but, also, now further promised to assist him in procuring a large permanent supply of water, as well as some sails and rigging, and, though it would involve no small embarrassment to himself, yet he would spare three of his best seamen for temporary deck-officers; so that without delay the ship might proceed to Concepcion, there fully to refit for Lima, her destined port.

Such generosity was not without its effect, even upon the invalid. His face lighted up; eager and hectic, he met the honest glance of his visitor. With gratitude he seemed overcome.

°*hawse-hole . . . cabin window:* that is, Don Benito had started his seafaring career as an officer, not as a common seaman

"This excitement is bad for master," whispered the servant, taking his arm, and with soothing words gently drawing him aside.

When Don Benito returned, the American was pained to observe that his hopefulness, like the sudden kindling in his cheek, was but febrile and transient.

Ere long, with a joyless mien, looking up towards the poop, the host invited his guest to accompany him there, for the benefit of what little breath of wind might be stirring.

As during the telling of the story, Captain Delano had once or twice started at the occasional cymbaling of the hatchet-polishers, wondering why such an interruption should be allowed, especially in that part of the ship, and in the ears of an invalid; and moreover, as the hatchets had anything but an attractive look, and the handlers of them still less so, it was, therefore, to tell the truth, not without some lurking reluctance, or even shrinking, it may be, that Captain Delano, with apparent complaisance, acquiesced in his host's invitation. The more so, since, with an untimely caprice of punctilio, rendered distressing by his cadaverous aspect, Don Benito, with Castilian bows, solemnly insisted upon his guest's preceding him up the ladder leading to the elevation; where, one on each side of the last step, sat for armorial supporters and sentries two of the ominous file. Gingerly enough stepped good Captain Delano between them, and in the instant of leaving them behind, like one running the gauntlet, he felt an apprehensive twitch in the calves of his legs.

But when, facing about, he saw the whole file, like so many organ-grinders, still stupidly intent on their work, unmindful of everything beside, he could not but smile at his late fidgety panic.

Presently, while standing with his host, looking forward upon the decks below, he was struck by one of those instances of insubordination previously alluded to. Three black boys, with two Spanish boys, were sitting together on the hatches, scraping a rude wooden platter, in which some scanty mess had recently been cooked. Suddenly, one of the black boys, enraged at a word dropped by one of his white companions, seized a knife, and, though called to forbear by one of the oakum-pickers, struck the lad over the head, inflicting a gash from which blood flowed.

In amazement, Captain Delano inquired what this meant. To which the pale Don Benito dully muttered, that it was merely the sport of the lad.

"Pretty serious sport, truly," rejoined Captain Delano. "Had such a thing happened on board the *Bachelors' Delight,* instant punishment would have followed."

At these words the Spaniard turned upon the American one of his sudden, staring, half-lunatic looks; then, relapsing into his torpor, answered, "Doubtless, doubtless, Señor."

Is it, thought Captain Delano, that this hapless man is one of those paper captains I've known, who by policy wink at what by power they cannot put down? I know no sadder sight than a commander who has little of command but the name.

"I should think, Don Benito," he now said, glancing towards the oakum-picker who had sought to interfere with the boys, "that you would find it advantageous to keep all your blacks employed, especially the younger ones, no matter at what useless task, and no matter what happens to the ship. Why, even with my little band, I find such a course indispensable. I once kept a crew on my quarter-deck thrumming° mats for my cabin, when, for three days, I had given up my ship—mats, men, and all—for a speedy loss owing to the violence of a gale, in which we could do nothing but helplessly drive before it."

"Doubtless, doubtless," muttered Don Benito.

"But," continued Captain Delano, again glancing upon the oakum-pickers and then at the hatchet-polishers, nearby, "I see you keep some, at least, of your host employed."

"Yes," was again the vacant response.

"Those old men there, shaking their pows from their pulpits," continued Captain Delano, pointing to the oakum-pickers, "seem to act the part of old dominies° to the rest, little heeded as their admonitions are at times. Is this voluntary on their part, Don Benito, or have you appointed them shepherds to your flock of black sheep?"

"What posts they fill, I appointed them," rejoined the Spaniard, in an acrid tone, as if resenting some supposed satiric reflection.

"And these others, these Ashantee° conjurors here," continued Captain Delano, rather uneasily eyeing the brandished steel of the hatchet-polishers, where, in spots, it had been brought to a shine, "this seems a curious business they are at, Don Benito?"

"In the gales we met," answered the Spaniard, "what of our general cargo was not thrown overboard was much damaged by the brine. Since coming into calm weather, I have had several cases of knives and hatchets daily brought up for overhauling and cleaning."

"A prudent idea, Don Benito. You are part owner of ship and cargo, I presume; but none of the slaves, perhaps?"

"I am owner of all you see," impatiently returned Don Benito, "except the main company of blacks, who belonged to my late friend, Alexandro Aranda."

As he mentioned this name, his air was heartbroken; his knees shook; his servant supported him.

°*thrumming:* roughening the surface of canvas by inserting short pieces of line in it °*dominies:* schoolmasters or ministers. In this case, Captain Delano seems to be thinking of ministers, for he speaks of them as "shaking their pows (heads) from their pulpits." °*Ashantee:* a district on the west coast of Africa

Thinking he divined the cause of such unusual emotion, to confirm his surmise, Captain Delano, after a pause, said: "And may I ask, Don Benito, whether—since a while ago you spoke of some cabin passengers—the friend, whose loss so afflicts you, at the outset of the voyage accompanied his blacks?' '

"Yes."

"But died of the fever?"

"Died of the fever. Oh, could I but———" Again quivering, the Spaniard paused.

"Pardon me," said Captain Delano, lowly, "but I think that, by a sympathetic experience, I conjecture, Don Benito, what it is that gives the keener edge to your grief. It was once my hard fortune to lose, at sea, a dear friend, my own brother, then supercargo.° Assured of the welfare of his spirit, its departure I could have borne like a man; but that honest eye, that honest hand—both of which had so often met mine—and that warm heart; all, all—like scraps to the dogs—to throw all to the sharks! It was then I vowed never to have for fellow-voyager a man I loved, unless, unbeknown to him, I had provided every requisite, in case of a fatality, for embalming his mortal part for interment on shore. Were your friend's remains now on board this ship, Don Benito, not thus strangely would the mention of his name affect you."

"On board this ship?" echoed the Spainard. Then, with horrified gestures, as directed against some spectre, he unconsciously fell into the ready arms of his attendant, who, with a silent appeal toward Captain Delano, seemed beseeching him not again to broach a theme so unspeakably distressing to his master.

This poor fellow now, thought the pained American, is the victim of that sad superstition which associates goblins with the deserted body of man, as ghosts with an abandoned house. How unlike are we made! What to me, in like case, would have been a solemn satisfaction, the bare suggestion, even, terrifies the Spaniard into this trance. Poor Alexandro Aranda! what would you say could you here see your friend—who, on former voyages, when you, for months, were left behind, has, I dare say, often longed, and longed, for one peep at you—now transported with terror at the least thought of having you anyway nigh him.

At this moment with a dreary graveyard toll, betokening a flaw, the ship's forecastle bell, smote by one of the grizzled oakum-pickers, proclaimed ten o'clock, through the leaden calm; when Captain Delano's attention was caught by the moving figure of a gigantic black, emerging from the general crowd below, and slowly advancing towards the elevated poop. An iron collar was about his neck, from which depended° a chain, thrice wound round his body; the terminating links padlocked together at a broad band of iron, his girdle.

°*supercargo:* ship's clerk and supply officer °*depended:* hung

"How like a mute Atufal moves," murmured the servant.

The black mounted the steps of the poop, and, like a brave prisoner, brought up to receive sentence, stood in unquailing muteness before Don Benito, now recovered from his attack.

At the first glimpse of his approach, Don Benito had started, a resentful shadow swept over his face; and, as with the sudden memory of bootless rage, his white lips glued together.

This is some mulish mutineer, thought Captain Delano, surveying, not without a mixture of admiration, the colossal form of the negro.

"See, he waits your question, master," said the servant.

Thus reminded, Don Benito, nervously averting his glance, as if shunning, by anticipation, some rebellious response, in a disconcerted voice, thus spoke:—

"Atufal, will you ask my pardon, now?"

The black was silent.

"Again, master," murmured the servant, with bitter upbraiding eyeing his countryman. "Again, master; he will bend to master yet."

"Answer," said Don Benito, still avering his glance, "say but the one word, *pardon*, and your chains shall be off."

Upon this, the black, slowly raising both arms, let them lifelessly fall, his links clanking, his head bowed; as much as to say, "No, I am content."

"Go," said Don Benito, with inkept and unknown emotion.

Deliberately as he had come, the black obeyed.

"Excuse me, Don Benito," said Captain Delano, "but this scene surprises me; what means it, pray?"

"It means that that negro alone, of all the band, has given me peculiar cause of offense. I have put him in chains; I———"

Here he paused; his hand to his head, as if there were a swimming there, or a sudden bewilderment of memory had come over him; but meeting his servant's kindly glance seemed reassured, and proceeded:—

"I could not scourge such a form. But I told him he must ask my pardon. As yet he has not. At my command, every two hours he stands before me."

"And how long has this been?"

"Some sixty days."

"And obedient in all else? And respectful?"

"Yes."

"Upon my conscience, then," exclaimed Captain Delano, impulsively, "he has a royal spirit in him, this fellow."

"He may have some right to it," bitterly returned Don Benito, "he says he was king in his own land."

"Yes," said the servant, entering a word, "those slits in Atufal's ears once held wedges of gold; but poor Babo here, in his own land, was only a poor slave; a black man's slave was Babo, who now is the white's."

Somewhat annoyed by these conversational familiarities, Captain Delano turned curiously upon the attendant, then glanced inquiringly at his master; but, as if long wonted to these little informalities, neither master nor man seemed to understand him.

"What, pray, was Atufal's offense, Don Benito?" asked Captain Delano; "if it was not something very serious, take a fool's advice, and, in view of his general docility, as well as in some natural respect for his spirit, remit him his penalty."

"No, no, master never will do that," here murmured the servant to himself, "proud Atufal must first ask master's pardon. The slave there carries the padlock, but master here carries the key."

His attention thus directed, Captain Delano now noticed for the first, that, suspended by a slender silken cord from Don Benito's neck, hung a key. At once, from the servant's muttered syllables, divining the key's purpose, he smiled and said:—"So, Don Benito—padlock and key—significant symbols, truly."

Biting his lip, Don Benito faltered.

Though the remark of Captain Delano, a man of such native simplicity as to be incapable of satire or irony, had been dropped in playful allusion to the Spaniard's singularly evidenced lordship over the black; yet the hypochondriac seemed some way to have taken it as a malicious reflection upon his confessed inability thus far to break, down, at least, on a verbal summons, the entrenched will of the slave. Deploring this supposed misconception, yet despairing of correcting it, Captain Delano shifted the subject; but finding his companion more than ever withdrawn, as if still sourly digesting the lees of the presumed affront above-mentioned, by and by Captain Delano likewise became less talkative, oppressed, against his own will, by what seemed the secret vindictiveness of the morbidly sensitive Spaniard. But the good sailor, himself of a quite contrary disposition, refrained, on his part, alike from the appearance as from the feeling of resentment, and if silent, was only so from contagion.

Presently the Spaniard, assisted by his servant, somewhat discourteously crossed over from his guest; a procedure which sensibly enough might have been allowed to pass from idle caprice of ill humour, had not master and man, lingering round the corner of the elevated skylight, begun whispering together in low voices. This was unpleasing. And more: the moody air of the Spaniard, which at times had not been without a sort of valetudinarian stateliness, now seemed anything but dignified; while the menial familiarity of the servant lost its original charm of simple-hearted attachment.

In his embarrassment, the visitor turned his face to the other side of the ship. By so doing, his glance accidentally fell on a young Spanish sailor, a coil of rope in his hand, just stepped from the deck to the first round of the mizzen-rigging.° Perhaps the man would not have been particularly noticed, were it not that, during his ascent to one of the yards, he, with a sort of covert intentness, kept his eye fixed on Captain Delano, from whom, presently, it passed, as if by a natural sequence, to the two whisperers.

His own attention thus redirected to that quarter, Captain Delano gave a slight start. From something in Don Benito's manner just then, it seemed as if the visitor had, at least partly, been the subject of the withdrawn consultation going on—a conjecture as little agreeable to the guest as it was little flattering to the host.

The singular alternations of courtesy and ill breeding in the Spanish captain were unaccountable, except on one of two suppositions—innocent lunacy, or wicked imposture.

But the first idea, though it might naturally have occurred to an indifferent observer, and, in some respect, had not hitherto been wholly a stranger to Captain Delano's mind, yet, now that, in an incipient way, he began to regard the strangers' conduct something in the light of an intentional affront, of course the idea of lunacy was virtually vacated. But if not a lunatic, what then? Under the circumstances, would a gentleman, nay, any honest boor, act the part now acted by his host? The man was an impostor. Some low-born adventurer, masquerading as an oceanic grandee; yet so ignorant of the first requisites of mere gentlemanhood as to be betrayed into the present remarkable indecorum. That strange ceremoniousness, too, at other times evinced, seemed not uncharacteristic of one playing a part above his real level. Benito Cereno—Don Benito Cereno—a sounding name. One, too, at that period, not unknown, in the surname, to supercargoes and sea captains trading along the Spanish Main, as belonging to one of the most enterprising and extensive mercantile families in all those provinces; several members of it having titles; a sort of Castilian Rothschild,° with a noble brother, or cousin, in every great trading town of South America. The alleged Don Benito was in early manhood, about twenty-nine or thirty. To assume a sort of roving cadetship in the maritime affairs of such a house, what more likely scheme for a young knave of talent and spirit? But the Spaniard was a pale invalid. Never mind. For even to the degree of simulating mortal disease, the craft of some tricksters had been known to attain. To think that, under the aspect of infantile weakness, the most savage energies might be couched—those velvets of the Spaniard but the silky paw to his fangs.

From no train of thought did these fancies come; not from within, but from without; suddenly, too, and in one throng, like hoar frost; yet as

---

°*mizzen-rigging:* permanent set of lines that support the mast nearest the stern (mizzen) on each side. Such rigging is also used as a means of getting up and down the mast °*Rothschild:* the name of a great international banking family, still very much extant

soon to vanish as the mild sun of Captain Delano's good nature regained its meridian.

Glacing over once more towards his host—whose sideface, revealed above the skylight, was now turned towards him—he was struck by the profile, whose clearness of cut was refined by the thinness, incident to ill health, as well as ennobled about the chin by the beard. Away with suspicion. He was a true off-shoot of a true hidalgo° Cereno.

Relieved by these and other better thoughts, the visitor, lightly humming a tune, now began indifferently pacing the poop, so as not to betray to Don Benito that he had at all mistrusted incivility, much less duplicity; for such mistrust would yet be proved illusory, and by the event; though, for the present, the circumstance which had provoked that distrust remained unexplained. But when that little mystery should have been cleared up, Captain Delano thought he might extremely regret it, did he allow Don Benito to become aware that he had indulged in ungenerous surmises. In short, to the Spaniard's black-letter text,° it was best, for a while, to leave open margin.

Presently, his pale face twitching and overcast, the Spaniard, still supported by his attendant, moved over towards his guest, when, with even more than his usual embarrassment, and a strange sort of intriguing intonation in his husky whisper, the following conversation began:—

Señor, may I ask how long you have lain at this isle?"

"Oh, but a day or two, Don Benito."

"And from what port are you last?"

"Canton."

"And there, Señor, you exchanged your sealskins for teas and silks, I think you said?"

"Yes. Silks, mostly."

"And the balance you took in specie,° perhaps?"

Captain Delano, fidgeting a little, answered—

"Yes; some silver; not a very great deal, though."

"Ah—well. May I ask how many men have you, Señor?"

Captain Delano slightly started, but answered—

"About five-and twenty, all told."

"And at present, Señor, all on board, I suppose?"

"All on board, Don Benito," replied the Captain, now with satisfaction.

"And will be tonight, Señor?"

At this last question, following so many pertinacious ones, for the soul of him Captain Delano could not but look very earnestly at the questioner, who, instead of meeting the glance, with every token of craven discomposure dropped his eyes to the deck; presenting an unworthy

---

°*hidalgo:* blue blood (Spanish) °*black-letter text:* early printing in imitation of hand manuscript; to modern eyes difficult to read °*specie:* coin; hard cash

contrast to his servant, who, just then, was kneeling at his feet, adjusting a loose shoe buckle; his disengaged face meantime, with humble curiosity, turned openly up into his master's downcast one.

The Spaniard, still with a guilty shuffle, repeated his question:

"And—and will be tonight, Señor?"

"Yes, for aught I know," returned Captain Delano—"but nay," rallying himself into fearless truth, "some of them talked of going off on another fishing party about midnight."

"Your ships generally go—go more or less armed, I believe, Señor?"

"Oh, a six-pounder or two, in case of emergency," was the intrepidly indifferent reply, "with a small stock of muskets, sealing-spears, and cutlasses, you know."

As he thus responded, Captain Delano again glanced at Don Benito, but the latter's eyes were averted; while abruptly and awkwardly shifting the subject, he made some peevish allusion to the calm, and then, without apology, once more, with his attendant, withdrew to the opposite bulwarks, where the whispering was resumed.

At this moment, and ere Captain Delano could cast a cool thought upon what had just passed, the young Spanish sailor, before mentioned, was seen descending from the rigging. In act of stooping over to spring inboard to the deck, his voluminous, unconfined frock, or shirt, of coarse woolen, much spotted with tar, opened out far down the chest, revealing a soiled undergarment of what seemed the finest linen, edged, about the neck, with a narrow blue ribbon, sadly faded and worn. At this moment the young sailor's eye was again fixed on the whisperers, and Captain Delano thought he observed a lurking significance in it, as if silent signs, of some Freemason° sort, had that instant been interchanged.

This once more impelled his own glance in the direction of Don Benito, and, as before, he could not but infer that himself formed the subject of the conference. He paused. The sound of the hatchet-polishing fell on his ears. He cast another swift side-look at the two. They had the air of conspirators. In connection with the late questionings, and the incident of the young sailor, these things now begat such return of involuntary suspicion, that the singular guilelessness of the American could not endure it. Plucking up a gay and humorous expression, he crossed over to the two rapidly, saying:—"Ha, Don Benito, your black here seems high in your trust; a sort of privy-counselor, in fact."

Upon this, the servant looked up with a good-natured grin, but the master started as from a venomous bite. It was a moment or two before the Spaniard sufficiently recovered himself to reply; which he did, at last, with cold constraint:—"Yes, Señor, I have trust in Babo."

°*Freemason:* literally, a member of the international and ancient lodge of freemasonry. Reference here is to the bonds of sympathy and the secret signs expressing the same that pass among Freemasons.

Here Babo, changing his previous grin of mere animal humor into an intelligent smile, not ungratefully eyed his master.

Finding that the Spaniard now stood silent and reserved, as if involuntarily, or purposely giving hint that his guest's proximity was inconvenient just then, Captain Delano, unwilling to appear uncivil even to incivility itself, made some trivial remark and moved off; again and again turning over in his mind the mysterious demeanor of Don Benito Cereno.

He had descended from the poop, and, wrapped in thought, was passing near a dark hatchway, leading down into the steerage, when, perceiving motion there, he looked to see what moved. The same instant there was a sparkle in the shadowy hatchway, and he saw one of the Spanish sailors, prowling there, hurriedly placing his hand in the bosom of his frock, as if hiding something. Before the man could have been certain who it was that was passing, he slunk below out of sight. But enough was seen of him to make it sure that he was the same young sailor before noticed in the rigging.

What was that which so sparkled? thought Captain Delano. It was no lamp—no match—no live coal. Could it have been a jewel? But how come sailors with jewels?—or with silk-trimmed undershirts either? Has he been robbing the trunks of the dead cabin-passengers? But if so, he would hardly wear one of the stolen articles on board ship here. Ah, ah—if, now, that was, indeed, a secret sign I saw passing between this suspicious fellow and his captain awhile since; if I could only be certain that, in my uneasiness, my senses did not deceive me, then———

Here, passing from one suspicious thing to another, his mind revolved the strange questions put to him concerning his ship.

By a curious coincidence, as each point was recalled, the black wizards of Ashantee would strike up with their hatchets, as in ominous comment on the white stranger's thoughts. Pressed by such enigmas and portents, it would have been almost against nature, had not, even into the least distrustful heart, some ugly misgivings obtruded.

Observing the ship, now helplessly fallen into a current, with enchanted sails, drifting with increased rapidity seaward; and noting that, from a lately intercepted projection of the land, the sealer was hidden, the stout mariner began to quake at thoughts which he barely durst confess to himself. Above all, he began to feel a ghostly dread of Don Benito. And yet, when he roused himself, dilated his chest, felt himself strong on his legs, and coolly considered it—what did all these phantoms amount to?

Had the Spaniard any sinister scheme, it must have reference not so much to him (Captain Delano) as to his ship (the *Bachelor's Delight*). Hence the present drifting away of the one ship from the other, instead of favoring any such possible scheme, was, for the time, at least, opposed to it. Clearly any suspicion, combining such contradictions, must need be delusive. Besides, was it not absurd to think of a vessel in distress—a vessel by sickness almost dismanned of her crew—a vessel whose inmates were parched for water—was it not a thousand times absurd that such a craft should, at present, be of a piratical character; or her commander, either for himself or those under him, cherish any desire but for speedy relief and refreshment? But then, might not general distress, and thirst in particular, be affected? And might not that same undiminished Spanish crew, alleged to have perished off to a remnant, be at that very moment lurking in the hold? On heartbroken pretense of entreating a cup of cold water, fiends in human form had got into lonely dwellings, nor retired until a dark deed had been done. And among the Malay pirates, it was no unusual thing to lure ships after them into their treacherous harbors, or entice boarders from a declared enemy at sea, by the spectacle of thinly manned or vacant decks, beneath which prowled a hundred spears with yellow arms ready to upthrust them through the mats.° Not that Captain Delano had entirely credited such things. He had heard of them—and now, as stories, they recurred. The present destination of the ship was the anchorage. There she would be near his own vessel. Upon gaining that vicinity, might not the *Sam Dominick,* like a slumbering volcano, suddenly let loose energies now hid?

He recalled the Spaniard's manner while telling his story. There was a gloomy hesitancy and subterfuge about it. It was just the manner of one making up his tale for evil purposes, as he goes. But if that story was not true, what was the truth? That the ship had unlawfully come into the Spaniard's possession? But in many of its details, especially in reference to the more calamitous parts, such as the fatalities among the seamen, the consequent prolonged beating about, the past sufferings from obstinate calms, and still continued suffering from thirst; in all these points, as well as others, Don Benito's story had corroborated not only the wailing ejaculations of the indiscriminate multitude, white and black, but likewise—what seemed impossible to be counterfeit—by the very expression and play of every human feature which Captain Delano saw. If Don Benito's story was, throughout, an invention, then every soul on board, down to the youngest negress, was his carefully drilled recruit in the plot: an incredible inference. And yet, if there was ground for mistrusting his veracity, that inference was a legitimate one.

But those questions of the Spaniard. There, indeed, one might pause. Did they not seem put with much the same object with which the burglar or assassin, by daytime, reconnoiters the walls of a house? But, with ill purposes, to solicit such information openly of the chief person en-

---

°*mats:* here, hatch coverings (sometimes made of plaited hemp or canvas, sometimes of wooden grating)

dangered, and so, in effect, setting him on his guard; how unlikely a procedure was that? Absurd, then, to suppose that those questions had been prompted by evil designs. Thus, the same conduct, which, in this instance, had raised the alarm, served to dispel it. In short, scarce any suspicion or uneasiness, however apparently reasonable at the time, which was not now, with equally apparent reason, dismissed.

At last he began to laugh at his former forebodings; and laugh at the strange ship for, in its aspect, someway siding with them, as it were; and laugh, too, at the odd-looking blacks, particularly those old scissors-grinders, the Ashantees; and those bed-ridden old knitting women, the oakum-pickers; and almost at the dark Spaniard himself, the central hobgoblin of all.

For the rest, whatever in a serious way seemed enigmatical, was now good-naturedly explained away by the thought that, for the most part, the poor invalid scarcely knew what he was about; either sulking in black vapors, or putting idle questions without sense of object. Evidently, for the present, the man was not fit to be intrusted with the ship. On some benevolent plea withdrawing the command from him, Captain Delano would yet have to send her to Concepción,° in charge of his second mate, a worthy person and good navigator—a plan not more convenient for the *San Dominick* than for Don Benito; for, relieved from all anxiety, keeping wholly to his cabin, the sick man, under the good nursing of his servant, would, probably, by the end of the passage, be in a measure restored to health, and with that he should also be restored to authority.

Such were the American's thoughts. They were tranquilizing. There was a difference between the idea of Don Benito's darkly preordaining Captain Delano's fate, and Captain Delano's lightly arranging Don Benito's. Nevertheless, it was not without something of relief that the good seaman presently perceived his whale-boat in the distance. Its absence had been prolonged by unexpected detention at the sealer's side, as well as its returning trip lengthened by the continual recession of the goal.

The advancing speck was observed by the blacks. Their shouts attracted the attention of Don Benito, who, with a return of courtesy, approaching Captain Delano, expressed satisfaction at the coming of some supplies, slight and temporary as they must necessarily prove.

Captain Delano responded; but while doing so, his attention was drawn to something passing on the deck below: among the crowd climbing the landward bulwarks, anxiously watching the coming boat, two blacks, to all appearances accidentally incommoded by one of the sailors, violently pushed him aside, which the sailor someway resenting, they dashed him to the deck, despite the earnest cries of the oakum-pickers.

°*Concepcion:* a major city of Chile

"Don Benito," said Captain Delano quickly, "do you see what is going on there? Look!"

But, seized by his cough, the Spaniard staggered, with both hands to his face, on the point of falling. Captain Delano would have supported him, but the servant was more alert, who, with one hand sustaining his master, with the other applied the cordial. Don Benito restored, the black withdrew his support, slipping aside a little, but dutifully remaining within call of a whisper. Such discretion was here evinced as quite wiped away, in the visitor's eyes, any blemish of impropriety which might have attached to the attendant, from the indecorous conferences before mentioned; showing, too, that if the servant were to blame, it might be more the master's fault than his own, since, when left to himself, he could conduct thus well.

His glance called away from the spectacle of disorder to the more pleasing one before him, Captain Delano could not avoid again congratulating his host upon possessing such a servant, who, though perhaps a little too forward now and then, must upon the whole be invaluable to one in the invalid's situation.

"Tell me, Don Benito," he added, with a smile—"I should like to have your man here, myself—what will you take for him? Would fifty doubloons be any object?"

"Master wouldn't part with Babo for a thousand doubloons," murmured the black, overhearing the offer, and taking it in earnest, and, with the strange vanity of a faithful slave, appreciated by his master, scorning to hear so paltry a valuation put upon him by a stranger. But Don Benito, apparently hardly yet completely restored, and again interrupted by his cough, made but some broken reply.

Soon his physical distress became so great, affecting his mind, too, apparently, that, as if to screen the sad spectacle, the servant gently conducted his master below.

Left to himself, the American, to while away the time till his boat should arrive, would have pleasantly accosted some one of the few Spanish seamen he saw; but recalling something that Don Benito had said touching their ill conduct, he refrained; as a shipmaster indisposed to countenance cowardice or unfaithfulness in seamen.

While, with these thoughts, standing with eye directed forward towards that handful of sailors, suddenly he thought that one or two of them returned the glance and with a sort of meaning. He rubbed his eyes, and looked again; but again seemed to see the same thing. Under a new form, but more obscure than any previous one, the old suspicions recurred, but, in the absence of Don Benito, with less of panic than before. Despite the bad account given of the sailors, Captain Delano resolved forthwith to accost one of them. Descending the poop, he made his way through the blacks, his movement drawing a queer cry from the oakum-pickers, prompted by whom, the negroes, twitching each other aside, divided before him; but, as if curious to see what was the object of this deliberate visit to their Ghetto, closing in behind, in tolerable order, followed the white stranger up. His progress thus proclaimed as by mounted kings-at-arms,° and escorted as by a Kaffir° guard of honor, Captain Delano, assuming a good-humored, off-handed air, continued to advance; now and then saying a blithe word to the negroes, and his eye curiously surveying the white faces, here and there sparsely mixed in with the blacks, like stray white pawns venturously involved in the ranks of the chessmen opposed.

While thinking which of them to select for his purpose, he chanced to observe a sailor seated on the deck engaged in tarring the strap of a large block, a circle of blacks squatted round him inquisitively.

The mean employment of the man was in contrast with something superior in his figure. His hand, black with continually thrusting it into the tar-pot held for him by a negro, seemed not naturally allied to his face, a face which would have been a very fine one but for its haggardness. Whether this haggardness had aught to do with criminality, could not be determined; since, as intense heat and cold, though unlike, produce like sensations, so innocence and guilt, when, through casual association with mental pain, stamping any visible impress, use one seal—a hacked one.

Not again that this reflection occurred to Captain Delano at the time, charitable man as he was. Rather another idea. Because observing so singular a haggardness combined with a dark eye, averted as in trouble and shame, and then again recalling Don Benito's confessed ill opinion of his crew, insensibly he was operated upon by certain general notions which, while disconnecting pain and abashment from virtue, invariably link them with vice.

If indeed, there be any wickedness on board this ship, thought Captain Delano, be sure that man there has fouled his hand in it, even as now he fouls it in the pitch. I don't like to accost him. I will speak to this other, this old Jack here on the windlass.

He advanced to an old Barcelona° tar, in ragged red breeches and dirty night-cap, cheeks trenched and bronzed, whiskers dense as thorn hedges. Seated between two sleepy-looking Africans, this mariner, like his younger shipmate, was employed upon some rigging—splicing a cable—the sleepy-looking blacks performing the inferior function of holding the outer parts of the ropes for him.

Upon Captain Delano's approach, the man at once hung his head below its previous level; the one necessary for business. It appeared as if he desired to be thought absorbed, with more than common fidelity, in his

---

°*kings-at-arms:* chief heralds °*Kaffir:* the name of a South African tribe °*Barcelona:* a Spanish seaport

task. Being addressed, he glanced up, but with what seemed a furtive, diffident air, which sat strangely enough on his weather-beaten visage, much as if a grizzly bear, instead of growling and biting, should simper and cast sheep's eyes. He was asked several questions concerning the voyage —questions purposely referring to several particulars in Don Benito's narrative, not previously corroborated by those impulsive cries greeting the visitor on the first coming on board. The questions were briefly answered, confirming all that remained to be confirmed of the story. The negroes about the windlass joined in with the old sailor; but, as they became talkative, he by degrees became mute, and at length quite glum, seemed morosely unwilling to answer more questions, and yet, all the while, this ursine air was somehow mixed with his sheepish one.

Despairing of getting into unembarrassed talk with such a centaur,° Captain Delano, after glancing round for a more promising countenance, but seeing none, spoke pleasantly to the blacks to make way for him; and so, amid various grins and grimaces, returned to the poop, feeling a little strange at first, he could hardly tell why, but upon the whole with regained confidence in Benito Cereno.

How plainly, thought he, did that old whiskerando yonder betray a consciousness of ill desert. No doubt, when he saw me coming, he dreaded lest I, appraised by his captain of the crew's general misbehavior, came with sharp words for him, and so down with his head. And yet —and yet, now that I think of it, that very fellow, if I err not, was one of those who seemed so earnestly eyeing me here awhile since. Ah, these currents spin one's head round almost as much as they do the ship. Ha, there now's a pleasant sort of sunny sight; quite sociable, too.

His attention had been drawn back to a slumbering negress, partly disclosed through the lacework of some rigging, lying, with youthful limbs carelessly disposed, under the lee of the bulwarks, like a doe in the shade of a woodland rock. Sprawling at her lapped breasts, was her wide-awake fawn, stark naked, its black little body half lifted from the deck, crosswise with its dam's; its hands, like two paws, clambering upon her; its mouth and nose ineffectually rooting to get at the mark; and meantime giving a vexatious half-grunt, blending with the composed snore of the negress.

The uncommon vigor of the child at length roused the mother. She started up, at a distance facing Captain Delano. But as if not at all concerned at the attitude in which she had been caught, delightedly she caught the child up, with maternal transports, covering it with kisses.

There's naked nature, now; pure tenderness and love, thought Captain Delano, well pleased.

This incident prompted him to remark the other negresses more

---

°*centaur:* one of a race half man and half horse; said to be irascible and gruff in temper (Greek mythology)

particularly than before. He was gratified with their manners: like most uncivilized women, they seemed at once tender of heart and tough of constitution; equally ready to die for their infants or fight for them. Unsophisticated as leopardesses; loving as doves. Ah! thought Captain Delano, these, perhaps, are some of the very women whom Ledyard° saw in Africa, and gave such a noble account of.

These natural sights somehow insensibly deepened his confidence and ease. At last he looked to see how his boat was getting on; but it was still pretty remote. He turned to see if Don Benito had returned; but he had not.

To change the scene, as well as to please himself with a leisurely observation of the coming boat, stepping over into the mizzen-chains, he clambered his way into the starboard quarter-gallery°—one of those abandoned Venetian-looking water-balconies previously mentioned—retreats cut off from the deck. As his foot pressed the half-damp, half-dry sea-mosses matting the place, and a chance phantom cats-paw°—an islet of breeze, unheralded, unfollowed—as this ghostly cat-paw came fanning his cheek; as his glance fell upon the row of small, round dead-lights—all closed like coppered eyes of the coffined—and the state-cabin door, once connecting with the gallery, even as the dead-lights had once looked out upon it, but now calked fast like a sarcophagus lid; and to a purple-back, tarred-over panel, threshold, and post; and he bethought him of the time, when that state-cabin and this state-balcony had heard the voices of the Spanish king's officers, and the forms of the Lima viceroy's° daughters had perhaps leaned where he stood—as these and other images flitted through his mind, as the cats-paw through the calm, gradually he felt rising a dreamy inquietude, like that of one who alone on the prairie feels unrest from the repose of the noon.

He leaned against the carved balustrade, again looking off toward his boat; but found his eye falling upon the ribbon grass, trailing along the ship's waterline, straight as a border of green box; and parterres° of seaweed, broad ovals and crescents, floating nigh and far, with what seemed long formal alleys between, crossing the terraces of swells, and sweeping round as if leading to the grottoes below. And overhanging all was the balustrade by his arm, which, partly stained with pitch and partly embossed with moss, seemed the charred ruin of some summer-house in a grand garden long running to waste.

°*Ledyard:* John Ledyard (1751-1788), a writer of travel books °*quarter-gallery:* a walkway along the side astern (or on the "quarter") of the ship. Melville goes on to suggest its likeness to the balconies that hang over the canals of Venice from the bankside houses. °*cat's-paw:* a light breeze that ruffles a comparatively small area of water surface °*the Lima viceroy:* the headquarters of the King's deputy, or viceroy, for all Spanish possessions in South America was once in Lima, Peru. °*parterrers:* ornamental garden arrangements

Trying to break one charm, he was but becharmed anew. Though upon the wide sea, he seemed in some far inland country; prisoner in some deserted château, left to stare at empty grounds, and peer out at vague roads, where never wagon or wayfarer passed.

But these enchantments were a little disenchanted as his eye fell on the corroded main-chains. Of an ancient style, massy and rusty in link, shackle and bolt, they seemed even more fit for the ship's present business than the one for which she had been built.

Presently he thought something moved nigh the chains. He rubbed his eyes, and looked hard. Groves of rigging were about the chains; and there, peering from behind a great stay,° like an Indian from behind a hemlock, a Spanish sailor, a marlinspike° in his hand, was seen, who made what seemed an imperfect gesture towards the balcony, but immediately, as if alarmed by some advancing step along the deck within, vanished into the recesses of the hempen forest, like a poacher.

What meant this? Something the man had sought to communicate, unbeknown to any one, even to his captain. Did the secret involve aught unfavorable to his captain? Were those previous misgivings of Captain Delano's about to be verified? Or, in his haunted mood at the moment, had some random, unintentional motion of the man, while busy with the stay, as if repairing it, been mistaken for a significant beckoning?

Not unbewildered, again he gazed off for his boat. But it was temporarily hidden by a rocky spur of the isle. As with some eagerness he bent forward, watching for the first shooting view of its beak, the balustrade gave way before him like charcoal. Had he not clutched an outreaching rope he would have fallen into the sea. The crash, though feeble, and the fall, though hollow, of the rotten fragments, must have been overheard. He glanced up. With sober curiosity peering down upon him was one of the old oakum-pickers, slipped from his perch to an outside boom; while below the old negro, and, invisible to him, reconnoitering from a port-hole like a fox from the mouth of its den, crouched the Spanish sailor again. From something suddenly suggested by the man's air, the mad idea now darted into Captain Delano's mind, that Don Benito's plea of indisposition, in withdrawing below, was but a pretense: that he was engaged there maturing his plot, of which the sailor, by some means gaining an inkling, had a mind to warn the stranger against; incited, it may be, by gratitude for a kind word on first boarding the ship. Was it from foreseeing some possible interference like this, that Don Benito had, beforehand, given such a bad character of his sailors, while praising the negroes; though, indeed, the former seemed as docile as the latter the contrary? The whites, too, by nature, were the shrewder race. A man with some evil design, would he not be likely to speak well

°*stay:* part of the standing rigging that holds the masts in place °*marlinspike:* pointed hand-tool used for splicing

of that stupidity which was blind to his depravity, and malign that intelligence from which it might not be hidden? Not unlikely, perhaps. But if the whites had dark secrets concerning Don Benito, could then Don Benito be any way in complicity with the blacks? But they were too stupid. Besides, who ever heard of a white so far a renegade as to apostatize from his very species almost, by leaguing in against it with negroes? These difficulties recalled former ones. Lost in their mazes, Captain Delano, who had now regained the deck, was uneasily advancing along it, when he observed a new face; an aged sailor seated cross-legged near the main hatchway. His skin was shrunk up with wrinkles like a pelican's empty pouch; his hair frosted; his countenance grave and composed. His hands were full of ropes, which he was working into a large knot. Some blacks were about him obligingly dipping the strands for him, here and there, as the exigencies of the operation demanded.

Captain Delano crossed over to him, and stood in silence surveying the knot; his mind, by a not uncongenial transition, passing from its own entanglements to those of the hemp. For intricacy, such a knot he had never seen in an American ship, nor indeed any other. The old man looked like an Egyptian priest, making Gordian knots° for the temple of Ammon. The knot seemed a combination of double-bowline-knot, treble-crown-knot, back-handed-well-knot, knot-in-and-out-knot, and jamming-knot.

At last, puzzled to comprehend the meaning of such a knot, Captain Delano addressed the knotter:—

"What are you knotting there, my man?"

"The knot," was the brief reply, without looking up.

"So it seems; but what is it for?"

"For some one else to undo," muttered back the old man, playing his fingers harder than ever, the knot being now nearly completed.

While Captain Delano stood watching him, suddenly the old man threw the knot towards him, saying in broken English—the first heard in the ship—something to this effect: "Undo it, cut it, quick." It was said lowly, but with such condensation of rapidity, that the long, slow words in Spanish, which had preceded and followed, almost operated as covers to the brief English between.

For a moment, knot in hand, and knot in head, Captain Delano stood mute; while, without further heeding him, the old man was now intent upon other ropes. Presently there was a slight stir behind Captain Delano. Turning, he saw the chained negro, Atufal, standing quietly there. The next moment the old sailor rose, muttering, and, followed by his subordi-

°*Gordian knots:* Allusion here is to the intricate knot tied on the order of Gordius, a king of ancient Phyrgia, who prophesied that the man who untied it would rule all Asia. According to legend, Alexander the Great "solved" the problem by cutting through the knot with his sword.

nate negroes, removed to the forward part of the ship, where in the crowd he disappeared.

An elderly negro, in a clout° like an infant's, and with a pepper and salt head, and a kind of attorney air, now approached Captain Delano. In tolerable Spanish, and with a good-natured, knowing wink, he informed him that the old knotter was simple-witted, but harmless; often playing his odd tricks. The negro concluded by begging the knot, for of course the stranger would not care to be troubled with it. Unconsciously, it was handed to him. With a sort of congé,° the negro received it, and, turning his back, ferreted into it like a detective custom-house officer after smuggled laces. Soon, with some African word, equivalent to pshaw, he tossed the knot overboard.

All this is very queer now, thought Captain Delano, with a qualmish sort of emotion; but, as one feeling incipient sea-sickness, he strove, by ignoring the symptoms, to get rid of the malady. Once more he looked off for his boat. To his delight, it was now again in view, leaving the rocky spur astern.

The sensation here experienced, after at first relieving his uneasiness, with unforeseen efficacy soon began to remove it. The less distant sight of that well-known boat—showing it, not as before, half blended with the haze, but with outline defined, so that its individuality, like a man's, was manifest; that boat, *Rover* by name, which, though now in strange seas, had often pressed the beach of Captain Delano's home, and, brought to its threshold for repairs, had familiarly lain there, as a Newfoundland dog; the sight of that household boat evoked a thousand trustful associations, which, contrasted with previous suspicions, filled him not only with lightsome confidence, but somehow with half humorous self-reproaches at his former lack of it.

"What, I, Amasa Delano—Jack of the Beach, as they called me when a lad—I, Amasa; the same that, duck-satchel° in hand, used to paddle along the water-side to the schoolhouse made from the old hulk—I, little Jack of the Beach, that used to go berrying with cousin Nat and the rest; I to be murdered here at the ends of the earth, on board a haunted pirate-ship by a horrible Spaniard? Too nonsensical to think of! Who would murder Amasa Delano? His conscience is clean. There is some one above. Fie, fie, Jack of the Beach! you are a child indeed; a child of the second childhood, old boy; you are beginning to dote and drool, I'm afraid."

Light of heart and foot, he stepped aft, and there was met by Don Benito's servant, who, with a pleasing expression, responsive to his own present feelings, informed him that his master had recovered from the effects of his coughing fit, and had just ordered him to go present his

---

°*clout:* a loin cloth like a baby's diapers °*congé:* gesture of farewell °*duck-satchel:* bag made of "duck" or light canvas, presumably used in this case to hold schoolbooks

compliments to his good guest, Don Amasa, and say that he (Don Benito) would soon have the happiness to rejoin him.

There now, do you mark that? again thought Captain Delano, walking the poop. What a donkey I was. This kind gentleman who here sends me his kind compliments, he, but ten minutes ago, dark-lantern in hand, was dodging round some old grindstone in the hold, sharpening a hatchet for me, I thought. Well, well; these long calms have a morbid effect on the mind, I've often heard, though I never believed it before. Ha! glancing towards the boat; there's *Rover;* good dog; a white bone in her mouth. A pretty big bone though, seems to me.—What? Yes, she has fallen afoul of the bubbling tide-rip there. It sets her the other way, too, for the time. Patience.

It was now about noon, though, from the greyness of everything, it seemed to be getting towards dusk.

The calm was confirmed. In the far distance away from the influence of land, the leaden ocean seemed laid out and leaded up, its course finished, soul gone, defunct. But the current from landward, where the ship was, increased; silently sweeping her further and further towards the tranced waters beyond.

Still, from his knowledge of those latitudes, cherishing hopes of a breeze, and a fair and fresh one, at any moment, Captain Delano, despite present prospects, buoyantly counted upon bringing the *San Dominick* safely to anchor ere night. The distance swept over was nothing; since, with a good wind, ten minutes' sailing would retrace more than sixty minutes' drifting. Meantime, one moment turning to mark *Rover* fighting the tide-rip, and the next to see Don Benito approaching, he continued walking the poop.

Gradually he felt a vexation arising from the delay of his boat; this soon merged into uneasiness; and at last—his eye falling continually, as from a stage-box into the pit, upon the strange crowd before and below him, and, by and by, recognizing there the face—now composed to indifference—of the Spanish sailor who had seemed to beckon from the main-chains—something of his old trepidations returned.

Ah, thought he—gravely enough—this is like the ague: because it went off, it follows not that it won't come back.

Though ashamed of the relapse, he could not altogether subdue it; and so, exerting his good nature to the utmost, insensibly he came to a compromise.

Yes, this is a strange craft; a strange history, too, and strange folks on board. But—nothing more.

By way of keeping his mind out of mischief till the boat should arrive, he tried to occupy it with turning over and over, in a purely speculative sort of way, some lesser peculiarities of the captain and crew. Among others, four curious points recurred:

First, the affair of the Spanish lad assailed with a knife by the slave boy; an act winked at by Don Benito. Second, the tyranny in Don Benito's treatment of Atufal, the black; as if a child should lead a bull of the Nile by the ring in his nose. Third, the trampling of the sailor by the two negroes; a piece of insolence passed over without so much as a reprimand. Fourth, the cringing submission to their master, of all the ship's underlings, mostly blacks; as if by the least inadvertence they feared to draw down his despotic displeasure.

Coupling these points, they seemed somewhat contradictory. But what then, thought Captain Delano, glancing towards his now nearing boat—what then? Why, Don Benito is a very capricious commander. But he is not the first of the sort I have seen; though it's true he rather exceedes any other. But as a nation—continued he in his reveries—these Spaniards are all an odd set; the very word Spaniard has a curious, conspirator, Guy-Fawkish° twang to it. And yet, I dare say, Spaniards in the main are as good folks as any in Duxbury, Massachusetts. Ah good! At last *Rover* has come.

As, with its welcome freight, the boat touched the side, the oakum-pickers, with venerable gestures, sought to restrain the blacks, who, at the sight of three gurried° water casks in its bottom, and a pile of wilted pumpkins in its bow, hung over the bulwarks in disorderly raptures.

Don Benito, with his servant, now appeared; his coming, perhaps, hastened by hearing the noise. Of him Captain Delano sought permission to serve out the water, so that all might share alike, and none injure themselves by unfair excess. But sensible, and, on Don Benito's account, kind as this offer was, it was received with what seemed impatience; as if aware that he lacked energy as a commander, Don Benito, with the true jealousy of weakness, resented as an affront any interference. So, at least, Captain Delano inferred.

In another moment the casks were being hoisted in, when some of the eager negroes accidentally jostled Captain Delano, where he stood by the gangway; so that, unmindful of Don Benito, yielding to the impulse of the moment, with good-natured authority he bade the blacks stand back; to enforce his words making use of a half-mirthful, half-menacing gesture. Instantly the blacks paused, just where they were, each negro and negress suspended in his or her posture, exactly as the word had found them—for a few seconds continuing so—while, as between the responsive posts of a telegraph, an unknown syllable ran from man to man among the perched oakum-pickers. While the visitor's attention was fixed by this scene, suddenly the hatchet-polishers half rose, and a rapid cry came from Don Benito.

°*Guy-Fawkish:* Reference is to Guy Fawkes (1570-1606), participant in a plot to blow up the Houses of Parliament in London. His name has been associated with conspiracy ever since. °*gurried:* lashed with ropes to facilitate handling and hoisting

Thinking that at the signal of the Spaniard he was about to be massacred, Captain Delano would have sprung for his boat, but paused, as the oakum-pickers, dropping down into the crowd with earnest exclamations, forced every white and every negro back, at the same moment, with gestures friendly and familiar, almost jocose, bidding him, in substance, not be a fool. Simultaneously the hatchet-polishers resumed their seats, quietly as so many tailors, and at once, as if nothing had happened, the work of hoisting in the casks was resumed, whites and blacks singing at the tackle.

Captain Delano glanced towards Don Benito. As he saw his meager form in the act of recovering itself from reclining in the servant's arms, into which the agitated invalid had fallen, he could not but marvel at the panic by which himself had been surprised, on the darting supposition that such a commander, who, upon a legitimate occasion, so trivial, too, as it now appeared, could lose all self-command, was, with energetic iniquity, going to bring about his murder.

The casks being on deck, Captain Delano was handed a number of jars and cups by one of the steward's aids, who, in the name of his captain, entreated him to do as he had proposed—dole out the water. He complied, with republican impartiality as to this republican element, which always seeks one level, serving the oldest white no better than the youngest black; excepting, indeed, poor Don Benito, whose condition, if not rank, demanded an extra allowance. To him, in the first place, Captain Delano presented a fair pitcher of the fluid; but, thirsting as he was for it, the Spaniard quaffed not a drop until after several grave bows and salutes. A reciprocation of courtesies which the sight-loving Africans hailed with clapping of hands.

Two of the less wilted pumpkins being reserved for the cabin table, the residue were minced up on the spot for the general regalement. But the soft bread, sugar, and bottled cider, Captain Delano would have given the whites alone, and in chief Don Benito; but the latter objected; which disinterestedness not a little pleased the American; and so mouthfuls all around were given alike to whites and blacks; excepting one bottle of cider, which Babo insisted upon setting aside for his master.

Here it may be observed that as, on the first visit of the boat, the American had not permitted his men to board the ship, neither did he now; being unwilling to add to the confusion of the decks.

Not uninfluenced by the peculiar good-humor at present prevailing, and for the time oblivious of any but benevolent thoughts, Captain Delano, who, from recent indications, counted upon a breeze within an hour or two at furthest, dispatched the boat back to the sealer, with orders for all the hands that could be spared immediately to set about rafting casks to the watering-place and filling them. Likewise he bade word be carried to his chief officer, that if, against present expectation, the ship was not brought to anchor by sunset, he need be under no concern; for as there was to be a full moon that night, he (Captain Delano) would remain on board ready to play the pilot, come the wind soon or late.

As the two Captains stood together, observing the departing boat—the servant, as it happened, having just spied a spot on his master's velvet sleeve, and silently engaged rubbing it out—the American expressed his regrets that the *San Dominick* had no boats; none, at least, but the unseaworthy old hulk of the long-boat, which, warped as a camel's skeleton in the desert, and almost as bleached, lay pot-wise inverted amidships, one side a little tipped, furnishing a subterraneous sort of den for family groups of the blacks, mostly women and small children; who, squatting on old mats below, or perched above in the dark dome, on the elevated seats, were descried, some distance within, like a social circle of bats, sheltering in some friendly cave; at intervals, ebon flights of naked boys and girls, three or four years old, darting in and out of the den's mouth.

"Had you three or four boats now, Don Benito," said Captain Delano, "I think that, by tugging at the oars, your negroes here might help along matters some. Did you sail from port without boats, Don Benito?"

"They were stove in the gales, Señor."

"That was bad. Many men, too, you lost then. Boats and men. Those must have been hard gales, Don Benito."

"Past all speech," cringed the Spaniard.

"Tell me, Don Benito," continued his companion with increased interest, "tell me, were these gales immediately off the pitch of Cape Horn?"

"Cape Horn?—who spoke of Cape Horn?"

"Yourself did, when giving me an account of your voyage," answered Captain Delano, with almost equal astonishment at this eating of his own words, even as he ever seemed eating his own heart, on the part of the Spaniard. "You yourself, Don Benito, spoke of Cape Horn," he emphatically repeated.

The Spaniard turned, in a sort of stooping posture, pausing an instant, as one about to make a plunging exchange of elements, as from air to water. At this moment a messenger, a white, hurried by, in the regular performance of his function carrying the last expired half-hour forward to the forecastle, from the cabin time-piece, to have it struck at the ship's large bell.

"Master," said the servant, discontinuing his work on the coat sleeve, and addressing the rapt Spaniard with a sort of timid apprehensiveness, as one charged with a duty, the discharge of which, it was foreseen, would prove irksome to the very person who had imposed it, and for whose benefit it was intended, "master told me never mind where he was, or how engaged, always to remind him, to a minute, when shaving time comes. Miguel has gone to strike the half-hour afternoon. It is *now*, master. Will master go into the cuddy°?"

"Ah—yes," answered the Spaniard, starting, as from dreams into realities; then turning upon Captain Delano, he said that ere long he would resume the conversation.

"Then if master means to talk more to Don Amasa," said the servant, "why not let Don Amasa sit by master in the cuddy, and master can talk, and Don Amasa can listen, while Babo here lathers and strops."

"Yes," said Captain Delano, not unpleased with this sociable plan, "yes, Don Benito, unless you had rather not, I will go with you."

"Be it so, Señor."

As the three passed aft, the American could not but think it another strange instance of his host's capriciousness, this being shaved with such uncommon punctuality in the middle of the day. But he deemed it more than likely that the servant's anxious fidelity had something to do with the matter; inasmuch as the timely interruption served to rally his master from the mood which had evidently been coming upon him.

The place called the cuddy was a light deck-cabin formed by the poop, a sort of attic to the large cabin below. Part of it had formerly been the quarters of the officers; but since their death all the partitionings had been thrown down, and the whole interior converted into one spacious and airy marine hall; for absence of fine furniture and picturesque disarray of odd appurtenances, somewhat answering to the wide, cluttered hall of some eccentric bachelor-squire in the country, who hangs his shooting-jacket and tobacco-pouch on deer antlers, and keeps his fishing-rod, tongs, and walking-stick in the same corner.

The similitude was heightened, if not originally suggested, by glimpses of the surrounding sea; since, in one aspect, the country and the ocean seem cousins-german.°

The floor of the cuddy was matted. Overhead, four or five old muskets were stuck into horizontal holes along the beams. On one side was a claw-footed old table lashed to the deck; a thumbed missal on it, and over it a small, meager crucifix attached to the bulkhead. Under the table lay a dented cutlass or two, with a hacked harpoon, among some melancholy old rigging, like a heap of poor friars' girdles. There were also two long, sharp, ribbed settees of Malacca cane, black with age, and uncomfortable to look at as inquisitors' racks, with a large, misshapen armchair, which, furnished with a rude barber's crotch at the back, working with a screw, seemed some grotesque engine of torment. A flag-locker was in one corner, open, exposing various colored bunting, some rolled up, others half unrolled, still others tumbled. Opposite was a cumbrous washstand, of black mahogany, all of one block, with a pedestal, like a font, and over it a railed shelf, containing combs, brushes, and other implements of the toilet. A torn hammock of stained grass swung near; the sheets tossed,

---

°*cuddy:* cabin °*cousins-german:* first cousins

and the pillow wrinkled up like a brow, as if whoever slept here slept but illy, with alternate visitations of sad thoughts and bad dreams.

The further extremity of the cuddy, overhanging the ship's stern, was pierced with three openings, windows or port-holes, according as men or cannon might peer, socially or unsocially, out of them. At present neither men nor cannon were seen, though huge ring-bolts and other rusty iron fixtures of the woodwork hinted of twenty-four-pounders.

Glancing towards the hammock as he entered, Captain Delano said, "You sleep here, Don Benito?"

"Yes, Señor, since we got into mild weather."

"This seems a sort of dormitory, sitting room, sail-loft, chapel, armory, and private closet all together, Don Benito," added Captain Delano, looking round.

"Yes, Señor; events have not been favorable to much order in my arrangements."

Here the servant, napkin on arm, made a motion as if waiting his master's good pleasure. Don Benito signified his readiness, when, seating him in the Malacca armchair, and for the guest's convenience drawing opposite one of the settees, the servant commenced operations by throwing back his master's collar and loosening his cravat.

There is something in the negro which, in a peculiar way, fits him for avocations about one's person. Most negroes are natural valets and hairdressers; taking to the comb and brush congenially as to the castanets, and flourishing them apparently with almost equal satisfaction. There is, too, a smooth tact about them in this employment, with a marvelous, noiseless, gliding briskness, not ungraceful in its way, singularly pleasing to behold, and still more so to be the manipulated subject of. And above all is the great gift of good humor. Not the mere grin or laugh is here meant. Those were unsuitable. But a certain easy cheerfulness, harmonious in every glance and gesture; as though God had set the whole negro to some pleasant tune.

When to this is added the docility arising from the unaspiring contentment of a limited mind, and that susceptibility of blind attachment sometimes inhering in indisputable inferiors, one readily perceives why those hypochondriacs, Johnson and Byron°—it may be, something like the hypochondriac Benito Cereno—took to their hearts, almost to the exclusion of the entire white race, their serving men, the negroes, Barber and Fletcher. But if there be that in the negro which exempts him from the inflicted sourness of the morbid or cynical mind, how, in his most prepossessing aspects, must he appear to a benevolent one? When at ease

---

°*those hypochondriacs, Johnson and Byron:* Dr. Samuel Johnson (1709-1784) was literary dictator of eighteenth-century London. George Gordon, Lord Byron (1788-1824) was one of the most notable among the English poets of the Romantic period. Both men tended to take a morbid concern with their health

with respect to exterior things, Captain Delano's nature was not only benign, but familiarly and humorously so. At home, he had often taken rare satisfaction in sitting in his door, watching some free man of color at his work or play. If on a voyage he chanced to have a black sailor, invariably he was on chatty and half-gamesome terms with him. In fact, like most men of a good, blithe heart, Captain Delano took to negroes, not philanthropically, but genially, just as other men to Newfoundland dogs.

Hitherto, the circumstances in which he found the *San Dominick* had repressed the tendency. But in the cuddy, relieved from his former uneasiness, and, for various reasons, more sociably inclined than at any previous period of the day, and seeing the colored servant, napkin on arm, so debonair about his master, in a business so familiar as that of shaving, too, all his old weakness for negroes returned.

Among other things, he was amused with an odd instance of the African love of bright colors and fine shows, in the black's informally taking from the flag-locker a great piece of bunting of all hues, and lavishly tucking it under his master's chin for an apron.

The mode of shaving among the Spaniards is a little different from what it is with other nations. They have a basin, specifically called a barber's basin, which on one side is scooped out, so as accurately to receive the chin, against which it is closely held in lathering; which is done, not with a brush, but with soap dipped in the water of the basin and rubbed on the face.

In the present instance salt water was user for lack of better; and the parts lathered were only the upper lip, and low down under the throat, all the rest being cultivated beard.

The preliminaries being somewhat novel to Captain Delano, he sat curiously eyeing them, so that no conversation took place, nor, for the present, did Don Benito appear disposed to renew any.

Setting down his basin, the negro searched among the razors, as for the sharpest, and having found it, gave it an additional edge by expertly stropping it on the firm, smooth, oily skin of his open palm; he then made a gesture as if to begin, but midway stood suspended for an instant, one hand elevating the razor, the other professionally dabbling among the bubbling suds on the Spaniard's lank neck. Not unaffected by the close sight of the gleaming steel, Don Benito nervously shuddered, his usual ghastliness was heightened by the lather, which lather, again, was intensified in its hue by the contrasting sootiness of the negro's body. Altogether the scene was somewhat peculiar, at least to Captain Delano, nor, as he saw the two thus postured, could he resist the vagary, that in the black he saw a headsman, and in the white a man at the block. But this was one of those antic conceits, appearing and vanishing in a breath, from which, perhaps, the best regulated mind is not always free.

Meantime the agitation of the Spaniard had a little loosened the bunting from around him, so that one broad fold swept curtainlike over the chair-arm to the floor, revealing, amid a profusion of armorial bars and groundcolors—black, blue, and yellow—a closed castle in a blood-red field diagonal with a lion rampant in a white.

"The castle and the lion," exclaimed Captain Delano—"why, Don Benito, this is the flag of Spain you use here. It's well it's only I, and not the King, that sees this," he added, with a smile, "but,"—turning towards the black— "it's all one, I suppose, so the colors be gay," which playful remark did not fail somewhat to tickle the negro.

"Now, master," he said, readjusting the flag, and pressing the head gently further back into the crotch of the chair; "now, master," and the steel glanced nigh that throat.

Again Don Benito faintly shuddered.

"You must not shake so, master. See, Don Amasa, master always shakes when I shave him. And yet master knows I never yet have drawn blood, though it's true, if master will shake so, I may some of these times. Now, master," he continued. "And now, Don Amasa, please go on with your talk about the gale, and all that; master can hear, and, between times, master can answer."

"Ah yes, these gales," said Captain Delano; "but the more I think of your voyage, Don Benito, the more I wonder, not at the gales, terrible as they must have been, but at the disastrous interval following them. For here, by your account, have you been these two months and more getting from Cape Horn to Santa Maria, a distance which I myself, with a good wind, have sailed in a few days. True, you had calms, and long ones, but to be becalmed for two months, that is, at least, unusual. Why Don Benito, had almost any other gentleman told me such a story, I should have been half disposed to a little incredulity."

Here an involuntary expression came over the Spaniard, similiar to that just before on the deck, and whether it was the start he gave, or a sudden gawky roll of the hull in the calm, or a momentary unsteadiness of the servant's hand, however, it was, just then the razor drew blood, spots of which stained the creamy lather under the throat: immediately the black barber drew back his steel, and, remaining in his professional attitude, back to Captain Delano, and face to Don Benito, held up the trickling razor, saying, with a sort of half humorous sorrow, "See, master—you shook so—here's Babo's first blood."

No sword drawn before James the First of England,° no assassination in that timid King's presence, could have produced a more terrified aspect than was now presented by Don Benito.

°*James the First of England:* Obsessedly fearful that he would be assassinated, James I (1566-1625) would not or could not endure the sight of blood or naked steel. (He died of natural causes.)

Poor fellow, thought Captain Delano, so nervous he can't even bear the sight of barber's blood; and this unstrung, sick man, is it credible that I should have imagined he meant to spill all my blood, who can't endure the sight of one little drop of his own? Surely, Amasa Delano, you have been beside yourself this day. Tell it not when you get home, sappy Amasa. Well, well, he looks like a murderer, doesn't he? More like as if himself were to be done for. Well, well, this day's experience shall be a good lesson.

Meantime, while these things were running through the honest seaman's mind, the servant had taken the napkin from his arm, and to Don Benito had said—"But answer Don Amasa, please, master, while I wipe this ugly stuff off the razor, and strop it again."

As he said the words, his face was turned half round, so as to be alike visible to the Spaniard and the American, and seemed, by its expression, to hint, that he was desirous, by getting his master to go on with the conversation, considerately to withdraw his attention from the recent annoying accident. As if glad to snatch the offered relief, Don Benito resumed, rehearsing to Captain Delano, that not only were the calms of unusual duration, but the ship had fallen in with obstinate currents; and other things he added, some of which were but repetitions of former statements, to explain how it came to pass that the passage from Cape Horn to Santa Maria had been so exceedingly long; now and then mingling with his words, incidental praises, less qualified than before, to the blacks, for their general good conduct. These particulars were not given consecutively, the servant, at convenient times, using his razor, and so, between the intervals of shaving, the story and panegryic went on with more than usual huskiness.

To Captain Delano's imagination, now again not wholly at rest, there was something so hollow in the Spaniard's manner, with apparently some reciprocal hollowness in the servant's dusky comment of silence, that the idea flashed across him, that possibly master and man, for some unknown purpose, were acting out, both in word and deed, nay, to the very tremor of Don Benito's limbs, some juggling play before him. Neither did the suspicion of collusion lack apparent support, from the fact of those whispered conferences before mentioned. But then, what could be the object of enacting this play of the barber before him? At last, regarding the notion as a whimsy, insensibly suggested, perhaps, by the theatrical aspect of Don Benito in his harlequin ensign, Captain Delano speedily banished it.

The shaving over, the servant bestirred himself with a small bottle of scented waters, pouring a few drops on the head, and then diligently rubbing; the vehemence of the exercise causing the muscles of his face to twitch rather strangely.

His next operation was with comb, scissors, and brush; going round and round, smoothing a curl here clipping an unruly whisker hair there, giving a graceful sweep to the temple-lock, with other impromptu touches evincing the hand of a master; while, like any resigned gentleman in barber's hands, Don Benito bore all, much less uneasily, at least, than he had done the razoring; indeed, he sat so pale and rigid now, that the negro seemed a Nubian sculptor finishing off a white statue-head.

All being over at last, the standard of Spain removed, tumbled up, and tossed back into the flag-locker, the negro's warm breath blowing away any stray hair which might have lodged down his master's neck; collar and cravat readjusted; a speck of lint whisked off the velvet lapel; all this being done, backing off a little space, and pausing with an expression of subdued self-complacency, the servant for a moment surveyed his master, as, in toilet at least, the creature of his own tasteful hands.

Captain Delano playfully complimented him upon his achievement; at the same time congratulating Don Benito.

But neither sweet waters, nor shampooing, nor fidelity, nor sociality, delighted the Spaniard. Seeing him relapsing into forbidding gloom, and still remaining seated, Captain Delano, thinking that his presence was undesired just then, withdrew, on pretense of seeing whether, as he had prophesied, any signs of a breeze were visible.

Walking forward to the main-mast, he stood awhile thinking over the scene, and not without some undefined misgivings, when he heard a noise near the cuddy, and turning, saw the negro, his hand to his cheek. Advancing, Captain Delano perceived that the cheek was bleeding. He was about to ask the cause, when the negro's wailing soliloquy enlightened him.

"Ah, when will master get better from his sickness; only the sour heart that sour sickness breeds made him serve Babo so; cutting Babo with the razor, because, only by accident, Babo had given master one little scratch; and for the first time in so many a day, too. Ah, ah, ah," holding his hand to his face.

It is possible, thought Captain Delano; was it to wreak in private his Spanish spite against this poor friend of his, that Don Benito, by his sullen manner, impelled me to withdraw? Ah, this slavery breeds ugly passions in man.—Poor fellow!

He was about to speak in sympathy to the negro, but with a timid reluctance he now reentered the cuddy. Presently master and man came forth; Don Benito leaning on his servant as if nothing had happened.

But a sort of love quarrel, after, all, thought Captain Delano.

He accosted Don Benito, and they slowly walked together. They had gone but a few paces, when the steward—a tall, rajah-looking mulatto, orientally set off with a pagoda turban formed by three or four Madras handkerchiefs wound about his head, tier on tier—approaching with a salaam, announced lunch in the cabin.

On their way thither, the two captains were preceded by the mulatto, who, turning round as he advanced, with continual smiles and bows, ushered them on, a display of elegance which quite completed the insignificance of the small bare-headed Babo, who, as if not unconscious of inferiority, eyed askance the graceful steward. But in part, Captain Delano imputed his jealous watchfulness to that peculiar feeling which the full-blooded African entertains from the adulterated one. As for the steward, his manner, if not bespeaking much dignity of self-respect, yet evidenced his extreme desire to please; which is doubly meritorious, as at once Christian and Chesterfieldian.°

Captain Delano observed with interest that while the complexion of the mulatto was hybrid, his physiognomy was European—classically so.

"Don Benito," whispered he, "I am glad to see this usher-of-the-golden-rod° of yours; the sight refutes an ugly remark once made to me by a Barbados planter; that when a mulatto has a regular European face, look out for him; he is a devil. But see, your steward here has features more regular than King George's of England; and yet there he nods, and bows, and smiles; a king, indeed—the king of kind hearts and polite fellows. What a pleasant voice he has, too."

"He has, Señor."

"But tell me, has he not, so far as you have known him, always proved a good, worthy fellow?" said Captain Delano, pausing, while with a final genuflection the steward disappeared into the cabin; "come, for the reason just mentioned, I am curious to know."

"Francesco is a good man," a sort of° sluggishly responded Don Benito, like a phlegmatic appreciator, who would neither find fault nor flatter.

"Ah, I thought so. For it were strange, indeed, and not very creditable to us white-skins, if a little of our blood mixed with the African's, should, far from improving the latter's quality, have the sad effect of pouring vitriolic acid into black broth; improving the hue, perhaps, but not the wholesomeness."

"Doubtless, doubtless, Señor, but,"—glancing at Babo—"not to speak of negroes, your planter's remark I have heard applied to the Spanish and Indian intermixtures in our provinces. But I know nothing about the matter," he listlessly added.

And here they entered the cabin.

The lunch was a frugal one. Some of Captain Delano's fresh fish and

°*Chesterfieldian:* Reference is to Philip Dormer Stanhope, fourth earl of Chesterfield (1694-1773), who was in his time and has remained the exemplar of polished correctness in manners. °*usher-of-the-golden-rod:* The "Gentlemen Usher of the Black Rod" is a major official in the household of the reigning English sovereign. The substitution of "golden" here is a clumsy joke on Delano's part in reference to the color of Francesco's skin. °*a sort of:* The meaning of this expression, despite various editorial emendations, remains obscure.

pumpkins, biscuit and salt beef, the reserved bottle of cider, and the *San Dominick's* last bottle of Canary.°

As they entered, Francesco, with two or three colored aids, was hovering over the table giving the last adjustments. Upon perceiving their master they withdrew, Francesco making a smiling congé, and the Spaniard, without condescending to notice it, fastidiously remarking to his companion that he relished not superfluous attendance.

Without companions, host and guest sat down, like a childless married couple, at opposite ends of the table, Don Benito waving Captain Delano to his place, and, weak as he was, insisting upon that gentleman being seated before himself.

The negro placed a rug under Don Benito's feet, and a cushion behind his back, and then stood behind, not his master's chair, but Captain Delano's. At first, this a little surprised the latter. But it was soon evident that, in taking his position, the black was still true to his master; since by facing him he could the more readily anticipate his slightest want.

"This is an uncommonly intelligent fellow of yours, Don Benito," whispered Captain Delano across the table.

"You say true, Señor."

During the repast, the guest again reverted to parts of Don Benito's story, begging further particulars here and there. He inquired how it was that the scurvy and fever should have committed such wholesale havoc upon the whites, while destroying less than half the blacks. As if this question reproduced the whole scene of plague before the Spaniard's eyes, miserably reminding him of his solitude in a cabin where before he had had so many friends and officers round him, his hand shook, his face became hueless, broken words escaped; but directly the sane memory of the past seemed replaced by insane terrors of the present. With starting eyes he stared before him at vacancy. For nothing was to be seen but the hand of his servant pushing the Canary over towards him. At length a few sips served partially to restore him. He made random reference to the different constitution of races, enabling one to offer more resistance to certain maladies than another. The thought was new to his companion.

Presently Captain Delano, intending to say something to his host concerning the pecuniary part of the business he had undertaken for him, especially—since he was strictly accountable to his owners—with reference to the new suit of sails, and other things of that sort; and naturally preferring to conduct such affairs in private, was desirous that the servant should withdraw; imagining that Don Benito for a few minutes could dispense with his attendance. He, however, waited awhile; thinking that, as the conversation proceeded, Don Benito, without being prompted, would perceive the propriety of the step.

°*Canary:* a sweet wine originally made in the Canary Islands

But it was otherwise. At last catching his host's eye, Captain Delano, with a slight backward gesture of his thumb, whispered, "Don Benito, pardon me, but there is an interference with the full expression of what I have to say to you."

Upon this the Spaniard changed countenance; which was imputed to his resenting the hint, as in some way a reflection upon his servant. After a moment's pause, he assured his guest that the black's remaining with them could be of no disservice; because since losing his officers he had made Babo (whose original office, it now appeared, had been captain of the slaves) not only his constant attendant and companion, but in all things his confidant.

After this, nothing more could be said; though, indeed, Captain Delano could hardly avoid some little tinge of irritation upon being left ungratified in so inconsiderable a wish, by one, too, for whom he intended such solid services. But it is only his querulousness, thought he; and so filling his glass he proceeded to business.

The price of the sails and other matters were fixed upon. But while this was being done, the American observed that, though his original offer of assistance had been hailed with hectic animation, yet now, when it was reduced to a business transaction, indifference and apathy were betrayed. Don Benito, in fact, appeared to submit to hearing the details more out of regard to common propriety, than from any impression that weighty benefit to himself and his voyage was involved.

Soon, his manner became still more reserved. The effort was vain to seek to draw him into social talk. Gnawed by his splenetic mood, he sat twitching his beard, while to little purpose the hand of his servant, mute as that on the wall, slowly pushed over the Canary.

Lunch being over, they sat down on the cushioned transom°; the servant placing a pillow behind his master. The long continuance of the calm had now affected the atmosphere. Don Benito sighed heavily, as if for breath.

"Why not adjourn to the cuddy?" said Captain Delano. "There is more air there." But the host sat silent and motionless.

Meantime his servant knelt before him, with a large fan of feathers. And Francesco coming in on tiptoes, handed the negro a little cup of aromatic waters, with which at intervals he chafed his master's brow; smoothing the hair along the temples as a nurse does a child's. He spoke no word. He only rested his eye on his master's, as if, amid all Don Benito's distress, a little to refresh his spirit by the silent sight of fidelity.

Presently the ship's bell sounded two o'clock; and through the cabin windows a slight rippling of the sea was discerned; and from the desired direction.

"There," exclaimed Captain Delano, "I told you so, Don Benito, look!"

°*transom:* window seat

He had risen to his feet, speaking in a very animated tone, with a view the more to rouse his companion. But though the crimson curtain of the stern-window near him that moment fluttered against his pale cheek, Don Benito seemed to have even less welcome for the breeze than the calm.

Poor fellow, thought Captain Delano, bitter experience has taught him that one ripple does not make a wind, any more than one swallow a summer. But he is mistaken for once. I will get his ship in for him, and prove it.

Briefly alluding to his weak condition, he urged his host to remain quietly where he was, since he (Captain Delano) would with pleasure take upon himself the responsibility of making the best use of the wind.

Upon gaining the deck, Captain Delano started at the unexpected figure of Atufal, monumentally fixed at the threshold, like one of those sculptured porters of black marble guarding the porches of Egyptian tombs.

But this time the start was, perhaps, purely physical. Atufal's presence, singularly attesting docility even in sullenness, was contrasted with that of the hatchet-polishers, who in patience evinced their industry; while both spectacles showed, that lax as Don Benito's general authority might be, still, whenever he chose to exert it, no man so savage or colossal but must, more or less, bow.

Snatching a trumpet° which hung from the bulwarks, with a free step Captain Delano advanced to the forward edge of the poop, issuing his orders in his best Spanish. The few sailors and many negroes, all equally pleased, obediently set about heading the ship towards the harbor.

While giving some directions about setting a lower stu'n-sail,° suddenly Captain Delano heard a voice faithfully repeating his orders. Turning, he saw Babo, now for the time acting, under the pilot, his original part of captain of the slaves. This assistance proved valuable. Tattered sails and warped yards were soon brought into some trim. And no brace or halyard was pulled but to the blithe songs of the inspirited negroes.

Good fellows, thought Captain Delano, a little training would make fine sailors of them. Why see, the very women pull and sing too. These must be some of those Ashantee negresses that make such capital soldiers, I've heard. But who's at the helm? I must have a good hand there.

He went to see.

The *San Dominick* steered with a cumbrous tiller, with large horizontal pulleys attached. At each pulley-end stood a subordinate black, and between them, at the tiller-head, the responsible post, a Spanish seaman, whose countenance evinced his due share in the general hopefulness and

---

°***trumpet:*** here, a speaking trumpet or megaphone °*stu'n-sail:* a studding sail; an auxiliary sail set for short maneuvering or to supplement the regular sail area

confidence at the coming of the breeze. He proved the same man who had behaved with so shame-faced an air on the windlass.

"Ah,—it is you, my man," exclaimed Captain Delano— "well, no more sheep's eyes now;—look straight forward and keep the ship so. Good hand, I trust? And want to get into the harbor, don't you?"

The man assented with an inward chuckle, grasping the tiller-head firmly. Upon this, unperceived by the American, the two blacks eyed the sailor intently.

Finding all right at the helm, the pilot went forward to the forecastle, to see how matters stood there.

The ship now had way enough to breast the current. With the approach of evening, the breeze would be sure to freshen.

Having done all that was needed for the present, Captain Delano, giving his last orders to the sailors, turned aft to report affairs to Don Benito in the cabin; perhaps additionally incited to rejoin him by the hope of snatching a moment's private chat while the servant was engaged upon deck.

From opposite sides, there were, beneath the poop, two approaches to the cabin; one further forward than the other, and consequently communicating with a longer passage. Marking the servant still above, Captain Delano, taking the nighest entrance—the one last named, and at whose porch Atufal still stood—hurried on his way, till, arrived at the cabin threshold, he paused an instant, a little to recover from his eagerness. Then, with the words of his intended business upon his lips, he entered. As he advanced toward the seated Spaniard, he heard another footstep, keeping time with his. From the opposite door, a salver in hand, the servant was likewise advancing.

"Confound the faithful fellow," thought Captain Delano; "what a vexatious coincidence."

Possibly, the vexation might have been something different, were it not for the brisk confidence inspired by the breeze. But even as it was, he felt a slight twinge, from a sudden indefinite association in his mind of Babo with Atufal.

"Don Benito," said he, "I give you joy; the breeze will hold, and will increase. By the way, your tall man and timepiece, Atufal, stands without. By your order, of course?"

Don Benito recoiled, as if at some bland satirical touch, delivered with such adroit garnish of apparent good breeding as to present no handle for retort. He is like one flayed° alive, thought Captain Delano; where may one touch him without causing a shrink?

The servant moved before his master, adjusting a cushion; recalled to civility, the Spaniard stiffly replied: "You are right. The slave appears

---

°*flayed:* skinned

where you saw him, according to my command; which is, that if at the given hour I am below, he must take his stand and abide my coming."

"Ah now, pardon me, but that is treating the poor fellow like an ex-king indeed. Ah, Don Benito," smiling, "for all the license you permit in some things, I fear lest, at bottom, you are a bitter hard master."

Again Don Benito shrank; and this time, as the good sailor thought, from a genuine twinge of his conscience.

Again conversation became constrained. In vain Captain Delano called attention to the now perceptible motion of the keel gently cleaving the sea; with lackluster eye, Don Benito returned words few and reserved.

By and by, the wind having steadily risen, and still blowing right into the harbor, bore the *San Dominick* swiftly on. Rounding a point of land, the sealer at distance came into open view.

Meantime Captain Delano had again repaired to the deck, remaining there some time. Having at last altered the ship's course, so as to give the reef a wide berth, he returned for a few moments below.

I will cheer up my poor friend, this time, thought he.

"Better and better, Don Benito," he cried as he blithely reentered: "there will soon be an end to your cares, at least for a while. For when, after a long, sad voyage, you know, the anchor drops into the haven all its vast weight seems lifted from the captain's heart. We are getting on famously, Don Benito. My ship is in sight: Look through this side-light here; there she is; all a-taunt-o! The *Bachelor's Delight*, my good friend. Ah, how this wind braces one up. Come, you must take a cup of coffee with me this evening. My old steward will give you as fine a cup as ever any sultan tasted. What say you, Don Benito, will you?"

At first, the Spaniard glanced feverishly up, casting a longing look towards the sealer, while with mute concern his servant gazed into his face. Suddenly the old ague of coldness returned, and dropping back to his cushions he was silent.

"You do not answer. Come, all day you have been my host; would you have hospitality all on one side?"

"I cannot go," was the response.

"What? It will not fatigue you. The ships will lie together as near as they can, without swinging foul. It will be little more than stepping from deck to deck; which is but as from room to room. Come, come, you must not refuse me."

"I cannot go," decisively and repulsively repeated Don Benito.

Renouncing all but the last appearance of courtesy, with a sort of cadaverous sullenness, and biting his thin nails to the quick, he glanced, almost glared, at his guest, as if impatient that a stranger's presence should interfere with the full indulgence of his morbid hour. Meantime the sound of the parted waters came more and more gurglingly and merrily in at the windows; as reproaching him for his dark spleen; as telling him that, sulk as he might, and go mad with it, nature cared not a jot; since, whose fault was it, pray?

But the foul mood was now at its depth, as the fair wind at its height.

There was something in the man so far beyond any mere unsociality or sourness previously evinced, that even the forbearing good nature of his guest could no longer endure it. Wholly at a loss to account for such demeanor, and deeming sickness with eccentricity, however extreme, no adequate excuse, well satisfied, too, that nothing in his own conduct could justify it, Captain Delano's pride began to be roused. Himself became reserved. But all seemed one to the Spaniard. Quitting him, therefore, Captain Delano once more went to the deck.

The ship was now within less than two miles of the sealer. The whale-boat was seen darting over the interval.

To be brief, the two vessels, thanks to the pilot's skill, ere long in neighborly style lay anchored together.

Before returning to his own vessel, Captain Delano had intended communicating to Don Benito the smaller details of the proposed services to be rendered. But, as it was, unwilling anew to subject himself to rebuffs, he resolved, now that he had seen the *San Dominick* safely moored, immediately to quit her, without further allusion to hospitality or business. Indefinitely postponing his ulterior plans, he would regulate his future actions according to future circumstances. His boat was ready to receive him; but his host still tarried below. Well, thought Captain Delano, if he has little breeding, the more need to show mine. He descended to the cabin to bid a ceremonious, and, it may be, tacitly rebukeful adieu. But to his great satisfaction, Don Benito, as if he began to feel the weight of that treatment with which his slighted guest had, not indecorously, retaliated upon him, now supported by his servant, rose to his feet, and grasping Captain Delano's hand, stood tremulous; too much agitated to speak. But the good augury hence drawn was suddenly dashed, by his resuming all his previous reserve, with augmented gloom, as, with half-averted eyes, he silently reseated himself on his cushions. With a corresponding return of his own chilled feelings, Captain Delano bowed and withdrew.

He was hardly midway in the narrow corridor, dim as a tunnel, leading from the cabin to the stairs, when a sound, as of the tolling for execution in some jail-yard, fell on his ears. It was the echo of the ship's flawed bell, striking the hour, drearily reverberated in this subterranean vault. Instantly, by a fatality not to be withstood, his mind, responsive to the portent, swarmed with superstitious suspicions. He paused. In images far swifter than these sentences, the minutes details of all his former distrusts swept through him.

Hitherto, credulous good nature had been too ready to furnish excuses for reasonable fears. Why was the Spaniard, so superfluously punctilious at times, now heedless of common propriety in not accompanying to the side his departing guest? Did indisposition forbid? Indisposition had not forbidden more irksome exertion that day. His last equivocal demeanor recurred. He had risen to his feet, grasped his guest's hand, motioned toward his hat; then, in an instant, all was eclipsed in sinister muteness and gloom. Did this imply one brief, repentant relenting at the final moment, from some iniquitous plot, followed by remorseless return to it? His last glance seemed to express a calamitous, yet acquiescent farewell to Captain Delano forever. Why decline the invitation to visit the sealer that evening? Or was the Spaniard less hardened than the Jew,° who refrained not from supping at the board of him whom the same night he meant to betray? What imported all those day-long enigmas and contradictions, except they were intended to mystify, preliminary to some stealthy blow? Atufal, the pretended rebel, but punctual shadow, that moment lurked by the threshold without. He seemed a sentry, and more. Who, by his own confession, had stationed him there? Was the negro now lying in wait?

The Spaniard behind—his creature before: to rush from darkness to light was the involuntary choice.

The next moment, with clenched jaw and hand, he passed Atufal, and stood unharmed in the light. As he saw his trim ship lying peacefully at anchor, and almost within ordinary call; as he saw his household boat, with familiar faces in it, patiently rising and falling on the short waves by the *San Dominick's* side; and then, glancing about the decks where he stood, saw the oakum-pickers still gravely plying their fingers; and heard the low, buzzing whistle and industrious hum of the hatchet-polishers, still bestirring themselves over their endless occupation; and more than all, as he saw the benign aspect of nature, taking her innocent repose in the evening; the screened sun in the quiet camp of the west shining out like the mild light from Abraham's tent°; as charmed eye and ear took in all these, with the chained figure of the black, clenched jaw and hand relaxed. Once again he smiled at the phantoms which had mocked him, and felt something like a tinge of remorse, that, by harboring them even for a moment, he should, by implication, have betrayed an atheist doubt of the ever-watchful Providence above.

There was a few minutes' delay, while, in obedience to his orders, the boat was being hooked along to the gangway. During this interval, a sort of saddened satisfaction stole over Captain Delano, at thinking of the kindly offices he had that day discharged for a stranger. Ah, thought he, after good actions one's conscience is never ungrateful, however much so the benefited party may be.

Presently, his foot, in the first act of descent into the boat, pressed the first round of the side-ladder, his face presented inward upon the

°*the Jew:* Judas Iscariot (*Matthew 26:25*) °*Abraham's tent:* *Genesis 18*

deck. In the same moment, he heard his name courteously sounded; and, to his pleased surprise, saw Don Benito advancing— an unwonted energy in his air, as if, at the last moment, intent upon making amends for his recent discourtesy. With instinctive good feeling, Captain Delano, withdrawing his foot, turned and reciprocally advanced. As he did so, the Spaniard's nervous eagerness increased, but his vital energy failed; so that, the better to support him, the servant, placing his master's hand on his naked shoulder, and gently holding it there, formed himself into a sort of crutch.

When the two captains met, the Spaniard again fervently took the hand of the American, at the same time casting an earnest glance into his eyes, but, as before, too much overcome to speak.

I have done him wrong, self-reproachfully thought Captain Delano; his apparent coldness has deceived me; in no instance has he meant to offend.

Meantime, as if fearful that the continuance of the scene might too much unstring his master, the servant seemed anxious to terminate it. And so still presenting himself as a crutch, and walking between the two captains, he advanced with them towards the gangway; while still, as if full of kindly contrition, Don Benito would not let go the hand of Captain Delano, but retained it in his, across the black's body.

Soon they were standing by the side, looking over into the boat, whose crew turned up their curious eyes. Waiting a moment for the Spaniard to relinquish his hold, the now embarrassed Captain Delano lifted his foot, to overstep the threshold of the open gangway; but still Don Benito would not let go his hand. And yet, with an agitated tone, he said, "I can go no further; here I must bid you adieu. Adieu, my dear, dear Don Amasa. Go—go!" suddenly tearing his hand loose, "go, and God guard you better than me, my best friend."

Not unaffected, Captain Delano would now have lingered; but catching the meekly admonitory eye of the servant, with a hasty farewell he descended into his boat, followed by the continual adieus of Don Benito, standing rooted in the gangway.

Seating himself in the stern, Captain Delano, making a last salute, ordered the boat shoved off. The crew had their oars on end. The bowsman pushed the boat a sufficient distance for the oars to be lengthwise dropped. The instant that was done, Don Benito sprang over the bulwarks, falling at the feet of Captain Delano; at the same time calling towards his ship, but in tones so frenzied, that none in the boat could understand him. But, as if not equally obtuse, three sailors, from three different and distant parts of the ship, splashed into the sea, swimming after their captain, as if intent upon his rescue.

The dismayed officer of the boat eagerly asked what this meant. To which, Captain Delano, turning a disdainful smile upon the unaccountable

Spaniard, answered that, for his part, he neither knew nor cared; but it seemed as if Don Benito had taken it into his head to produce the impression among his people that the boat wanted to kidnap him. "Or else—give way for your lives," he wildly added, starting at a clattering hubbub in the ship, above which rang the tocsin of the hatchet-polishers; and seizing Don Benito by the throat he added, "this plotting pirate means murder!" Here, in apparent verification of the words, the servant, a dagger in his hand, was seen on the rail overhead, poised, in the act of leaping, as if with desperate fidelity to befriend his master to the last; while, seemingly to aid the black, the three white sailors were trying to clamber into the hampered bow. Meantime, the whole host of negroes, as if inflamed at the sight of their jeopardized captain, impended in one sooty avalanche over the bulwarks.

All this, with what preceded, and what followed, occurred with such involutions of rapidity, that past, present, and future seemed one.

Seeing the negro coming, Captain Delano had flung the Spaniard aside, almost in the very act of clutching him, and, by the unconscious recoil, shifting his place, with arms thrown up, so promptly grappled the servant in his descent, that with dagger presented at Captain Delano's heart, the black seemed of purpose to have leaped there as to his mark. But the weapon was wrenched away, and the assailant dashed down into the bottom of the boat, which now, with disentangled oars, began to speed through the sea.

At this juncture, the left hand of Captain Delano, on one side, again clutched the half-reclining Don Benito, heedless that he was in a speechless faint, while his right foot, on the other side, ground the prostrate negro; and his right arm pressed for added speed on the after oar, his eye bent forward, encouraging his men to their utmost.

But here, the officer of the boat, who had at last succeeded in beating off the towing sailors, and was now, with face turned aft, assisting the bowsman at his oar, suddenly called to Captain Delano, to see what the black was about; while a Portuguese oarsman shouted to him to give heed to what the Spaniard was saying.

Glancing down at his feet, Captain Delano saw the freed hand of the servant aiming with a second dagger—a small one, before concealed in his wool—with this he was snakishly writhing up from the boat's bottom, at the heart of his master, his countenance lividly vindictive, expressing the centered purpose of his soul; while the Spaniard, half-choked, was vainly shrinking away, with husky words, incoherent to all but the Portuguese.

That moment, across the long-benighted mind of Captain Delano, a flash of revelation swept, illuminating, in unanticipated clearness, his host's whole mysterious demeanor, with every enigmatic event of the day, as well as the entire past voyage of the *San Dominick*. He smote Babo's hand down, but his own heart smote him harder. With infinite pity he withdrew his hold from Don Benito. Not Captain Delano, but Don Benito, the black in leaping into the boat, had intended to stab.

Both the black's hands were held, as, glancing up towards the *San Dominick,* Captain Delano, now with scales dropped from his eyes, saw the negroes, not in misrule, not in tumult, not as if frantically concerned for Don Benito, but with mask torn away, flourishing hatchets, and knives, in ferocious piratical revolt. Like delirious black dervishes, the six Ashantees danced on the poop. Prevented by their foes from springing into the water, the Spanish boys were hurrying up to the topmost spars, while such of the few Spanish sailors, not already in the sea, less alert, were descried, helplessly mixed in, on deck, with the blacks.

Meantime Captain Delano hailed his own vessel, ordering the ports up, and the guns run out. But by this time the cable of the *San Dominick* had been cut; and the fag-end,° in lashing out, whipped away the canvas shroud about the beak, suddenly revealing, as the bleached hull swung round towards the open ocean, death for the figure-head, in a human skeleton; chalky comment on the chalked words below, "*Follow your leader.*" At the sight, Don Benito, covering his face, wailed: "'Tis he, Aranda! my murdered, unburied friend!"

Upon reaching the sealer, calling for ropes, Captain Delano bound the negro, who made no resistance, and had him hoisted to the deck. He would then have assisted the now almost helpless Don Benito up the side; but Don Benito, wan as he was, refused to move, or be moved, until the negro should have been first put below out of view. When, presently assured that it was done, he no more shrank from the ascent.

The boat was immediately dispatched back to pick up the three swimming sailors. Meantime, the guns were in readiness, though, owing to the *San Dominick* having glided somewhat astern of the sealer, only the aftermost one could be brought to bear. With this, they fired six times; thinking to cripple the fugitive ship by bringing down her spars. But only a few inconsiderable ropes were shot away. Soon the ship was beyond the gun's range, steering broad out of the bay; the blacks thickly clustering round the bowsprit, one moment with taunting cries towards the whites, the next with upthrown gestures hailing the now dusky moors of ocean—cawing crows escaped from the hand of the fowler.

The first impulse was to slip the cables and give chase. But, upon second thoughts, to pursue with whale-boat and yawl seemed more promising.

Upon inquiring of Don Benito what firearms they had on board the *San Dominick,* Captain Delano was answered that they had none that could be used; because, in the earlier stages of the mutiny, a cabin-

---

°*fag-end:* a frayed, untwisted end of rope

passenger, since dead, had secretly put out of order the locks of what few muskets there were. But with all his remaining strength, Don Benito entreated the American not to give chase, either with ship or boat; for the negroes had already proved themselves such desperadoes, that, in case of a present assault, nothing but a total massacre of the whites could be looked for. But, regarding this warning as coming from one whose spirit had been crushed by misery, the American did not give up his design.

The boats were got ready and armed. Captain Delano ordered his men into them. He was going himself when Don Benito grasped his arm.

"What! have you saved my life, Señor, and are you now going to throw away your own?"

The officers also, for reasons connected with their interests and those of the voyage, and a duty owing to the owners, strongly objected against their commander's going. Weighing their remonstrances a moment, Captain Delano felt bound to remain; appointing his chief mate—an athletic and resolute man, who had been a privateer'sman—to head the party. The more to encourage the sailors, they were told, that the Spanish captain considered his ship good as lost; that she and her cargo, including some gold and silver, were worth more than a thousand doubloons. Take her, and no small part should be theirs. The sailors replied with a shout.

The fugitives had now almost gained an offing.° It was nearly night; but the moon was rising. After hard, prolonged pulling, the boats came up on the ship's quarters, at a suitable distance laying upon their oars to discharge their muskets. Having no bullets to return, the negroes sent their yells. But, upon the second volley, Indian-like, they hurled their hatchets. One took off a sailor's fingers. Another struck the whale-boat's bow, cutting off the rope there, and remaining stuck in the gunwale like a woodman's axe. Snatching it, quivering from its lodgment, the mate hurled it back. The returned gauntlet now stuck in the ship's broken quarter-gallery, and so remained.

The negroes giving too hot a reception, the whites kept a more respectful distance. Hovering now just out of reach of the hurtling hatchets, they, with a view to the close encounter which must soon come, sought to decoy the blacks into entirely disarming themselves of their most murderous weapons in a hand-to-hand fight, by foolishly flinging them, as missiles, short of the mark, into the sea. But, ere long, perceiving the stratagem, the negroes desisted, though not before many of them had to replace their lost hatchets with handspikes; an exchange which, as counted upon, proved, in the end, favorable to the assailants.

Meantime, with a strong wind, the ship still clove the water; the boats alternately falling behind, and pulling up, to discharge fresh volleys.

°*offing:* a distance; here, a significant distance

The fire was mostly directed towards the stern, since there, chiefly, the negroes, at present, were clustering. But to kill or maim the negroes was not the object. To take them, with the ship, was the object. To do it, the ship must be boarded; which could not be done by boats while she was sailing so fast.

A thought now struck the mate. Observing the Spanish boys still aloft, high as they could get, he called to them to descend to the yards, and cut adrift the sails. It was done. About this time, owing to causes hereafter to be shown, two Spaniards, in the dress of sailors, and conspicuously showing themselves, were killed; not by volleys, but by deliberate marksman's shots; while, as it afterwards appeared, by one of the general discharges, Atufal, the black, and the Spaniard at the helm likewise were killed. What now, with the loss of the sails, and loss of leaders, the ship became unmanageable to the negroes.

With creaking masts, she came heavily round to the wind; the prow slowly swinging into view of the boats, its skeleton gleaming in the horizontal moonlight, and casting a gigantic ribbed shadow upon the water. One extended arm of the ghost seemed beckoning the whites to avenge it.

"Follow your leader!" cried the mate; and, one on each bow, the boats boarded. Sealing-spears and cutlasses crossed hatchets and hand-spikes. Huddled upon the longboat amidships, the negresses raised a wailing chant, whose chorus was the clash of the steel.

For a time, the attack wavered; the negroes wedging themselves to beat it back; the half-repelled sailors, as yet unable to gain a footing, fighting as troopers in the saddle, one leg sideways flung over the bulwarks, and one without, playing their cutlasses like carter's whips. But in vain. They were almost overborne, when, rallying themselves into a squad as one man, with a huzza, they sprang inboard, where, entangled, they involuntarily separated again. For a few breath's space, there was a vague, muffled, inner sound, as of submerged swordfish rushing hither and thither through shoals of blackfish. Soon, in a reunited band, and joined by the Spanish seamen, the whites came to the surface, irresistibly driving the negroes toward the stern. But a barricade of casks and sacks, from side to side, had been thrown up by the main-mast. Here the negroes faced about, and though scorning peace or truce, yet fain would have had respite. But, without pause, overleaping the barrier, the unflagging sailors again closed. Exhausted, the blacks now fought in despair. Their red tongues lolled, wolf-like, from their black mouths. But the pale sailors teeth were set; not a word was spoken; and in five minutes more, the ship was won.

Nearly a score of the negroes were killed. Exclusive of those by the balls, many were mangled; their wounds— mostly inflicted by the long-edged sealing-spears, resembling those shaven ones of the English at Preston Pans,° made by the poled scythes of the Highlanders. On the other side, none were killed, though several were wounded; some severely, including the mate. The surviving negroes were temporarily secured, and the ship, towed back into the harbor at midnight, once more lay anchored.

Omitting the incidents and arrangements ensuing, suffice it that, after two days spent in refitting, the ships sailed in company for Concepción, in Chile, and thence for Lima, in Peru; where, before the vice-regal courts, the whole affair, from the beginning, underwent investigation.

Though, midway on the passage, the ill-fated Spaniard, relaxed from constraint, showed some signs of regaining health with free will; yet, agreeably to his own foreboding, shortly before arriving at Lima, he relapsed, finally becoming so reduced as to be carried ashore in arms. Hearing of his story and plight, one of the many religious institutions of the City of Kings opened an hospitable refuge to him, where both physician and priest were his nurses, and a member of the order volunteered to be his one special guardian and consoler, by night and by day.

The following extracts, translated from one of the official Spanish documents, will, it is hoped, shed light on the preceding narrative, as well as, in the first place, reveal the true port of departure and true history of the *San Dominick's* voyage, down to the time of her touching at the island of Santa Maria. But, ere the extracts come, it may be well to preface them with a remark.

The document selected, from among many others, for partial translation, contains the deposition of Benito Cereno; the first taken in the case. Some disclosures therein were, at the time, held dubious for both learned and natural reasons. The tribunal inclined to the opinion that the deponent, not undisturbed in his mind by recent events, raved of some things which could never have happened. But subsequent depositions of the surviving sailors, bearing out the revelations of their captain in several of the strangest particulars, gave credence to the rest. So that the tribunal, in its final decision, rested its capital sentences upon statements which, had they lacked confirmation, it would have deemed it but duty to reject.

> *I, Don José de Abos and Padilla,* His Majesty's Notary for the Royal Revenue, and Register of this Province, and Notary Public of the Holy Crusade of this Bishoprick, etc.
>
> Do certify and declare, as much as is requisite in law, that, in the criminal cause commenced the twenty-fourth of the month of September, in the year seventeen hundred and ninety-nine, against the negroes of the ship *San Dominick*, the following declaration before me was made:

°*Preston Pans:* A battle was fought there in 1745 between British army units and Scottish irregulars who supported the cause of the Stuart Pretender.

Declaration of the first Witness, *Don Benito Cereno.*

The same day and month and year, His Honor, Doctor Juan Martinez de Rozas, Councilor of the Royal Audience of this Kingdom, and learned in the law of this Intendency, ordered the captain of the ship *San Dominick,* Don Benito Cereno, to appear; which he did in his litter, attended by the monk Infelez; of whom he received the oath, which he took by God, our Lord, and a Sign of the Cross; under which he promised to tell the truth of whatever he should know and should be asked;—and being interrogated agreeably to the tenor of the act, commencing the process, he said, that on the twentieth of May last, he set sail with his ship from the port of Valparaiso, bound to that of Callao; loaded with the produce of the country beside thirty cases of hardware and one hundred and sixty blacks, of both sexes, mostly belonging to Don Alexandro Aranda, gentleman, of the City of Mendoza; that the crew of the ship consisted of thirty-six men, beside the persons who went as passengers; that the negroes were in part as follows:

[*Here, in the original, follows a list of some fifty names, descriptions, and ages, compiled from certain recovered documents of Aranda's and also from recollections of the deponent, from which portions only are extracted.*]

—One, from about eighteen to nineteen years, named José, and this was the man that waited upon his master, Don Alexandro, and who speaks well the Spanish, having served him four or five years; * * * a mulatto, named Francesco, the cabin steward, of a good person and voice having sung in the Valparaiso churches, native of the province of Buenos Aires, aged about thirty-five years. * * * A smart negro, named Dago, who had been for many years a grave-digger among the Spaniards, aged forty-six years. * * * Four old negroes, born in Africa, from sixty to seventy, but sound, calkers by trade, whose names are as follows:—the first was named Mure, and he was killed (as was also his son named Diamelo); the second, Nacta; the third, Yola, likewise killed; the fourth, Ghofan; and six full-grown negroes, aged from thirty to forty-five, all raw, and born among the Ashantees—Matinqui, Yau, Lecbe, Mapenda, Yambaio, Akim, four of whom were killed; * * * a powerful negro named Atufal, who being supposed to have been a chief in Africa, his owner set great store by him. * * * And a small negro of Senegal, but some years among the Spaniards, aged about thirty, which negro's name was Babo; * * * that he does not remember the names of the others, but that still expecting the residue of Don Alexandro's papers will be found, will then take due account of them all and remit to the court; * * * and thirty-nine women and children of all ages.

[*The catalogue over, the deposition goes on:*]

* * * That all the negroes slept upon deck, as is customary in this navigation, and none wore fetters, because the owner, his friend Aranda, told him that they were all tractable; * * * that on the seventh day after leaving port, at three o'clock in the morning, all the Spaniards being asleep except two officers of the watch, who were the boatswain, Juan Robles, and the carpenter, Juan Bautista Gayete, and the helmsman and his boy, the negroes revolted suddenly, wounded dangerously the boatswain and the carpenter, and successively killed eighteen men of those who were sleeping upon deck, some with handspikes and hatchets, and others by throwing them alive overboard, after tying them; that of the Spaniards upon deck, they left about seven, as he thinks, alive and tied, to maneuver the ship, and three or four more, who hid themselves, remained also alive. Although in the act of revolt the negroes made themselves masters of the hatchway, six or seven wounded went through it to the cockpit, without any hindrance on their part; that during the act of revolt, the mate and another person, whose name he does not recollect, attempted to come up through the hatchway, but being quickly wounded, were obliged to return to the cabin; that the deponent resolved at break of day to come up the companion-way, where the negro Babo was, being the ringleader, and Atufal, who assisted him, and having spoken to them, exhorted them to cease committing such atrocities, asking them, at the same time, what they wanted and intended to do, offering, himself, to obey their commands; that notwithstanding this, they threw, in his presence, three men, alive and tied, overboard; that they told the deponent to come up, and that they would not kill him; which having done, the negro Babo asked him whether there were in those seas any negro countries where they might be carried, and he answered them, No; that the negro Babo afterwards told him to carry them to Senegal,° or to the neighboring islands of St. Nicholas; and he answered, that this was impossible, on account of the great distance, the necessity involved of rounding Cape Horn, the bad condition of the vessel, the want of provisions, sails, and water; but that the negro Babo replied to him he must carry them in any way; that they would do and conform themselves to anything the deponent should require as to eating and drinking; that after a long conference, being absolutely compelled to please them, for they threatened to kill all the whites if they were not, at all events, carried to Senegal, he told them that what was most wanting for the voyage was water; that they would go near the coast to take it, and thence they would proceed on their course; that the negro Babo agreed to it; and the deponent steered towards the intermediate ports, hoping to meet some Spanish or foreign vessel that would save them; that within ten or eleven days they saw the land, and continued their course by it in the vinciity of Nasca;

°*Senegal:* district on the west coast of Africa

that the deponent observed that the negroes were now restless and mutinous, because he did not effect the taking in of water, the negro Babo having required, with threats, that it should be done, without fail, the following day; he told him he saw plainly that the coast was steep, and the rivers designated in the maps were not to be found, with other reasons suitable to the circumstances; that the best way would be to go to the island of Santa Maria, where they might water easily, it being a solitary island, as the foreigners did; that the deponent did not go to Pisco, that was near, nor make any other port of the coast, because the negro Babo had intimated to him several times, that he would kill all the whites the very moment he should perceive any city, town, or settlement of any kind on the shores to which they should be carried: that having determined to go to the island of Santa Maria, as the deponent had planned, for the purpose of trying whether, on the passage or near the island itself, they could find any vessel that should favor them, or whether he could escape from it in a boat to the neighboring coast of Arauco, to adopt the necessary means he immediately changed his course, steering for the island; that the negroes Babo and Atuful held daily conferences, in which they discussed what was necessary for their design of returning to Senegal, whether they were to kill all the Spaniards, and particularly the deponent; that eight days after parting from the coast of Nasca, the deponent being on the watch a little after daybreak, and soon after the negroes had their meeting, the negro Babo came to the place where the deponent was, and told him that he had determined to kill his master, Don Alexandro Aranda, both because he and his companions could not otherwise be sure of their liberty, and that to keep the seamen in subjection, he wanted to prepare a warning of what road they should be made to take did they or any of them oppose him; and that, by means of the death of Don Alexandro, that warning would best be given; but, that what this last meant, the deponent did not at the time comprehend, nor could not, further than the death of Don Alexandro was intended; and moreover the negro Babo proposed to the deponent to call the mate Raneds, who was sleeping in the cabin, before the thing was done, for fear, as the deponent understood it, that the mate, who was a good navigator, should not be killed with Don Alexandro and the rest; that the deponent, who was the friend, from youth, of Don Alexandro, prayed and conjured, but all was useless; for the negro Babo answered him that the thing could not be prevented, and that all the Spaniards risked their death if they should attempt to frustrate his will in this matter, or any other; that, in this conflict, the deponent called the mate, Raneds, who was forced to go apart, and immediately the negro Babo commanded the Ashantee Matinqui and the Ashantee Lecbe to go and commit the murder; that those two went down with hatchets to the berth of Don Alexandro; that, yet half alive and mangled, they dragged him on deck; that they were going to throw him overboard in that state, but the negro Babo stopped them, bidding the murder be completed on the deck before him, which was done, when, by his orders, the body was carried below, forward; that nothing more was seen of it by the deponent for three days; * * * that Don Alonzo Sidonia, an old man, long resident at Valparaiso, and lately appointed to a civil office in Peru, whither he had taken passage, was at the time sleeping in the berth opposite Don Alexandro's; that awakening at his cries, surprised by them, and at the sight of the negroes with their bloody hatchets in their hands, he threw himself into the sea through a window which was near him, and was drowned, without it being in the power of the deponent to assist or take him up; * * * that a short time after killing Aranda, they brought upon deck his cousin-german, of middle-age, Don Francisco Masa, of Mendoza, and the young Don Joaquin, Marques of Aramboalaza, then lately from Spain, with his Spanish servant Ponce, and the three young clerks of Aranda, José Morairi, Lorenzo Bargas, and Hermenegildo Gandix, all of Cadiz; that Don Joaquin and Hermenegildo Gandix, the negro Babo, for purposes hereafter to appear, preserved alive; but Don Francisco Masa, José Morairi, and Lorenzo Bargas, with Ponce the servant, beside the boatswain, Juan Robles, the boatswain's mates, Manuel Viscaya and Roderigo Hurta, and four of the sailors, the negro Babo ordered to be thrown alive into the sea, although they made no resistance, nor begged for anything else but mercy; that the boatswain Juan Robles, who knew how to swim, kept the longest above water, making acts of contrition, and, in the last words he uttered, charged this deponent to cause mass to be said for his soul to our Lady of Succor; * * * that, during the three days which followed, the deponent uncertain what fate had befallen the remains of Don Alexandro, frequently asked the negro Babo where they were, and, if still on board, whether they were to be preserved for interment ashore, entreating him so to order it; that the negro Babo answered nothing till the fourth day, when at sunrise, the deponent coming on deck, the negro Babo showed him a skeleton, which had been substituted for the ship's proper figurehead—the image of Cristobal Colon,° the discoverer of the New World; that the negro Babo asked him whose skeleton that was, and whether from its whiteness, he should not think of it a white's; that, upon discovering his face the negro Babo, coming close, said words to this effect: "Keep faith with the blacks from here to Senegal, or you shall in spirit, as now in body, follow your leader," pointing to the prow; * * * that the same morning the negro Babo took by succession each Spaniard forward, and asked him whose skeleton that was, and whether, from its whiteness, he should not think it a white's; that each Spaniard covered his face; that then to each the negro Babo repeated the words in the first place said to the deponent; * * * that they (the Spaniards), being then assembled aft, the negro Babo harangued them, saying that he had now done all; that the deponent (as navigator for the negroes) might pursue his course, warning him

°*Cristobal Colon:* Columbus

and all of them that they should, soul and body, go the way of Don Alexandro, if he saw them (the Spaniards) speak or plot anything against them (the negroes), a threat which was repeated every day; that, before the events last mentioned, they had tied the cook to throw him overboard, for it is not known what thing they heard him speak, but finally the negro Babo spared his life, at the request of the deponent; that a few days after, the deponent, endeavoring not to omit any means to preserve the lives of the remaining whites, spoke to the negroes peace and tranquillity, and agreed to draw up a paper, signed by the deponent and the sailors who could write, as also by the negro Babo, for himself and all the blacks, in which the deponent obliged himself to carry them to Senegal, and they not to kill any more, and he formally to make over to them the ship, with the cargo, with which they were for that time satisfied and quieted * * * But the next day, the more surely to guard against the sailors' escape, the negro Babo commanded all the boats to be destroyed but the long-boat, which was unseaworthy, and another, a cutter in good condition, which knowing it would yet be wanted for towing the water casks, he had it lowered down into the hold. * * *

[*Various particulars of the prolonged and perplexed navigation ensuing here follow, with incidents of a calamitous calm, from which portion one passage is extracted, to wit:*]

—That on the fifth day of the calm, all on board suffered much from the heat, and want of water, and five having died in fits, and mad, the negroes became irritable, and for a chance gesture, which they deemed suspicious—though it was harmless—made by the mate, Raneds, to the deponent in the act of handing a quadrant, they killed him, but that for this they afterwards were sorry, the mate being the only remaining navigator on board, except the deponent.

* * *

—That omitting other events which daily happened, and which can only serve, uselessly to recall past misfortunes and conflicts, after seventy-three days' navigation, reckoned from the time they sailed from Nasca, during which they navigated under a scanty allowance of water, and were afflicted with the calms before mentioned, they at last arrived at the island of Santa Maria, on the seventeenth of the month of August, at about six o'clock in the afternoon, at which hour they cast anchor very near the American ship, *Bachelor's Delight,* which lay in the same bay, commanded by the generous Captain Amasa Delano; but at six o'clock in the morning, they had already descried the port, and the negroes became uneasy, as soon as at distance they saw the ship, not having expected to see one there; that the negro Babo pacified them, assuring them that no fear need be had; that straightway he ordered the figure on the bow to be covered with canvas, as for repairs, and had the decks a little set in order; that for a time the negro Babo and the negro Atufal conferred; that the negro Atufal was for sailing away, but the negro Babo would not, and, by himself, cast about what to do; that at last he came to the deponent, proposing to him to say and do all that the deponent declares to have said and done to the American captain; * * * that the negro Babo warned him that if he varied in the least, or uttered any word, or gave any look that should give the least intimation of the past events or present state, he would instantly kill him, with all his companions, showing a dagger, which he carried hid, saying something which, as he understood it, meant that that dagger would be alert as his eyes; that the negro Babo then announced the plan to all his companions, which pleased them; that he then, the better to disguise the truth, devised many expedients, in some of them uniting deceit and defense; that of this sort was the device of the six Ashantees before named, who were his bravoes°; that them he stationed on the break of the poop, as if to clean certain hatchets (in cases, which were part of the cargo), but in reality to use them, and distribute them at need, and at a given word he told them; that, among other devices, was the device of presenting Atufal, his right hand man, as chained, though in a moment the chains could be dropped; that in every particular he informed the deponent what part he was expected to enact in every device, and what story he was to tell on every occasion, always threatening him with instant death if he varied in the least: that, conscious that many of the negroes would be turbulent, the negro Babo appointed the four aged negroes who were calkers, to keep what domestic order they could on the decks; that again and again he harangued the Spaniards and his companions, informing them of his intent, and of his devices, and of the invented story that this deponent was to tell; charging them lest any of them varied from that story; that these arrangements were made and matured during the interval of two or three hours, betwen their first sighting the ship and the arrival on board of Captain Amasa Delano; that this happened about half-past seven o'clock in the morning, Captain Amasa Delano coming in his boat, and all gladly receiving him; that the deponent, as well as he could force himself, acting then the part of principal owner, and a free captain of the ship, told Captain Amasa Delano, when called upon, that he came from Buenos Aires, bound to Lima, with three hundred negroes; that off Cape Horn, and in a subsequent fever, many negroes had died; that also, by similar casualties, all the sea officers and the greatest part of the crew had died.

* * *

°*bravoes:* henchmen; strong-arm men

[*And so the deposition goes on, circumstantially recounting the fictitious story dictated to the deponent by Babo, and through the deponent imposed upon Captain Delano; and also recounting the friendly offers of Captain Delano, with other things, but all of which is here omitted. After the fictitious story, etc., the deposition proceeds:*]

—that that generous Captain Amasa Delano remained on board all the day, till he left the ship anchored at six o'clock in the evening, deponent speaking to him always of his pretended misfortunes, under the fore-mentioned principles, without having had it in his power to tell a single word, or give him the least hint, that he might know the truth and state of things; because the negro Babo, performing the office of an officious servant with all the appearance of submission of the humble slave, did not leave the deponent one moment; that this was in order to observe the deponent's actions and words, for the negro Babo understands well the Spanish; and besides, there were thereabout some others who were constantly on the watch, and likewise understood the Spanish; * * * that upon one occasion, while deponent was standing on the deck conversing with Amasa Delano, by a secret sign the negro Babo drew him (the deponent) aside, the act appearing as if originating with the deponent; that then, he being draw aside, the negro Babo proposed to him to gain from Amasa Delano full particulars about his ship, and crew, and arms; that the deponent asked "For what?"; that the negro Babo answered he might conceive; that, grieved at the prospect of what might overtake the generous Captain Amasa Delano, the deponent at first refused to ask the desired questions, and used every argument to induce the negro Babo to give up this new design; that the negro Babo showed the point of his dagger; that, after the information had been obtained, the negro Babo again drew him aside, telling him that that very night he (the deponent) would be captain of two ships, instead of one, for that, great part of the American's ship's crew being to be absent fishing, the six Ashantees without any one else, would easily take it; that at this time he said other things to the same purpose; that no entreaties availed; that, before Amasa Delano's coming on board, no hint had been given touching the capture of the American ship; that to prevent this project the deponent was powerless; * * * —that in some things his memory is confused, he cannot distinctly recall every event; * * * that as soon as they had cast anchor at six o'clock in the evening, as has before been stated, the American Captain took leave, to return to his vessel; that upon a sudden impulse, which the deponent believes to have come from God and his angels, he, after the farewell had been said, followed the generous Captain Amasa Delano as far as the gunwale, where he stayed, under pretense of taking leave, until Amasa Delano should have been seated in his boat; that on shoving off, the deponent sprang from the gunwale into the boat and fell into it, he knows not how, God guarding him; that—

[*Here, in the original, follows the account of what further happened at the escape, and how the* San Dominick *was retaken, and of the passage to the coast; including in the recital many expressions of "eternal gratitude" to the "generous Captain Amasa Delano." The deposition then proceeds with recapitulatory remarks, and a partial renumeration of the Negroes, making record of their individual part in the past events, with a view to furnishing, according to command of the court, the data whereon to found the criminal sentences to be pronounced. From this portion is the following*:]

—That he believes that all the negroes, though not in the first place knowing to the design of revolt, when it was accomplished, approved it. * * * That the negro José, eighteen years old, and in the personal service of Don Alexandro, was the one who communicated the information to the negro Babo about the state of things in the cabin, before the revolt; that this is known, because, in the preceding nights, he used to come from his berth, which was under his master's, in the cabin, to the deck where the ringleader and his associates were, and had secret conversations with the negro Babo, in which he was several times seen by the mate; that one night, the mate drove him away twice; * * * that this same negro José was the one who, without being commanded to do so by the negro Babo, as Lecbe and Martinqui were, stabbed his master, Don Alexandro, after he had been dragged half-lifeless to the deck * * * that the mulatto steward, Francesco, was of the first band of revolters, that he was, in all things, the creature and tool of the negro Babo; that, to make his court, he, just before a repast in the cabin, proposed, to the negro Babo, poisoning a dish for the generous Captain Amasa Delano; this is known and believed, because the negroes have said it; but that the negro Babo, having another design, forbade Francesco; * * * that the Ashantee Lecbe was one of the worst of them; for that, on the day the ship was retaken, he assisted in the defense of her, with a hatchet in each hand, with one of which he wounded, in the breast, the chief mate of Amasa Delano, in the first act of boarding; this all knew; that, in sight of the deponent, Lecbe struck with a hatchet, Don Francisco Masa, when, by the negro Babo's orders, he was carrying him to throw him overboard alive, beside participating in the murder, before mentioned, of Don Alexandro Aranda, and others of the cabin-passengers; that, owing to the fury with which the Ashantees fought in the engagement with the boats, but this Lecbe and Yau survived; that Yau was bad as Lecbe; that Yau was the man who, by Babo's command, willingly prepared the skeleton of Don Alexandro, in a way the negroes afterwards told the deponent, but which he, so long as reason is left him, can never divulge; that Yau and Lecbe were the two who, in a calm by night, riveted the skeleton to the bow; this also the negroes told him; that the negro Babo was he who traced the inscription below it; that the negro Babo was the plotter from first to last; he ordered every murder, and was the helm and keel of the revolt; that Atufal was his lieutenant in all; but Atufal, with his own hand, committed no murder; nor did the negro Babo; * * * that Atufal was shot, being killed in the fight with the boats, ere boarding; * * * that the negresses, of age, were knowing to the revolt, and testified themselves satisfied at the death of their master, Don Alexandro; that, had the negroes not restrained them, they would have tortured to death, instead of simply killing, the Spaniards slain by command of the negro Babo; that the negresses used their utmost influence to have the deponent made away with; that, in the various acts of murder, they sang songs and danced—not gaily, but solemnly; and before the engagement with the boats, as well as during the action, they sang melancholy songs to the negroes, and that this melancholy tone was more inflaming than a different one would have been, and was so intended; that all this is believed, because the negroes have said it;—that of the thirty-six men of the crew, exclusive of the passengers (all of whom are now dead), which the deponent had knowledge of, six only remained alive, with four cabin-boys and ship-boys, not included with the crew; * * * —that the negroes broke an arm of one of the cabin-boys and gave him strokes with hatchets.

[*Then follow various random disclosures referring to various periods of time. The following are extracted:*]

—That during the presence of Captain Amasa Delano on board, some attempts were made by the sailors, and one by Hermenegildo Gandix, to convey hints to him of the true state of affairs; but that these attempts were ineffectual, owing to fear of incurring death, and furthermore, owing to the devices which offered contradictions to the true state of affairs, as well as owing to the generosity and piety of Amasa Delano incapable of sounding such wickedness; * * * that Luys Galgo, a sailor about sixty years of age, and formerly of the King's navy, was one of those who sought to convey tokens to Captain Amasa Delano; but his intent, though undiscovered, being suspected, he was, on a pretense, made to retire out of sight, and at last into the hold and there was made away with. This the negroes have since said; * * * that one of the ship-boys feeling, from Captain Amasa Delano's presence, some hopes of release, and not having enough prudence, dropped some chance word respecting his expectations, which being overheard and understood by a slave-boy with whom he was eating at the time, the latter struck him on the head with a knife, inflicting a bad wound, but of which the boy is now healing; that likewise, not long before the ship was brought to anchor, one of the seamen, steering at the time, endangered himself by letting the blacks remark some expression in his countenance, arising from a similar cause to the above; but this sailor, by his heedful after conduct, escaped; * * * that these statements are made to show the court that from the beginning to the end of the revolt, it was impossible for the deponent and his men to act otherwise than they did; * * * —that the third clerk,

Hermenegildo Gandix, who before had been forced to live among the seamen, wearing a seaman's habit, and in all respects appearing to be one for the time, he, Gandix, was killed by a musket ball fired through mistake from the boats before boarding; having in his fright run up the mizzen-rigging, calling to the boats—"don't board," lest upon their boarding the negroes should kill him; that this inducing the Americans to believe he some way favored the cause of the negroes, they fired two balls at him, so that he fell wounded from the rigging, and was drowned in the sea; * * * —that the young Don Joaquin, Marques de Aramboalaza, like Hermenegildo Gandix, the third clerk, was degraded to the office and appearance of a common seaman; that upon one occasion when Don Joaquin shrank, the negro Babo commanded the Ashantee Lecbe to take tar and heat it, and pour it upon Don Joaquin's hands; * * * —that Don Joaquin was killed owing to another mistake of the Americans, but one impossible to be avoided, as upon the approach of the boats, Don Joaquin, with a hatchet tied edge out and upright to his hand, was made by the negroes to appear on the bulwarks; whereupon, seen with arms in his hands, and in a questionable attitude, he was shot for a renegade seaman; * * * that on the person of Don Joaquin was found secreted a jewel, which, by papers that were discovered, proved to have been meant for the shrine of our Lady of Mercy in Lima; a votive offering, beforehand prepared and guarded, to attest to his gratitude, when he should have landed in Peru, his last destination for the safe conclusion of his entire voyage from Spain; * * * —that the jewel, with the other effects of the late Don Joaquin, is in the custody of the Hospital de Sacerdotes, awaiting the disposition of the honorable court; * * * —that, owing to the condition of the deponent, as well as the haste in which the boats departed for the attack, the Americans were not forewarned that there were, among the apparent crew, a passenger and one of the clerks disguised by the negro Babo; * * * —that, beside the negroes killed in the action, some were killed after the capture and reanchoring at night, when shackled to the ring-bolts on deck; that these deaths were committed by the sailors, ere they could be prevented. That as soon as informed of it, Captain Amasa Delano used all his authority, and in particular with his own hand, struck down Martinez Gola, who, having found a razor in the pocket of an old jacket of his, which one of the shackled negroes had on, was aiming it at the negro's throat; that the noble Captain Amasa Delano also wrenched from the hand of Bartholomew Barlo a dagger, secreted at the time of the massacre of the whites, with which he was in the act of stabbing a shackled negro, who, the same day, with another negro, had thrown him down and jumped upon him; * * * —that, for all the events befalling through so long a time, during which the ship was in the hands of the negro Babo, he cannot here give account; but that, what he has said is the most substantial of what occurs to him at present, and is the truth under the oath which he has taken; which declaration he affirmed and ratified, after hearing it read to him.

He said that he is twenty-nine years of age, and broken in body and mind; that when finally dismissed by the court, he shall not return home to Chile, but betake himself to the monastery on Mount Agonia without; and signed with his honor, and crossed himself, and, for the time, departed as he came, in his litter, with the monk Infelez, to the Hospital de Sacerdotes.

Benito Cereno.

Dr. Rozas.

If the Deposition of Benito Cereno served as the key to fit into the lock of the complications which precede it, then, as a vault whose door has been flung back, the *San Dominick's* hull lies open today.

Hitherto the nature of this narrative, besides rendering the intricacies in the beginning unavoidable, has more or less required that many things, instead of being set down in the order of occurrence, should be retrospectively, or irregularly given; this last is the case with the following passages, which will conclude the account.

During the long, mild voyage to Lima, there was, as before hinted, a period during which the sufferer a little recovered his health, or, at least in some degree, his tranquility. Ere the decided relapse which came, the two captains had many cordial conversations—their fraternal unreserve in singular contrast with former withdrawments.

Again and again it was repeated, how hard it had been to enact the part forced on the Spaniard by Babo.

"Ah, my dear friend," Don Benito once said, 'at those very times you thought me so morose and ungrateful, nay, when, as you now admit, you have thought me plotting your murder, at those very times my heart was frozen; I could not look at you, thinking of what, both on board this ship and your own, hung, from other hands, over my kind benefactor. And as God lives, Don Amasa, I know not whether desire for my own safety alone could have nerved me to that leap into your boat, had it not been for the thought that, did you, unenlightened, return to your ship, you, my best friend, with all who might be with you, stolen upon, that night, in your hammocks, would never in this world have wakened again. Do but think how you walked this deck, how you sat in this cabin, every inch of ground mined into honeycombs under you. Had I dropped the least hint, made the least advance towards an understanding between us; death, explosive death—yours as mine—would have ended the scene."

"True, true," cried Captain Delano, starting, "you have saved my life, Don Benito, more than I yours; saved it, too, against my knowledge and will."

"Nay, my friend," rejoined the Spaniard, courteous even to the point of religion, "God charmed your life, but you saved mine. To think of some things you did—those smilings and chattings, rash pointings and gesturings. For less than these, they slew my mate, Raneds; but you had the Prince of Heaven's safe conduct through all ambuscades."

"Yes, all is owing to Providence, I know: but the temper of my mind that morning was more than commonly pleasant, while the sight of so much suffering, more apparent than real, added to my good nature, compassion, and charity, happily interweaving the three. Had it been otherwise, doubtless, as you hint, some of my interferences might have ended unhappily enough. Besides, those feelings I spoke of enabled me to get the better of momentary distrust, at times when acuteness might have cost me my life, without saving another's. Only at the end did my suspicions get the better of me, and you know how wide of the mark they then proved."

"Wide, indeed," said Don Benito, sadly; "you were with me all day; stood with me, sat with me, talked with me, looked at me, ate with me, drank with me; and yet, your last act was to clutch for a monster, not only an innocent man, but the most pitiable of all men. To such degree may malign machinations and deceptions impose. So far may even the best man err, in judging the conduct of one with the recesses of whose condition he is not acquainted. But you were forced to it; and you were in time undeceived. Would that, in both respects, it was so ever, and with all men."

"You generalize, Don Benito; and mournfully enough. But the past is passed; why moralize upon it? Forget it. See, yon bright sun has forgotten it all, and the blue sea, and the blue sky; these have turned over new leaves."

"Because they have no memory," he dejectedly replied; "because they are not human."

"But these mild trades° that now fan your cheek, do they not come with a humanlike healing to you? Warm friends, steadfast friends are the trades."

"With their steadfastness they but waft me to my tomb, Señor," was the foreboding response.

"You are saved," cried Captain Delano, more and more astonished and pained; "you are saved: what has cast such a shadow upon you?"

"The negro."

There was silence, while the moody man sat, slowly and unconsciously gathering his mantle about him, as if it were a pall.

There was no more conversation that day.

But if the Spaniard's melancholy sometimes ended in muteness upon topics like the above, there were others upon which he never spoke at all; on which, indeed, all his old reserves were piled. Pass over the worst, and, only to elucidate, let an item or two of these be cited. The dress, so

---

°*trades:* the trade winds, winds around the equator that "trade" directions; they blow north from the southern hemisphere and south from the northern hemisphere

precise and costly, worn by him on the day whose events have been narrated, had not willingly been put on. And that silver-mounted sword, apparent symbol of despotic command, was not, indeed, a sword, but the ghost of one. The scabbard, artificially stiffened, was empty.

As for the black—whose brain, not body, had schemed and led the revolt, with the plot—his slight frame, inadequate to that which it held, had at once yielded to the superior muscular strength of his captor, in the boat. Seeing all was over, he uttered no sound, and could not be forced to. His aspect seemed to say, since I cannot do deeds, I will not speak words. Put in irons in the hold, with the rest, he was carried to Lima. During the passage, Don Benito did not visit him. Nor then, nor at any time after would he look at him. Before the tribunal he refused. When pressed by the judges he fainted. On the testimony of the sailors alone rested the legal identity of Babo.

Some months after, dragged to the gibbet at the tail of a mule, the black met his voiceless end. The body was burned to ashes; but for many days, the head, that hive of subtlety, fixed on a pole in the Plaza, met, unabashed, the gaze of the whites; and across the Plaza looked towards St. Bartholomew's church, in whose vaults slept then, as now, the recovered bones of Aranda: and across the Rimac bridge looked towards the monstery, on Mount Agonia without; where, three months after being dismissed by the court, Benito Cereno, borne on the bier, did, indeed, follow his leader.

° ° °

OTHER SUGGESTED WORKS

James Baldwin, "Many Thousands Gone," from *Notes of A Native Son*
W.E.B. DuBois, *The Souls of Black Folk*
Ralph Ellison, *Invisible Man*
William Faulkner, *Light In August*
Mark Twain, *Huckleberry Finn*

QUESTIONS

1a. Robert Hayden has stated that he sees no reason "why a Negro poet should be limited to 'racial utterance'," and many of his poems have no racial overtones. What, if any, "racial utterance" do you find in "Tour 5"? Who are the "phantoms, highwaymen, slaves and armies"? What is meant by "static villages whose names are all that's left of Choctaw, Chickasaw"?

b. The words "Confederate sentinels," "enemy," "menace," "shrill gorgon silence," and "taut civility" all suggest hostility. Who is hostile, toward whom, and why?

c. Who are the "wordless and remote" children? Why do they wave? How do they fit into the landscape?

d. What do you think is the meaning of the title of the poem?

2a. A number of voices speak in "Middle Passage," offering lines from hymns, prayers, eyewitness accounts of the voyage, and comments by the poet. How do you distinguish among these voices? Describe each speaker, giving his experience and point of view.

b. Why does Hayden use different voices to tell the story of the mutiny? There are figures in the poem who do not speak. Why does the poet choose not to have them give their version of the journey? How would the story differ if it were told by Cinquez?

c. What is meant by "voyage through death to life upon these shores"? How does the meaning of this phrase change as it is repeated throughout the poem?

d. What is the tone of the poem? Is there any chance of misunderstanding the poet's sympathies? Is the uprising justified? When might a mutiny be justified?

e. What is the effect of including lines from the hymn, "Jesus, Savior, Pilot Me?" Why are hymns and prayers included?

f. Find examples in the poem that illustrate the gulf between word and deed, for example between what the captors claim to be their attitude toward the slaves and their actual treatment of them. How are the captors affected by slavery?

3a. Compare Melville's account of a mutiny to Hayden's in "Middle Passage." In what respects are the circumstances (conditions on the ship, relationships between blacks and whites, final outcome) similar and in what respects different?

b. What were the weather conditions on the morning of Captain Delano's discovery of the *San Dominick*? Who describes the "grey mantles," "grey fowl," "masks," "vapors," "the ship that shows no colors," etc? What is meant by "shadows present foreshadowing deeper shadows to come"?

c. Describe Captain Delano's character. What are his views on strangers, blacks, Europeans, ship captaincies, philanthropy, the nature of good and evil? How do you account for his inability to comprehend the truth of the situation? Is he simply naive, even stupid? Does he ever understand what Don Benito understands? Discuss.

d. Describe Benito Cereno's character. Compare his views on the subjects listed above to those of Delano.

e. Find examples of stereotypes in the story. Who uses these images, Delano or Melville? What, if any, nonstereotypical images of blacks do you find in the story?

f. *Benito Cereno* has been described as a riddle or puzzle. It seems clear that at least two readings are necessary to sift through its complexity. How do specific images change upon a second reading? Give examples of phrases or scenes that take on new meaning?

g. Describe Babo's character. Do any of the stereotypes fit him? Is he clever? Is he evil? Why doesn't he speak after he is captured?

h. Whom do you admire in this story? List traits that are admirable in Delano, Cereno, and Babo. Who do you think is most changed by the events of the story?

i. What is the evil at work in this story? What does Benito Cereno learn during the course of the story? How does he learn it? Does Delano learn anything? If so, what does he learn? If not, why not?

j. Why does Benito Cereno answer, "The Negro," to Delano's question as to what has cast a shadow upon him? What do you think he means by the answer?

4. How are the eyewitnesses in "Middle Passage" and *Benito Cereno* affected by the slave uprisings? Would you attribute their different responses to differences in the characters of Babo and Cinquez? From the accounts given, how much do you know about these two slave leaders?

5. Both "Middle Passage" and *Benito Cereno* are based on actual slave mutinies, and their major characters represent historic figures. Why do you think Melville and Hayden were interested in writing interpretations of these events? Although *Benito Cereno* is not an abolitionist tract, Melville was involved in the movement to abolish slavery, and he has been criticized for apparent ambiguities in the story. How might the story be interpreted as pro-slavery or as not anti-slavery? Are there ambiguities in Hayden's poem? Why, or why not?

6. Many writers describe the presence of black people in the United States as a shadow cast upon the nation's image of itself. List ways in which the shadow imagery is used in the works included in Part I.

PART II

The Mask

And there are buds that cannot bloom at all in light.
—Countee Cullen, from "From the Dark Tower"

The Mask

Amasa Delano's visions of blacks on board the *San Dominick* include familiar stereotypes: the devoted servant, the victim, the exotic primitive, the savage beast. Some of these black people are wearing masks in order to fool the American. Masks are used both to conceal and to disguise what is hidden from view. As a cover, a mask shields only the one who wears it; as a disguise, it serves to fool the viewer, to transform the wearer into something he is not. In Greek drama, masks are offered as an aid to the audience in identifying the characters; in that sense, a mask is a tool of recognition, a means of confirming an identity. By contrast, in African cultures, a mask is only successful if it does *not* resemble a real person or anything known. One expects, one hopes for a lack of recognition. This second, African use of the mask can frequently be found in black writing and its purposes and ambiguities are numerous.

Unfortunately for the mask wearer, one cannot always control the effect of the mask upon one's own identity. Too often, one risks taking on the characteristics one purports to be mocking or loses touch with the real self behind the mask. It is important when considering the selections that follow to look for evidence that a mask is being worn, to try to characterize the features of the mask, and to determine whether it is possible to distinguish between the mask and the wearer. It is also important to consider the ways in which the mask is used by those who look upon it. Is it necessary, and if so, why? Whose purposes does it serve? Finally, look for evidence that black people are beginning to cast off their masks, to lay down the vestiges of a tradition that once enslaved them.

° ° °

A Shield: the Heart Inviolate

In the selections that follow most of the characters who wear masks seem to do so in order to hide themselves from view. Their masks defend them against known enemies, usually white people who would inflict pain either directly by oppressing black people or indirectly by refusing to see them.

One of the earliest black poets to gain national recognition, Paul Laurence Dunbar wrote two kinds of poetry, dialect and standard English. Though he has been criticized for simply reflecting what white's wanted to read about black people, Dunbar was capable of insightful comment on the situation of blacks. Claude McKay was a major figure in the Harlem Renaissance of the 1920s. A Jamaican, McKay came to the United States in 1912, and his first American volume of poetry, *Harlem Shadows*, was published in 1922. Stephen Crane, best known for his novel, *The Red Badge of Courage*, wrote a collection of stories about a township called Whilomville, which he modeled after Port Jervis, New York. Among these stories are "The Monster," a novelette about a black man who becomes disfigured during an act of heroism, and "The Knife," which explored the roles forced upon blacks.

Sherwood Anderson, whose major work is *Winesburg, Ohio*, was one of a number of white writers influenced by the Harlem Renaissance. His black characters tend to fit the stereotype of the exotic primitive in sharp contrast to the white world which Anderson saw as oppressed by technology and the puritan ethic. William Faulkner's "Pantaloon in Black" is from his collection of stories, *Go Down, Moses*. Perhaps more than any other 20th-century white writer, Faulkner was willing to confront the complexity of relationships between black and white people in America.

° ° °

WE WEAR THE MASK

Paul Laurence Dunbar (1872-1906)

We wear the mask that grins and lies,
It hides our cheeks and shades our eyes,—
This debt we pay to human guile;
With torn and bleeding hearts we smile,
And mouth with myriad subtleties.

Why should the world be overwise,
In counting all our tears and sighs?
Nay, let them only see us, while
   We wear the mask.

We smile, but, O great Christ, our cries
To Thee from tortured souls arise.
We sing, but oh, the clay is vile
Beneath our feet, and long the mile;
But let the world dream otherwise,
   We wear the mask.

OUTCAST

Claude McKay (1891-1948)

For the dim regions whence my fathers came
My spirit, bondaged by the body, longs,
Words felt, but never heard, my lips would frame;
My soul would sing forgotten jungle songs.
I would go back to darkness and to peace,
But the great western world holds me in fee,
And I may never hope for full release
While to its alien gods I bend my knee.
Something in me is lost, forever lost,
Some vital thing has gone out of my heart,
And I must walk the way of life a ghost
Among the sons of earth, a thing apart.

For I was born, far from my native clime,
Under the white man's menace, out of time.

THE WHITE HOUSE

Claude McKay

Your door is shut against my tightened face,
And I am sharp as steel with discontent;
But I possess the courage and the grace
To bear my anger proudly and unbent.
The pavement slabs burn loose beneath my feet,
A chafing savage, down the decent street;
And passion rends my vitals as I pass,
Where boldly shines your shuttered door of glass.
Oh, I must search for wisdom every hour,
Deep in my wrathful bosom sore and raw,
And find in it the superhuman power
To hold me to the letter of your law!
Oh, I must keep my heart inviolate
Against the potent poison of your hate.

THE KNIFE

Stephen Crane (1871-1900)

I

Si Byrant's place was on the shore of the lake, and his garden patch, shielded from the north by a bold little promontory and a higher ridge inland, was accounted the most successful and surprising in all Whilomville township. One afternoon Si was working in the garden patch, when Doctor Trescott's man, Peter Washington, came trudging slowly along the road, observing nature. He scanned the white man's fine agricultural results. "Take your eye off them there melons, you rascal," said Si, placidly.

The Negro's face widened in a grin of delight. "Well, Mist' Bryant, I raikon I ain't on'y make m'se'f covertous er-lookin' at dem yere mellums, sure'nough. Dey suhtainly is grand."

"That's all right," responded Si, with affected bitterness of spirit. "That's all right. Just don't you admire 'em too much, that's all."

Peter chuckled and chuckled. "Ma Lode! Mist' Bryant, y-y-you don' think I'm gwine come prowlin' in dish yer gawden?"

"No, I know you hain't," said Si, with solemnity. "B'cause, if you did, I'd shoot you so full of holes you couldn't tell yourself from a sponge."

"Um—no, seh! No, seh! I don' raikon you'll get chance at Pete, Mist' Bryant. No, seh. I'll take an' run 'long an' rob er bank 'fore I'll come foolishin' 'roun *your* gawden, Mist' Bryant."

Bryant, gnarled and strong as an old tree, leaned on his hoe and laughed a Yankee laugh. His mouth remained tightly closed, but the sinister lines which ran from the sides of his nose to the meetings of his lips developed to form a comic oval, and he emitted a series of grunts, while his eyes gleamed merrily and his shoulders shook. Peter, on the contrary, threw back his head and guffawed thunderously. The effete joke in regard to an American Negro's fondness for watermelons was still an admirable pleasantry to them, and this was not the first time they had engaged in badinage over it. In fact, this venerable survival had formed between them a friendship of casual roadside quality.

Afterward Peter went on up the road. He continued to chuckle until he was far away. He was going to pay a visit to old Alek Williams, a Negro who lived with a large family in a hut clinging to the side of a mountain. The scattered colony of Negroes which hovered near Whilomville was of interesting origin, being the result of some contrabands who had drifted as far north as Whilomville during the great civil war. The descendants of these adventurers were mainly conspicuous for their bewildering number and the facility which they possessed for adding even to this number. Speaking, for example, of the Jacksons—one couldn't hurl a stone into the hills about Whilomville without having it land on the roof of a hut full of Jacksons. The town reaped little in labor from these curious suburbs. There were a few men who came in regularly to work in gardens, to drive teams, to care for horses, and there were a few women who came in to cook or to wash. These latter had usually drunken husbands. In the main the colony loafed in high spirits, and the industrious minority gained no direct honor from their fellows, unless they spent their earnings on raiment, in which case they were naturally treated with distinction. On the whole, the hardships of these people were the wind, the rain, the snow, and any other physical difficulties which they could cultivate. About twice a year the lady philanthropists of Whilomville went up against them, and came away poorer in goods but rich in complacence. After one of these attacks the colony would preserve a comic air of rectitude for two days, and then relapse again to the genial irresponsibility of a crew of monkeys.

Peter Washington was one of the industrious class who occupied a position of distinction, for he surely spent his money on personal decoration. On occasion he would dress better than the Mayor of Whilomville himself, or at least in more colors, which was the main thing to the minds of his admirers. His ideal had been the late gallant Henry Johnson, whose conquests in Watermelon Alley, as well as in the hill shanties, had proved him the equal if not the superior of any Pullman car porter in the country. Perhaps Peter had too much Virginia laziness and humor in him to be a wholly adequate successor to the fastidious Henry Johnson, but, at any rate, he admired his memory so attentively as to be openly termed a dude by envious people.

On this afternoon he was going to call on old Alek Williams because Alek's eldest girl was just turned seventeen and, to Peter's mind, was a triumph of beauty. He was not wearing his best clothes, because on his last visit Alek's half-breed hound Susie had taken occasion to forcefully extract a quite large and valuable part of the visitor's trousers. When Peter arrived at the end of the rocky field which contained old Alek's shanty he stooped and provided himself with several large stones, weighing them carefully in his hand, and finally continuing his journey with three stones of about eight ounces each. When he was near the house, three gaunt hounds, Rover and Carlo and Susie, came sweeping down upon him. His impression was that they were going to climb him as if he were a tree, but at the critical moment they swerved and went growling and snapping around him, their heads low, their eyes malignant. The afternoon caller waited until Susie presented her side to him; then he heaved one of his eight-ounce rocks. When it landed, her hollow ribs gave forth a drum-like sound, and she was knocked sprawling, her legs in the air. The other hounds at once fled in horror, and she followed as soon as she was able, yelping at the top of her lungs. The afternoon caller resumed his march.

At the wild expressions of Susie's anguish old Alek had flung open the door and come hastily into the sunshine. "Yah, you Suse, come erlong outa dat now. What fer you—Oh, how do, how do, Mist' Wash'ton—how do?"

"How do, Mist' Willums? I done foun' it necessa'y fer ter damnearkill dish yer dawg a' yourn, Mist' Willums."

"Come in, come in, Mist' Wash'ton. Dawg no'count, Mist' Wash'ton." Then he turned to address the unfortunate animal "Hu't, did it? Hu't? 'Pears like you gwine lun some saince by time somebody brek yer back. 'Pears like I gwine club yer inter er frazzle 'fore you fin' out some saince. G'w'on 'way f'm yah!"

As the old man and his guest entered the shanty a body of black children spread out in crescent-shape formation and observed Peter with awe. Fat old Mrs. Williams greeted him turbulently, while the eldest girl, Mollie, lurked in a corner and giggled with finished imbecility, gazing at the visitor with eyes that were shy and bold by turns. She seemed at times absurdly over-confident, at times foolishly afraid; but her giggle consistently endured. It was a giggle on which an irascible but right-minded judge would have ordered her forthwith to be buried alive.

Amid a great deal of hospitable gabbling, Peter was conducted to the best chair out of the three that the house contained. Enthroned therein, he made himself charming in talk to the old people, who beamed upon him joyously. As for Mollie, he affected to be unaware of her existence. This may have been a method for entrapping the sentimental interest of that young gazelle, or it may be that the giggle had worked upon him.

He was absolutely fascinating to the old people. They could talk like rotary snow-ploughs, and he gave them every chance, while his face was illumined with appreciation. They pressed him to stay for supper, and he consented, after a glance at the pot on the stove which was too furtive to be noted.

During the meal old Alek recounted the high state of Judge Hagenthorpe's kitchen garden, which Alek said was due to his unremitting industry and fine intelligence. Alek was a gardener, whenever impending starvation forced him to cease temporarily from being a lily of the field.

"Mist' Bryant he suhtainly got er grand gawden," observed Peter.

"Dat so, dat so, Mist' Wash'ton," assented Alek. "He got fine gawden."

"Seems like I nev' *did* see sech mellums, big as er bar'l, layin' dere. I don't raikon an'body in dish yer county kin hol' it with Mist' Bryant when comes ter mellums."

"Dat so, Mist' Wash'ton."

They did not talk of watermelons until their heads held nothing else, as the phrase goes. But they talked of watermelons until, when Peter started for home that night over a lonely road, they held a certain dominant position in his mind. Alek had come with him as far as the fence, in order to protect him from possible attack by the mongrels. There they had cheerfully parted, two honest men.

The night was dark, and heavy with moisture. Peter found it uncomfortable to walk rapidly. He merely loitered on the road. When opposite Si Bryant's place he paused and looked over the fence into the garden. He imagined he could see the form of a huge melon lying in dim stateliness not ten yards away. He looked at the Bryant house. Two windows, downstairs, were lighted. The Bryants kept no dog, old Si's favorite child having once been bitten by a dog, and having since died, within that year, of pneumonia.

Peering over the fence, Peter fancied that if any low-minded night prowler should happen to note the melon, he would not find it difficult to possess himself of it. This person would merely wait until the lights were out in the house, and the people presumably asleep. Then he would climb the fence, reach the melon in a few strides, sever the stem with his ready knife, and in a trice be back in the road with his prize. There need be no noise, and, after all, the house was some distance.

Selecting a smooth bit of turf, Peter took a seat by the roadside. From time to time he glanced at the lighted window.

II

When Peter and Alek had said good-bye, the old man turned back in the rocky field and shaped a slow course toward that high dim light which marked the little window of his shanty. It would be incorrect to say that Alek could think of nothing but watermelons. But it was true that Si Bryant's watermelon patch occupied a certain conspicuous position in his thoughts.

He sighed; he almost wished that he was again a conscienceless pickaninny, instead of being one of the most ornate, solemn, and look-at-me-sinner deacons that ever graced the handle of a collection basket. At this time it made him quite sad to reflect upon his granite integrity. A weaker man might perhaps bow his moral head to the temptation, but for him such a fall was impossible. He was a prince of the church, and if he had been nine princes of the church he could not have been more proud. In fact, religion was to the old man a sort of personal dignity. And he was on Sundays so obtrusively good that you could see his sanctity through a door. He forced it on you until you would have felt its influence even in a forecastle.

It was clear in his mind that he must put watermelon thoughts from him, and after a moment he told himself, with much ostentation, that he had done so. But it was cooler under the sky than in the shanty, and as he was not sleepy, he decided to take a stroll down to Si Bryant's place and look at the melons from a pinnacle of spotless innocence. Reaching the road, he paused to listen. It would not do to let Peter hear him, because that graceless rapscallion would probably misunderstand him. But, assuring himself that Peter was well on his way, he set out, walking briskly until he was within four hundred yards of Bryant's place. Here he went to the side of the road, and walked thereafter on the damp, yielding turf. He made no sound.

He did not go on to that point in the main road which was directly opposite the watermelon patch. He did not wish to have his ascetic contemplation disturbed by some chance wayfarer. He turned off along a short lane which led to Si Bryant's barn. Here he reached a place where he could see, over the fence, the faint shapes of the melons.

Alek was affected. The house was some distance away, there was no dog, and doubtless the Bryants would soon extinguish their lights and go to bed. Then some poor lost lamb of sin might come and scale the fence, reach a melon in a moment, sever the stem with his ready knife, and in a trice be back in the road with his prize. And this poor lost lamb of sin might even be a bishop, but no one would ever know it. Alek singled out with his eye a very large melon, and thought that the lamb would prove his judgment if he took that one.

He found a soft place in the grass, and arranged himself comfortably. He watched the lights in the windows.

III

It seemed to Peter Washington that the Bryants absolutely consulted their own wishes in regard to the time for retiring; but at last he saw the lighted windows fade briskly from left to right, and after a moment a window on the second floor blazed out against the darkness. Si was going to bed. In five minutes this window abruptly vanished, and all the world was night.

Peter spent the ensuing quarter-hour in no mental debate. His mind was fixed. He was here, and the melon was there. He would have it. But an idea of being caught appalled him. He thought of his position. He was the beau of his community, honored right and left. He pictured the consternation of his friends and the cheers of his enemies if the hands of the redoutable Si Bryant should grip him in his shame.

He arose and, going to the fence, listened. No sound broke the stillness, save the rhythmical incessant clicking of myriad insects and the guttural chanting of the frogs in the reeds at the lake-side. Moved by sudden decision, he climbed the fence and crept silently and swiftly down upon the melon. His open knife was in his hand. There was the melon, cool, fair to see, as pompous in its fatness as the cook in a monastery.

Peter put out a hand to steady it while he cut the stem. But at the instant he was aware that a black form had dropped over the fence lining the lane in front of him and was coming stealthily toward him. In a palsy of terror he dropped flat upon the ground, not having strength enough to run away. The next moment he was looking into the amazed and agonized face of old Alek Williams.

There was a moment of loaded silence, and then Peter was overcome by a mad inspiration. He suddenly dropped his knife and leaped upon Alek. "I got che!" he hissed. "I got che! I got che!" The old man sank down as limp as rags. "I got che! I got che! Steal Mist' Bryant's mellums, hey?"

Alek, in a low voice, began to beg. "Oh, Mist' Peter Wash'ton, don' go fer ter be too ha'd on er ole man! I nev' come yere fer ter steal 'em. 'Deed I didn't, Mist' Wash'ton! I come yere jes fer ter *feel'*em. Oh, please, Mist' Wash'ton—"

"Come erlong outa yere, you ol' rip," said Peter, "an' don' trumple on dese yer baids. I gwine put you w'ah you won' ketch col'."

Without difficulty he tumbled the whining Alek over the fence to the roadway and followed him with sheriff-like expedition. He took him by the scruff. "Come erlong, deacon. I raikon I gwine put you w'ah you kin pray, deacon. Come erlong, deacon."

The emphasis and reiteration of his layman's title in the church produced a deadly effect upon Akel. He felt to his marrow the heinous crime into which this treacherous night had betrayed him. As Peter marched his prisoner up the road toward the mouth of the lane, he continued his remarks: "Come erlong, deacon. Nev' see er man so anxious-like erbout er mellum-paitch, deacon. Seem like you jes' must see 'em er-growin' an' *feel* em, deacon. Mist' Bryant he'll be s'prised, deacon, findin' out you come fer ter *feel* his mellums. Come erlong, deacon. Mist' Bryant he expectin' some ole rip like you come soon."

They had almost reached the lane when Alek's cur Susie, who had followed her master, approached in the silence which attends dangerous dogs; and seeing indications of what she took to be war, she appended herself swiftly but firmly to the calf of Peter's left leg. The mêlée was short, but spirited. Alek had no wish to have his dog complicate his already serious misfortunes, and went manfully to the defense of his captor. He procured a large stone, and by beating this with both hands down upon the resounding skull of the animal, he induced her to quit her grip. Breathing heavily, Peter dropped into the long grass at the roadside. He said nothing.

"Mist' Wash'ton," said Alek at last, in a quavering voice, "I raikon I gwine wait yere see what you gwine do ter me."

Whereupon Peter passed into a spasmodic state, in which he rolled to and fro and shook.

"Mist' Wash'ton, I hope dish yer dog ain't gone an' give you fitses?"

Peter sat up suddenly. "No, she ain't," he answered; "but she gin me er big skeer; an' fer yer 'sistance with er cobblestone, Mist' Willums, I tell you what I gwine do—I tell you what I gwine do." He waited an impressive moment. "I gwine 'lease you!"

Old Alek trembled like a little bush in a wind. "Mist' Wash'ton?"

Quoth Peter, deliberately, "I gwine 'lease you."

The old man was filled with a desire to negotiate this statement at once, but he felt the necessity of carrying off the event without an appearance of haste. "Yes, seh; thank 'e, seh; thank 'e, Mist' Wash'ton. I raikon I ramble home pressenly."

He waited an interval, and then dubiously said, "Good-evenin', Mist' Wash'ton."

"Good-evenin', deacon. Don' come foolin' roun' *feelin'* no mellums, and I say troof. Good-evenin', deacon."

Alek took off his hat and made three profound bows. "Thank 'e, seh. Thank 'e, seh. Thank 'e, seh."

Peter underwent another severe spasm, but the old man walked off toward his home with a humble and contrite heart.

IV

The next morning Alek proceeded from his shanty under the complete but customary illusion that he was going to work. He trudged manfully along until he reached the vicinity of Si Bryant's place. Then, by stages, he relapsed into a slink. He was passing the garden patch under full steam when, at some distance ahead of him, he saw Si Bryant leaning casually on the garden fence.

"Good-mornin', Alek."

"Good-mawnin', Mist' Bryant," answered Alek, with a new deference. He was marching on, when he was halted by a word—"Alek!"

He stopped. "Yes, seh."

"I found a knife this mornin' in th' road," drawled Si, "an' I thought maybe it was yourn."

Improved in mind by this divergence from the direct line of attack, Alek stepped up easily to look at the knife. "No, seh," he said, scanning it as it lay in Si's palm, while the cold steel-blue eyes of the white man looked down into his stomach, "'tain't no knife er mine." But he knew the knife. He knew it as if it had been his mother. And at the same moment a spark flashed through his head and made wise his understanding. He knew everything. "'Tain't much of er knife, Mist' Bryant," he said, deprecatingly.

"'Tain't much of a knife, I know that," cried Si, in sudden heat, "but I found it this mornin' in my watermelon patch—hear?"

"Watahmellum paitch?" yelled Alek, not astounded.

"Yes, in my watermelon patch," sneered Si, "an' I think you know something about it, too!"

"Me?" cried Alek. "Me?"

"Yes—you!" said Si, with icy ferocity. "Yes—you!" He had become convinced that Alek was not in any way guilty, but he was certain that the old man knew the owner of the knife, and so he pressed him at first on criminal lines. "Alek, you might as well own up now. You've been meddlin' with my watermelons!"

"Me?" cried Alek again. "Yah's *ma* knife. I done cah'e it foh yeahs."

Bryant changed his ways. "Look here, Alek," he said, confidentially: "I know you and you know me, and there ain't no use in any more skirmishin'. *I* know that *you* know whose knife that is. Now whose is it?"

This challenge was so formidable in character that Alek temporarily quailed and began to stammer. "Er—now—Mist' Bryant—you—you—frien' er mine—"

"I know I'm a friend of yours, but," said Bryant, inexorably, "who owns this knife?"

Alek gathered unto himself some remnants of dignity and spoke with reproach: "Mist' Bryant, dish yer knife ain' mine."

"No," said Bryant, "it ain't. But you know who it belongs to, an' I want you to tell me—quick."

"Well, Mist' Bryant," answered Alek, scratching his wool, "I won't say 's I *do* know who b'longs ter dish yer knife, an' I won't say 's I *don't*."

Bryant again laughed his Yankee laugh, but this time there was little humor in it. It was dangerous.

Alek, seeing that he had got himself into hot water by the fine diplomacy of his last sentence, immediately began to flounder and totally submerge himself. "No, Mist' Bryant," he repeated, "I won't say 's I *do* know who b'longs ter dish yer knive, an' I won't say 's I *don't*." And he began to parrot this fatal sentence again and again. It seemed wound about his tongue. He could not rid himself of it. Its very power to make trouble for him seemed to originate the mysterious Afric reason for its repetition.

"Is he a very close friend of yourn?" said Bryant, softly.

"F-frien'?" stuttered Alek. He appeared to weigh this question with much care. "Well, seems like he *was* er frien', an' then agin, it seems like he—"

"It seems like he *wasn't*?" asked Bryant.

"Yes, seh, jest so, jest so," cried Alek. "Sometimes it seems like he *wasn't*. Then again—" He stopped for profound meditation.

The patience of the white man seemed inexhaustible. At length his low and oily voice broke the stillness. "Oh, well, of course if he's a friend of yourn, Alek! You know I wouldn't want to make no trouble for a friend of yourn."

"Yes, seh," cried the Negro at once. "He's er frien' er mine. He is dat."

"Well, then, it seems as if about the only thing to do is for you to tell me his name so's I can send him his knife, and that's all there is to it."

Alek took off his hat, and in perplexity ran his hand over his wool. He studied the ground. But several times he raised his eyes to take a sly peep at the imperturbable visage of the white man. "Y-y-yes, Mist' Bryant.—I raikon dat's erbout all what kin be done. I gwine tell you who b'longs ter dish yer knife."

"Of course," said the smooth Bryant, "it ain't a very nice thing to have to do, but—"

"No, seh," cried Alek, brightly; "I'm gwine tell you, Mist' Bryant. I gwine tell you erbout dat knife. Mist' Bryant," he asked solemnly, "does you know who b'longs ter dar knife?"

"No, I—"

"Well, I gwine tell. I gwine tell who. Mist' Bryant—" The old man drew himself to a stately pose and held forth his arm. "I gwine tell who. Mist' Bryant, *dish yer knife blongs ter Sam Jackson!*"

Bryant was startled into indignation. "Who in hell is Sam Jackson?" he growled.

"He's a nigger," said Alek, impressively, "and he wuks in er lumber-yawd up yere in Hoswego."

From SHERWOOD ANDERSON'S NOTEBOOK: NOTES OUT OF A MAN'S LIFE

Sherwood Anderson (1876-1941)

NOTE 4

When I am not writing all my instincts lead me to go where men are working with their hands. Formerly I also worked with my hands, touched to some purpose wood, iron, brass, brick, stone, the earth. That one should get money by writing, painting, making music is in some way false.

I love rich delicate fabrics and carpets, love to touch such things with my fingers but why should I possess them?

As an outcast in the world of men, working my way from place to place, I was uncomfortable but happy.

In the south, where I now live, it seems to me the Negroes, who do all the hard work, are the sweetest people.

I cannot approach the Negro, cannot speak intimately with him. Such an attempt on my part would arouse the suspicions of both whites and blacks.

I stand aside, make myself as much as I can a part of the wharves, the streets, the fields where these men and women work.

Others feel as I feel. A southern woman writer, of what is called a distinguished family down here, whispered to me across a dinner table. "What, if you were not yourself, would you like to be?" I had asked her, making conversation.

"Above all things I should like to be a Negro woman," she said.

I talked to a southern man, the son of a planter. For a long time he had been at work on a novel. It was smart and clever. That was not what he wanted it to be. "If there is ever an art produced in the American south it must come from the Negro," he said.

I dress in as fine linen as I can afford, wear bright ties, loud socks, carry a cane. The Negroes on the docks among whom I spend so much of my time like me so. I can see the looks of approval pass from eye to eye. We have something in common. Together we love bright gaudy colors, food, the earth, the sky, the river. We love song and laughter, night, drink, and lust.

NOTE 9

As to this matter of a man's relations to other men and to women. Directly—being a man—I have no relation to anything. I play—am of no direct importance. It may be that I sometimes fertilize another man or woman, mentally or physically. That seems to me quite accidental. If the thing were not done by me someone else might do it.

The woman who has a child, carrying it in her body, thrusting it forth in pain, can walk feeling a direct relation between herself and trees, grasses, animals. I am much less the animal, being male. Often I pitch off into the world of fancy, losing, for the time being, all direct connection with the physical world.

I visit China, the South Seas, the frozen North. I talk to men, make love to women, play with children. I am, in fancy and during one day, a dozen other men. I live inside them, pick up objects with their fingers, think their thoughts, feel what they feel.

If I could stay quite completely in the world of fancy or in the physical world I might be satisfied. I stay in neither.

I am a candle blown by the wind. Soon I shall go out.

I go to the river where men are loading ships. I sit watching two strong Negroes who are putting great timbers into the hold of a ship. What they touch with their great black fingers is something definite. I am envious of them.

In fancy I can build a whole city of beautiful houses. I can sail a ship on stormy seas, can lift great stones—but my fancies, that can come so swiftly and quickly, are as quickly blown away.

I sleep in a room in the midst of books. I write books. In one night, when I am sleepless, enough fancies come to me to make a whole library of books.

They come and go. Nothing stays. I produce nothing of any permanence. Men like me, feeling keenly this impermanence, have invented heaven and hell. "Better roast forever in hell than to disappear like a candle blown out," they say.

But the vision of heaven and hell is also a fancy.

The Negro working on the docks is envious of me sitting and thinking. I am envious of him rolling the great timbers. He thinks me an aristocrat and I think him an aristocrat.

What would I not give to accomplish something definite—related to trees, the earth, the sky, the seas!

What would I not give to be a man, not the shadow of a man!

NOTE 23

If some white artist could go among the Negroes and live with them much beautiful stuff might be got. The trouble is that no American white man could do it without self-consciousness. The best thing is to stand aside, listen and wait. If I can be impersonal in the presence of black laborers, watch the dance of bodies, hear the song, I may learn something.

NOTE 24

A dream—I saw a tall fine-looking man with a light coming from his forehead. Everything hung suspended in space. A beautiful, rather sensual-looking woman, quite naked, was half turned, in just the position taken by a baseball pitcher about to throw a ball.

Later, I saw Negro women framed by windows as pictures are framed. There were no buildings, just the framed windows floating in space.

At each window was a Negro woman and they were all old. They were old house servants, field hands, cotton pickers. As I saw each face the woman's whole story was revealed. Years of labor close down to the soil, the soil running through the fingers. When they were young women, nights sitting by a river or by a bayou. Dark earth-floored cabins. The big house of the whites, with lights shining in the distance.

Sometimes the Negro men were violent. They took knives and cut each other.

At other times many Negroes sat on the ground together and sang.

The connection between the man with the light in his forehead, the naked white woman and the faces of aged Negro women was not much. There are no direct connections made in such dreams. One feels sensuality, wonder, interest, quite naturally—is unashamed, does not try to be logical.

It may be that thus the Negro gets life. As for myself I leave the fact that I have such dreams to the psychoanalysts.

NOTE 25

A friend of mine was on a boat coming from the South Seas. On the boat was another American, from the South, from the State of Mississippi. As the night was hot and they could not sleep they sat on the deck talking.

The talk turned to Negro life in the American South and the Southerner told a tale.

When he was a young man he, the Southerner, went with another young man to hunt. In the late afternoon they came out of a canebrake and up onto a levee facing the Mississippi River.

At that moment a buggy came tearing along the levee top. It was driven by a young white woman of the neighborhood and she was terribly excited. She kept lashing the horse with a buggy whip and when she saw the white men she screamed.

The white men managed to stop the horse and inquired the reason for her terror. A Negro man had come alone out of the canebrake a half mile below.

She had been frightened. Many terrible things, she reminded them, had happened in the South.

The young white men ran along the levee, their guns in their hands. When they came to the Negro, a man of thirty-five and the father of a family, they presented their guns and made him march before them into the canebrake. They kept swearing, "You black son of a bitch." As they tied him securely to a tree he kept protesting. What had he done? "You know well enough, you black son of a bitch."

When they had him tied one of them took his hunting knife and cut off an ear. Then he handed the knife to his friend who took the other ear. They were collecting souvenirs of the occasion.

The Negro man was left tied in the canebrake several hours. It was very hot and the mosquitoes came in swarms. Later, other Negroes came and cut him loose.

The two young men dried the ears and kept them. The man on the boat, when he had told the story, went down to his cabin to get his dried ear and show it. He seemed to think it—my friend said—a symbol of the superiority of the whites.

PANTALOON IN BLACK

William Faulkner (1897-1962)

1

He stood in the worn, faded clean overalls which Mannie herself had washed only a week ago, and heard the first clod strike the pine box. Soon he had one of the shovels himself, which in his hands (he was better than six feet and weighed better than two hundred pounds) resembled the toy shovel a child plays with at the shore, its half cubic foot of flung dirt no more than the light gout of sand the child's shovel would have flung. Another member of his sawmill gang touched his arm and said, "Lemme have hit, Rider." He didn't even falter. He released one hand in midstroke and flung it backward, striking the other across the chest, jolting him back a step, and restored the hand to the moving shovel, flinging the dirt with that effortless fury so that the mound seemed to be rising of its own volition, not built up from above but thrusting visibly upward out of the earth itself, until at last the grave, save for its rawness, resembled any other marked off without order about the barren plot by shards of pottery and broken bottles and old brick and other objects insignificant to sight but actually of a profound meaning and fatal to touch, which no white man could have read. Then he straightened up and with one hand flung the shovel quivering upright in the mound like a javelin and turned and began to walk away, walking on even when an old woman came out of the meagre clump of his kin and friends and a few old people who had known him and his dead wife both since they were born, and grasped his forearm. She was his aunt. She had raised him. He could not remember his parents at all.

"Whar you gwine?" she said.

"Ah'm goan home," he said.

"You dont wants ter go back dar by yoself," she said. "You needs to eat. You come on home and eat."

"Ah'm goan home," he repeated, walking out from under her hand, his forearm like iron, as if the weight on it were no more than that of a fly, the other members of the mill gang whose head he was giving way quietly to let him pass. But before he reached the fence one of them overtook him; he did not need to be told it was his aunt's messenger.

"Wait, Rider," the other said. "We gots a jug in de bushes—" Then the other said what he had not intended to say, what he had never conceived of himself saying in circumstances like these, even though everybody knew it—the dead who either will not or cannot quit the earth yet al-

---

though the flesh they once lived in has been returned to it, let the preachers tell and reiterate and affirm how they left it not only without regret but with joy, mounting toward glory: "You dont wants ter go back dar. She be wawkin yit."

He didn't pause, glancing down at the other, his eyes red at the inner corners in his high, slightly backtilted head. "Lemme lone, Acey," he said. "Doan mess wid me now," and went on, stepping over the three-strand wire fence without even breaking his stride, and crossed the road and entered the woods. It was middle dusk when he emerged from them and crossed the last field, stepping over that fence too in one stride, into the lane. It was empty at this hour of Sunday evening—no family in wagon, no rider, no walkers churchward to speak to him and carefully refrain from looking after him when he had passed—the pale, powder-light, powder-dry dust of August from which the long week's marks of hoof and wheel had been blotted by the strolling and unhurried Sunday shoes, with somewhere beneath them, vanished but not gone, fixed and held in the annealing dust, the narrow, splay-toed prints of his wife's bare feet where on Saturday afternoons she would walk to the commissary to buy their next week's supplies while he took his bath; himself, his own prints, setting the period now as he strode on, moving almost as fast as a smaller man could have trotted, his body breasting the air her body had vacated, his eyes touching the objects—post and tree and field and house and hill—her eyes had lost.

The house was the last one in the lane, not his but rented from Carothers Edmonds, the local white landowner. But the rent was paid promptly in advance, and even in just six months he had refloored the porch and rebuilt and roofed the kitchen, doing the work himself on Saturday afternoon and Sunday with his wife helping him, and bought the stove. Because he made good money: saw-milling ever since he began to get his growth at fifteen and sixteen and now, at twenty-four, head of the timber gang itself because the gang he headed moved a third again as much timber between sunup and sundown as any other moved, handling himself at times out of the vanity of his own strength logs which ordinarily two men would have handled with canthooks; never without work even in the old days when he had not actually needed the money, when a lot of what he wanted, needed perhaps, didn't cost money—the women bright and dark and for all purposes nameless he didn't need to buy and it didn't matter to him what he wore and there was always food for him at any hour of day or night in the house of his aunt who didn't even want to take the two dollars he gave her each Saturday—so there had been only the Saturday and Sunday dice and whiskey that had to be paid for until that day six months ago when he saw Mannie, whom he had known all his life, for the first time and said to himself: "Ah'm thu wid all dat," and they married and he rented the cabin from Carothers Edmonds and built a fire on the hearth on their wedding night as the tale told how Uncle Lucas Beauchamp, Edmonds' oldest tenant, had done on his forty-five years ago and which had burned ever since; and he would rise and dress and eat his breakfast by lamplight to walk the four miles to the mill by sunup, and exactly one hour after sundown he would enter the house again, five days a week, until Saturday. Then the first hour would not have passed noon when he would mount the steps and knock, not on post or doorframe but on the underside of the gallery roof itself, and enter and ring the bright cascade of silver dollars onto the scrubbed table in the kitchen where his dinner simmered on the stove and the galvanised tub of hot water and the baking powder can of soft soap and the towel made of scalded flour sacks sewn together and his clean overalls and shirt waited, and Mannie would gather up the money and walk the half-mile to the commissary and buy their next week's supplies and bank the rest of the money in Edmonds' safe and return and they would eat once again without haste or hurry after five days—the sidemeat, the greens, the cornbread, the buttermilk from the well-house, the cake which she baked every Saturday now that she had a stove to bake in.

But when he put his hand on the gate it seemed to him suddenly that there was nothing beyond it. The house had never been his anyway, but now even the new planks and sills and shingles, the hearth and stove and bed, were all a part of the memory of somebody else, so that he stopped in the half-open gate and said aloud, as though he had gone to sleep in one place and then waked suddenly to find himself in another: "Whut's Ah doin hyar?" before he went on. Then he saw the dog. He had forgotten it. He remembered neither seeing nor hearing it since it began to howl just before dawn yesterday—a big dog, a hound with a strain of mastiff from somewhere (he had told Mannie a month after they married: "Ah needs a big dawg. You's de onliest least thing whut ever kep up wid me one day, leff alone fo weeks.") coming out from beneath the gallery and approaching, not running but seeming rather to drift across the dusk until it stood lightly against his leg, its head raised until the tips of his fingers just touched it, facing the house and making no sound; whereupon, as if the animal controlled it, had lain guardian before it during his absence and only this instant relinquished, the shell of planks and shingles facing him solidified, filled, and for the moment he believed that he could not possibly enter it. "But Ah needs to eat," he said. "Us bofe needs to eat," he said, moving on though the dog did not follow until he turned and cursed it. "Come on hyar!" he said. "Whut you skeered of? She lacked you too, same as me," and they mounted the steps and crossed the porch and entered the house—the dusk-filled single room where all those six months were now crammed and crowded into one instant of time until there was no space left for air to breathe, crammed and crowded about the hearth where the fire which was to have lasted to the end of them, before which in the days before he was able to buy the stove he would enter after his four-mile walk from the mill and find her, the shape of her narrow back and haunches squatting, one narrow spread hand shielding her face from the blaze over which the other hand held the skillet, had already fallen to a dry, light soilure of dead ashes when the sun rose yesterday—and himself standing there while the last of light died about the strong and indomitable beating of his heart and the deep steady arch and collapse of his chest which walking fast over the rough going of woods and fields had not increased and standing still in the quiet and fading room had not slowed down.

Then the dog left him. The light pressure went off his flank; he heard the click and hiss of its claws on the wooden floor as it surged away and he thought at first that it was fleeing. But it stopped just outside the front door, where he could see it now, and the upfling of its head as the howl began, and then he saw her too. She was standing in the kitchen door, looking at him. He didn't move. He didn't breathe nor speak until he knew his voice would be all right, his face fixed too not to alarm her. "Mannie," he said. "Hit's awright. Ah aint afraid." Then he took a step toward her, slow, not even raising his hand yet, and stopped. Then he took another step. But this time as soon as he moved she began to fade. He stopped at once, not breathing again, motionless, willing his eyes to see that she had stopped too. But she had not stopped. She was fading, going. "Wait," he said, talking as sweet as he had ever heard his voice speak to a woman: "Den lemme go wid you, honey." But she was going. She was going fast now, he could actually feel between them the insuperable barrier of that very strength which could handle alone a log which would have taken any two other men to handle, of the blood and bones and flesh too strong, invincible for life, having learned at least once with his own eyes how tough, even in sudden and violent death, not a young man's bones and flesh perhaps but the will of that bone and flesh to remain alive, actually was.

Then she was gone. He walked through the door where she had been standing, and went to the stove. He did not light the lamp. He needed no light. He had set the stove up himself and built the shelves for the dishes, from among which he took two plates by feel and from the pot sitting cold on the cold stove he ladled onto the plates the food which his aunt had brought yesterday and of which he had eaten yesterday though now he did not remember when he had eaten it nor what it was, and carried the plates to the scrubbed bare table beneath the single small fading window and drew two chairs up and sat down, waiting again until he knew his voice would be what he wanted it to be. "Come on hyar, now," he said roughly. "Come on hyar and eat yo supper. Ah aint gonter have no—" and ceased, looking down at his plate, breathing the strong, deep pants, his chest arching and collapsing until he stopped it presently and held himself motionless for perhaps a half minute, and raised a spoonful of the cold and glutinous peas to his mouth. The congealed and lifeless mass seemed to bounce on contact with his lips. Not even warmed from mouth-heat, peas and spoon spattered and rang upon the plate; his chair crashed backward and he was standing, feeling the muscles of his jaw beginning to drag his mouth open, tugging upward the top half of his head. But he stopped that too before it became sound, holding himself again while he rapidly scraped the food from his plate onto the other and took it up and left the kitchen, crossed the other room and the gallery and set the plate on the bottom step and went on toward the gate.

The dog was not there, but it overtook him within the first half mile. There was a moon then, their two shadows flitting broken and intermittent among the trees or slanted long and intact across the slope of pasture or old abandoned fields upon the hills, the man moving almost as fast as a horse could have moved over that ground, altering his course each time a lighted window came in sight, the dog trotting at heel while their shadows shortened to the moon's curve until at last they trod them and the last far lamp had vanished and the shadows began to lengthen on the other hand, keeping to heel even when a rabbit burst from almost beneath the man's foot, then lying in the gray of dawn beside the man's prone body, beside the labored heave and collapse of the chest, the loud harsh snoring which sounded not like groans of pain but like someone engaged without arms in prolonged single combat.

When he reached the mill there was nobody there but the fireman—an older man just turning from the woodpile, watching quietly as he crossed the clearing, striding as if he were going to walk not only through the boiler shed but through (or over) the boiler too, the overalls which had been clean yesterday now draggled and soiled and drenched to the knees with dew, the cloth cap flung onto the side of his head, hanging peak downward over his ear as he always wore it, the whites of his eyes rimmed with red and with something urgent and strained about them. "Whar yo bucket?" he said. But before the fireman could answer he had stepped past him and lifted the polished lard pail down from a nail in a post. "Ah just wants a biscuit," he said.

"Eat hit all," the fireman said. "Ah'll eat outen de yuthers' buckets at dinner. Den you gawn home and go to bed. You don't looks good."

"Ah aint come hyar to look," he said, sitting on the ground, his back against the post, the open pail between his knees, cramming the food into his mouth with his hands, wolfing it—peas again, also gelid and cold, a fragment of yesterday's Sunday fried chicken, a few rough chunks of this morning's fried sidemeat, a biscuit the size of a child's cap—indiscriminate, tasteless. The rest of the crew was gathering now, with voices and sounds of movement outside the boiler shed; presently the white foreman rode into the clearing on a horse. He did not look up, setting the empty pail aside, rising, looking at no one, and went to the branch and lay on his stomach and lowered his face to the water, drawing the water into himself with the same deep, strong, troubled inhalations that he had snored with, or as when he had stood in the empty house at dusk yesterday, trying to get air.

Then the trucks were rolling. The air pulsed with the rapid beating of the exhaust and the whine and clang of the saw, the trucks rolling one by one up to the skidway, he mounting the trucks in turn, to stand balanced on the load he freed, knocking the chocks out and casting loose the shackle chains and with his cant-hook squaring the sticks of cypress and gum and oak one by one to the incline and holding them until the next two men of his gang were ready to receive and guide them, until the discharge of each truck became one long rumbling roar punctuated by grunting shouts and, as the morning grew and the sweat came, chanted phrases of song tossed back and forth. He did not sing with them. He rarely ever did, and this morning might have been no different from any other—himself man-height again above the heads which carefully refrained from looking at him, stripped to the waist now, the shirt removed and the overalls knotted about his hips by the suspender straps, his upper body bare except for the handkerchief about his neck and the cap clapped and clinging somehow over his right ear, the mounting sun sweat-glinted steel-blue on the midnight-colored bunch and slip of muscles until the whistle blew for noon and he said to the two men at the head of the skidway: "Look out. Git out de way," and rode the log down the incline, balanced erect upon it in short rapid backward-running steps above the headlong thunder.

His aunt's husband was waiting for him—an old man, as tall as he was, but lean, almost frail, carrying a tin pail in one hand and a covered plate in the other; they too sat in the shade beside the branch a short distance from where the others were opening their dinner pails. The bucket contained a fruit jar of buttermilk packed in a clean damp towsack. The covered dish was a peach pie, still warm. "She baked hit fer you dis mawin," the uncle said. "She say fer you to come home." He didn't answer, bent forward a little, his elbows on his knees, holding the pie in both hands, wolfing at it, the syrupy filling smearing and trickling down his chin, blinking rapidly as he chewed, the whites of his eyes covered a little more by the creeping red. "Ah went to yo house last night, but you want dar. She sont me. She wants you to come on home. She kept de lamp burnin all last night fer you."

"Ah'm awright," he said.

"You aint awright. De Lawd guv, and He tuck away. Put yo faith and trust in Him. And she kin help you."

"Whut faith and trust?" he said. "Whut Mannie ever done ter Him? Whut He wanter come messin wid me and——"

"Hush!" the old man said. "Hush!"

Then the trucks were rolling again. Then he could stop needing to invent to himself reasons for his breathing, until after a while he began to believe he had forgot about breathing since now he could not hear it himself above the steady thunder of the rolling logs; whereupon as soon as he found himself believing he had forgotten it, he knew that he had not, so that instead of tipping the final log onto the skidway he stood up and cast his cant-hook away as if it were a burnt match and in the dying reverberation of the last log's rumbling descent he vaulted down between the two slanted tracks of the skid, facing the log which still lay on the truck. He had done it before—taken a log from the truck on his hands, balanced, and turned with it and tossed it onto the skidway, but never with a stick of this size, so that in a complete cessation of all sound save the pulse of the exhaust and the light free-running whine of the disengaged saw since every eye there, even that of the white foreman, was upon him, he nudged the log to the edge of the truckframe and squatted and set his palms against the underside of it. For a time there was no movement at all. It was as if the unrational and inanimate wood had invested, mesmerised the man with some of its own primal inertia. Then a voice said quietly: "He got hit. Hit's off de truck," and they saw the crack and gap of air, watching the infinitesimal straightening of the braced legs until the knees locked, the movement mounting infinitesimally through the belly's insuck, the arch of the chest, the neck cords, lifting the lip from the white clench of teeth in passing, drawing the whole head backward and only the bloodshot fixity of the eyes impervious to it, moving on up the arms and the straightening elbows until the balanced log was higher than his head. "Only he aint gonter turn wid dat un," the same voice said. "And when he try to put hit back on de truck, hit gonter kill him." But none of them moved. Then—there was no gathering of supreme effort—the log seemed to leap suddenly backward over his head of its own volition, spinning, crashing and thundering down the incline; he turned and stepped over the slanting track in one stride and walked through them as they gave way and went on across the clearing toward the woods even though the foreman called after him: "Rider!" and again: "You, Rider!"

At sundown he and the dog were in the river swamp four miles away—another clearing, itself not much larger than a room, a hut, a hovel partly of planks and partly of canvas, an unshaven white man standing in the door beside which a shotgun leaned, watching him as he approached, his hand extended with four silver dollars on the palm. "Ah wants a jug," he said.

"A jug?" the white man said. "You mean a pint. This is Monday. Aint you all running this week?"

"Ah laid off," he said. "Whar's my jug?" waiting, looking at nothing apparently, blinking his bloodshot eyes rapidly in his high, slightly back-tilted head, then turning, the jug hanging from his crooked middle finger against his leg, at which moment the white man looked suddenly and sharply at his eyes as though seeing them for the first time—the eyes which had been strained and urgent this morning and which now seemed to be without vision too and in which no white showed at all—and said,

"Here. Gimme that jug. You don't need no gallon. I'm going to give you that pint, give it to you. Then you get out of here and stay out. Dont come back until—" Then the white man reached and grasped the jug, whereupon the other swung it behind him, sweeping his other arm up and out so that it struck the white man across the chest.

"Look out, white folks," he said. "Hit's mine. Ah done paid you."

The white man cursed him. "No you aint. Here's your money. Put that jug down, nigger."

"Hit's mine," he said, his voice quiet, gentle even, his face quiet save for the rapid blinking of the red eyes. "Ah done paid for hit," turning on, turning his back on the man and the gun both, and recrossed the clearing to where the dog waited beside the path to come to heel again. They moved rapidly on between the close walls of impenetrable cane-stalks which gave a sort of blondness to the twilight and possessed something of that oppression, that lack of room to breathe in, which the walls of his house had had. But this time, instead of fleeing it, he stopped and raised the jug and drew the cob stopper from the fierce duskreek of uncured alcohol and drank, gulping the liquid solid and cold as ice water, without either taste or heat until he lowered the jug and the air got in. "Hah," he said. "Dat's right. Try me. Try me, big boy. Ah gots something hyar now dat kin whup you."

And, once free of the bottom's unbreathing blackness, there was the moon again, his long shadow and that of the lifted jug slanting away as he drank and then held the jug poised, gulping the silver air into his throat until he could breathe again, speaking to the jug: "Come on now. You always claim you's a better man den me. Come on now. Prove it." He drank again, swallowing the chill liquid tamed of taste or heat either while the swallowing lasted, feeling it flow solid and cold with fire, past then enveloping the strong steady panting of his lungs until they too ran suddenly free as his moving body ran in the silver solid wall of air he breasted. And he was all right, his striding shadow and the trotting one of the dog travelling swift as those of two clouds along the hill; the long cast of his motionless shadow and that of the lifted jug slanting across the slope and he watched the frail figure of his aunt's husband toiling up the hill.

"Dey tole me at de mill you was gone," the old man said. "Ah knowed whar to look. Come home, son. Dat ar cant help you."

"Hit done awready hope me," he said. "Ah'm awready home. Ah'm snakebit now and pizen cant hawm me."

"Den stop and see her. Leff her look at you. Dat's all she axes: just leff her look at you—" But he was already moving. "Wait!" the old man cried. "Wait!"

"You cant keep up," he said, speaking into the silver air, breasting aside the silver solid air which began to flow past him almost as fast as it would have flowed past a moving horse. The faint frail voice was already lost in the night's infinitude, his shadow and that of the dog scudding the free miles, the deep strong panting of his chest running free as air now because he was all right.

Then, drinking, he discovered suddenly that no more of the liquid was entering his mouth. Swallowing, it was no longer passing down his throat, his throat and mouth filled now with a solid and unmoving column which without reflex or revulsion sprang, columnar and intact and still retaining the mold of his gullet, outward glinting in the moonlight, splintering, vanishing into the myriad murmur of the dewed grass. He drank again. Again his throat merely filled solidly until two icy rills ran from his mouth-corners; again the intact column sprang silvering, glinting, shivering, while he panted the chill of air into his throat, the jug poised before his mouth while he spoke to it: "Awright. Ah'm ghy try you again. Soon as you makes up yo mind to stay whar I puts you, Ah'll leff you alone." He drank, filling his gullet for the third time and lowered the jug one instant ahead of the bright intact repetition, panting, indrawing the cool of air until he could breathe. He stoppered the cob carefully back into the jug and stood, panting, blinking, the long cast of his solitary shadow slanting away across the hill and beyond, across the mazy infinitude of all the night-bound earth. "Awright," he said. "Ah just misread de sign wrong. Hit's done done me all de help Ah needs. Ah'm awright now. Ah doan needs no mo of hit."

He could see the lamp in the window as he crossed the pasture, passing the black-and-silver yawn of the sandy ditch where he had played as a boy with empty snuff-tins and rusted harness-buckles and fragments of trace-chains and now and then an actual wheel, passing the garden patch where he had hoed in the spring days while his aunt stood sentry over him from the kitchen window, crossing the grassless yard in whose dust he had sprawled and crept before he learned to walk. He entered the house, the room, the light itself, and stopped in the door, his head backtilted a little as if he could not see, the jug hanging from his crooked finger, against his leg. "Unc Alec say you wanter see me," he said.

"Not just to see you," his aunt said. "To come home, whar we kin help you."

"Ah'm awright," he said. "Ah doan needs no help."

"No," she said. She rose from the chair and came and grasped his arm as she had grasped it yesterday at the grave. Again, as on yesterday, the forearm was like iron under her hand. "No! When Alec come back and tole me how you had wawked off de mill and de sun not half down, Ah knowed why and whar. And dat cant help you."

"Hit done awready hope me. Ah'm awright now."

"Dont lie to me," she said. "You aint never lied to me. Dont lie to me now."

Then he said it. It was his own voice, without either grief or amazement, speaking quietly out of the tremendous panting of his chest which in a moment now would begin to strain at the walls of this room too. But he would be gone in a moment.

"Nome," he said, "Hit aint done me no good."

"And hit cant! Cant nothing help you but Him! Ax Him! Tole Him about hit! He wants to hyar you and help you!"

"Efn He God, Ah dont needs to tole Him. Efn He God, He awready know hit. Awright. Hyar Ah is. Leff Him come down hyar and do me some good."

"On yo knees!" she cried. "On yo knees and ax Him!" But it was not his knees on the floor, it was his feet. And for a space he could hear her feet too on the planks of the hall behind him and her voice crying after him from the door: "Spoot! Spoot!"—crying after him across the moon-dappled yard the name he had gone by in his childhood and adolescence, before the men he worked with and the bright dark nameless women he had taken in course and forgotten until he saw Mannie that day and said, "Ah'm thu wid all dat," began to call him Rider.

It was just after midnight when he reached the mill. The dog was gone now. This time he could not remember when nor where. At first he seemed to remember hurling the empty jug at it. But later the jug was still in his hand and it was not empty, although each time he drank now the two icy runnels streamed from his mouth-corners, sopping his shirt and overalls until he walked constantly in the fierce chill of the liquid tamed now of flavor and heat and odor too even when the swallowing ceased. "Sides that," he said, "Ah wouldn't thow nothin at him. Ah mout kick him efn he needed hit and was close enough. But Ah wouldn't ruint no dog chunkin hit."

The jug was still in his hand when he entered the clearing and paused among the mute soaring of the moon-blond lumber-stacks. He stood in the middle now of the unimpeded shadow which he was treading again as he had trod it last night, swaying a little, blinking about at the stacked lumber, the skidway, the piled logs waiting for tomorrow, the boiler-shed all quiet and blanched in the moon. And then it was all right. He was moving again. But he was not moving, he was drinking, the liquid cold and swift and tasteless and requiring no swallowing, so that he could not tell if it were going down inside or outside. But it was all right. And now he was moving, the jug gone now and he didn't know the when or where of that either. He crossed the clearing and entered the boiler shed and went on through it, crossing the junctureless backloop of time's trepan, to the door of the tool-room, the faint glow of the lantern beyond the plank-joints, the surge and fall of living shadow, the mutter of voices, the mute click and scutter of the dice, his hand loud on the barred door, his voice loud too: "Open hit. Hit's me. Ah'm snakebit and bound to die."

Then he was through the door and inside the tool-room. They were the same faces—three members of his timber gang, three or four others of the mill crew, the white night-watchman with the heavy pistol in his hip pocket and the small heap of coins and worn bills on the floor before him, one who was called Rider and was Rider standing above the squatting circle, swaying a little, blinking, the dead muscles of his face shaped into smiling while the white man stared up at him. "Make room, gamblers," he said. "Make room. Ah'm snakebit and de pizen cant hawm me."

"You're drunk," the white man said. "Get out of here. One of you niggers open the door and get him out of here."

"Dass awright, boss-man," he said, his voice equable, his face still fixed in the faint rigid smiling beneath the blinking of the red eyes; "Ah aint drunk. Ah just cant wawk straight fer dis yar money weighin me down."

Now he was kneeling too, the other six dollars of his last week's pay on the floor before him, blinking, still smiling at the face of the white man opposite, then, still smiling, he watched the dice pass from hand to hand around the circle as the white man covered the bets, watching the soiled and palm-worn money in front of the white man gradually and steadily increase, watching the white man cast and win two doubled bets in succession then lose one for twenty-five cents, the dice coming to him at last, the cupped snug clicking of them in his fist. He spun a coin into the center.

"Shoots a dollar," he said, and cast, and watched the white man pick up the dice and flip them back to him. "Ah lets hit lay," he said. "Ah'm snakebit. Ah kin pass wid anything," and cast, and this time one of the negroes flipped the dice back. "Ah lets hit lay," he said, and cast, and moved as the white man moved, catching the white man's wrist before his hand reached the dice, the two of them squatting, facing each other above the dice and the money, his left hand grasping the white man's wrist, his face still fixed in the rigid and deadened smiling, his voice equable, almost deferential: "Ah kin pass even wid miss-outs. But dese hyar yuther boys—" until the white man's hand sprang open and the second pair of dice clattered onto the floor beside the first two and the white man wrenched free and sprang up and back and reached the hand backward toward the pocket where the pistol was.

The razor hung between his shoulder-blades from a loop of cotton string round his neck inside his shirt. The same motion of the hand which brought the razor forward over his shoulder flipped the blade open and freed it from the cord, the blade opening on until the back edge of it lay across the knuckles of his fist, his thumb pressing the handle into his closing fingers, so that in the second before the half-drawn pistol exploded he actually struck at the white man's throat not with the blade but with a sweeping blow of his fist, following through in the same motion so that not even the first jet of blood touched his hand or arm.

2

After it was over—it didn't take long; they found the prisoner on the following day, hanging from the bell-rope in a negro schoolhouse about two miles from the sawmill, and the coroner had pronounced his verdict of death at the hands of a person or persons unknown and surrendered the body to its next of kin all within five minutes—the sheriff's deputy who had been officially in charge of the business was telling his wife about it. They were in the kitchen. His wife was cooking supper. The deputy had been out of bed and in motion ever since the jail delivery shortly before midnight of yesterday and had covered considerable ground since, and he was spent now from lack of sleep and hurried food at hurried and curious hours and, sitting in a chair beside the stove, a little hysterical too.

"Them damn niggers," he said. "I swear to godfrey, it's a wonder we have as little trouble with them as we do. Because why? Because they aint human. They look like a man and they walk on their hind legs like a man, and they can talk and you can understand them and you think they are understanding you, at least now and then. But when it comes to the normal human feelings and sentiments of human beings, they might just as well be a damn herd of wild buffaloes. Now you take this one today——"

"I wish you would," his wife said harshly. She was a stout woman, handsome once, graying now and with a neck definitely too short, who looked not harried at all but composed in fact, only choleric. Also, she had attended a club rook-party that afternoon and had won the first, the fifty-cent, prize until another member had insisted on a recount of the scores and the ultimate throwing out of one entire game. "Take him out of my kitchen, anyway. You sheriffs! Sitting around that courthouse all day long, talking. It's no wonder two or three men can walk in and take prisoners out from under your very noses. They would take your chairs and desks and window sills too if you ever got your feet and backsides off of them that long."

"It's more of them Birdsongs than just two or three," the deputy said. "There's forty-two active votes in that connection. Me and Maydew taken the poll-list and counted them one day. But listen—" The wife turned from the stove, carrying a dish. The deputy snatched his feet rapidly out of the way as she passed him, passed almost over him, and went into the dining room. The deputy raised his voice a little to carry the increased distance: "His wife dies on him. All right. But does he grieve? He's the biggest and busiest man at the funeral. Grabs a shovel before they even got the box into the grave they tell me, and starts throwing dirt onto her faster than a slip scraper could have done it. But that's all right—" His wife came back. He moved his feet again and altered his voice again to the altered range: "—maybe that's how he felt about her. There aint any law against a man rushing his wife into the ground, provided he never had nothing to do with rushing her to the cemetery too. But here the next day he's the first man back at work except the fireman, getting back to the mill before the fireman had his fire going, let alone steam up; five minutes earlier and he could even have helped the fireman wake Birdsong up so Birdsong could go home and go back to bed again, or he could even have cut Birdsong's throat then and saved everybody trouble.

"So he comes to work, the first man on the job, when McAndrews and everybody else expected him to take the day off since even a nigger couldn't want no better excuse for a holiday than he had just buried his wife, when a white man would have took the day off out of pure respect no matter how he felt about his wife, when even a little child would have had sense enough to take a day off when he would still get paid for it too. But not him. The first man there, jumping from one log truck to another before the starting whistle quit blowing even, snatching up ten-foot cypress logs by himself and throwing them around like matches. And then, when everybody had finally decided that that's the way to take him, the way he wants to be without by-your-leave or much obliged or goodbye to McAndrews or nobody else, gets himself a whole gallon of bust-skull white-mule whisky, comes straight back to the mill and to the same crap game where Birdsong has been running crooked dice on them mill niggers for fifteen years, goes straight to the same game where he has been peacefully losing a probably steady average ninety-nine percent of his pay ever since he got big enough to read the spots on them miss-out dice, and cuts Birdsong's throat clean to the neckbone five minutes later." The wife passed him again and went to the dining room. Again he drew his feet back and raised his voice:

"So me and Maydew go out there. Not that we expected to do any good, as he had probably passed Jackson, Tennessee, about daylight; and besides; the simplest way to find him would be just to stay close behind them Birdsong boys. Of course there wouldn't be nothing hardly worth bringing back to town after they did find him, but it would close the case. So it's by the merest chance that we go by his house; I dont even remember why we went now, but we did; and there he is. Sitting behind the barred front door with a open razor on one knee and a loaded shotgun on the other? No. He was asleep. A big pot of field peas et clean empty on the stove, and him laying in the back yard asleep in the broad sun with just his head under the edge of the porch in the shade and a dog that looked like a cross between a bear and a Polled Angus steer yelling fire and murder from the back door. And we wake him and he sets up and says, 'Awright, white folks. Ah done it. Jest dont lock me up,' and Maydew says, 'Mr Birdsong's kinfolks aint going to lock you up neither. You'll have plenty of fresh air when they get hold of you,' and he says, 'Ah done it. Jest dont lock me up' —advising, instructing the sheriff not to lock him up; he done it all right and it's too bad but it aint convenient for him to be cut off from the fresh air at the moment. So we loaded him into the car, when here come the old woman—his ma or aunt or something—panting up the road at a dog-trot, wanting to come with us too, and Maydew trying to explain to her what would maybe happen to her too if them Birdsong kin catches us before we can get him locked up, only she is coming anyway, and like Maydew says, her being in the car too might be a good thing if the Birdsongs did happen to run into us, because after all interference with the law cant be condoned even if the Birdsong connection did carry that beat for Maydew last summer.

"So we brought her along too and got him to town and into the jail all right and turned him over to Ketcham and Ketcham taken him on up stairs and the old woman coming too, right on up to the cell, telling Ketcham, 'Ah tried to raise him right. He was a good boy. He aint never been in no trouble till now. He will suffer for what he done. But dont let the white folks get him,' until Ketcham says, 'You and him ought to thought of that before he started barbering white men without using the lather first.' So he locked them both up in the cell because he felt like Maydew did, that her being in there with him might be a good influence on the Birdsong boys if anything started if he should happen to be running for sheriff or something when Maydew's term was up. So Ketcham come on back down stairs and pretty soon the chain gang come in and went on up to the bull pen and he thought things had settled down for a while when all of a sudden he begun to hear the yelling, not howling: yelling, though there wasn't no words in it, and he grabbed his pistol and run back up stairs to the bull pen where the chain gang was and Ketcham could see into the cell where the old woman was kind of squinched down in one corner and where that nigger had done tore that iron cot clean out of the floor it was bolted to and was standing in the middle of the cell, holding the cot over his head like it was a baby's cradle, yelling, and says to the old woman, 'Ah aint goan hurt you,' and throws the cot against the wall and comes and grabs holt of that steel barred door and rips it out of the wall, bricks hinges and all, and walks out of the cell toting the door over his head like it was a gauze window-screen, hollering. 'It's awright. It's awright. Ah aint trying to git away.'

"Of course Ketcham could have shot him right there, but like he said, if it wasn't going to be the law, then them Birdsong boys ought to have the first lick at him. So Ketcham dont shoot. Instead, he jumps in behind where them chain gang niggers was kind of backed off from that steel door, hollering, 'Grab him! Throw him down!' except the niggers hung back at first too until Ketcham gets in where he can kick the ones he can reach, batting at the others with the flat of the pistol until they rush him. And Ketcham says that for a full minute that nigger would grab them as they come in and fling them clean across the room like they was rag dolls, saying, 'Ah aint tryin to git out. Ah aint tryin to git out,' until at last they pulled him down—a big mass of nigger heads and arms and legs boiling around on the floor and even then Ketcham says every now and then a nigger would come flying out and go sailing through the air across the room, spraddled out like a flying squirrel and with his eyes sticking out like car headlights, until at last they had him down and Ketcham went in and begun peeling away niggers until he could see him laying there under the pile of them, laughing, with tears big as glass marbles running across his face and down past his ears and making a kind of popping sound on the floor like somebody dropping bird eggs, laughing and laughing and saying, 'Hit look lack Ah just cant quit thinking. Look lack Ah just cant quit.' And what do you think of that?"

"I think if you eat any supper in this house you'll do it in the next five minutes," his wife said from the dining room. "I'm going to clear this table then and I'm going to the picture show."

° ° °

A Face to Meet a Face

A mask can serve as a disguise, an attempt to make the wearer seem like someone else. In the selections that follow, black people can be found showing themselves in altered forms, sometimes aggressively, often rejecting the myths that surround them.

Hart Crane is best known for his long, unfinished poem, "The Bridge" (1930), celebrating "the myth of America." "Black Tambourine," which appears here, is from his collection of lyrics, *White Buildings*. Maya Angelou is a poet, whose recent work includes *Oh Pray My Wings Are Gonna Fit Me Well.* The title of her autobiography, *I Know Why the Caged Bird Sings*, is taken from a Paul Laurence Dunbar poem. Born in New York City in 1937, William Melvin Kelley has published four novels, the best known being *A Different Drummer*, and a number of short stories. Dudley Randall is a Detroit resident, poet, and founder of Broadside Press. Langston Hughes, a librarian whose work spans the period from the Harlem Renaissance of the 1920s to the civil rights movement of the 1960s, wrote poems, short stories, a novel, essays, plays, and children's fiction. Born and raised in the Midwest, Hughes traveled extensively as a young man, settling finally in Harlem, with which he is identified.

BLACK TAMBOURINE

Hart Crane (1899-1932)

The interests of a black man in a cellar
Mark tardy judgment on the world's closed door.
Gnats toss in the shadow of a bottle,
And a roach spans a crevice in the floor.

Aesop,° driven to pondering, found
Heaven with the tortoise and the hare;
Fox brush° and sow ear top his grave
And mingling incantations on the air.

The black man, forlorn in the cellar,
Wanders in some mid-kingdom, dark, that lies,
Between his tambourine, stuck on the wall,
And, in Africa, a carcass quick with flies.

From I KNOW WHY THE CAGED BIRD SINGS

Maya Angelou (1928-)

Chapter 2

When Bailey was six and I a year younger, we used to rattle off the times tables with the speed I was later to see Chinese children in San Francisco employ on their abacuses. Our summer-gray pot-bellied stove bloomed rosy red during winter, and became a severe disciplinarian threat if we were so foolish as to indulge in making mistakes.

Uncle Willie used to sit, like a giant black Z (he had been crippled as a child), and hear us testify to the Lafayette County Training Schools' abilities. His face pulled down on the left side, as if a pulley had been attached to his lower teeth, and his left hand was only a mite bigger than Bailey's, but on the second mistake or on the third hesitation his big overgrown right hand would catch one of us behind the collar, and in the same moment would thrust the culprit toward the dull red heater, which throbbed like a devil's toothache. We were never burned, although once I might have been when I was so terrified I tried to jump onto the stove to

---

°*Aesop:* fable writer; a black slave who lived in the 6th century B.C. °*fox brush:* the tail of a fox

remove the possibility of its remaining a threat. Like most children, I thought if I could face the worst danger voluntarily, and *triumph,* I would forever have power over it. But in my case of sacrificial effort I was thwarted. Uncle Willie held tight to my dress and I only got close enough to smell the clean dry scent of hot iron. We learned the times tables without understanding their grand principle, simply because we had the capacity and no alternative.

The tragedy of lameness seems so unfair to children that they are embarrassed in its presence. And they, most recently off nature's mold, sense that they have only narrowly missed being another of her jokes. In relief at the narrow escape, they vent their emotions in impatience and criticism of the unlucky cripple.

Momma related times without end, and without any show of emotion, how Uncle Willie had been dropped when he was three years old by a woman who was minding him. She seemed to hold no rancor against the baby-sitter, nor for her just God who allowed the accident. She felt it necessary to explain over and over again to those who knew the story by heart that he wasn't "born that way."

In our society, where two-legged, two-armed strong Black men were able at best to eke out only the necessities of life, Uncle Willie, with his starched shirts, shined shoes and shelves full of food, was the whipping boy and butt of jokes of the underemployed and underpaid. Fate not only disabled him but laid a double-tiered barrier in his path. He was also proud and sensitive. Therefore he couldn't pretend that he wasn't crippled, nor could he deceive himself that people were not repelled by his defect.

Only once in all the years of trying not to watch him, I saw him pretend to himself and others that he wasn't lame.

Coming home from school one day, I saw a dark car in our front yard. I rushed in to find a strange man and woman (Uncle Willie said later they were schoolteachers from Little Rock) drinking Dr. Pepper in the cool of the Store. I sensed a wrongness around me, like an alarm clock that had gone off without being set.

I knew it couldn't be the strangers. Not frequently, but often enough, travelers pulled off the main road to buy tobacco or soft drinks in the only Negro store in Stamps. When I looked at Uncle Willie, I knew what was pulling my mind's coattails. He was standing erect behind the counter, not leaning forward or resting on the small shelf that had been built for him. Erect. His eyes seemed to hold me with a mixture of threats and appeal.

I dutifully greeted the strangers and roamed my eyes around for his walking stick. It was nowhere to be seen. He said, "Uh . . . this this . . . this . . . uh, my niece. She's . . . uh . . . just come from school." Then to the couple—"You know . . . how, uh, children are . . . th-th-these days . . . they play all d-d-day at school and c-c-can't wait to get home and pl-play some more."

The people smiled, very friendly.

He added, "Go on out and pl-play, Sister."

The lady laughed in a soft Arkansas voice and said, "Well, you know, Mr. Johnson, they say, you're only a child once. Have you children of your own?"

Uncle Willie looked at me with an impatience I hadn't seen in his face even when he took thirty minutes to loop the laces over his high-topped shoes. "I . . . I thought I told you to go . . . go outside and play."

Before I left I saw him lean back on the shelves of Garret Snuff, Prince Albert and Spark Plug chewing tobacco.

"No, ma'am . . . no ch-children and no wife." He tried a laugh. "I have an old m-m-mother and my brother's t-two children to l-look after."

I didn't mind his using us to make himself look good. In fact, I would have pretended to be his daughter if he wanted me to. Not only did I not feel any loyalty to my own father, I figured that if I had been Uncle Willie's child I would have received much better treatment.

The couple left after a few minutes, and from the back of the house I watched the red car scare chickens, raise dust and disappear toward Magnolia.

Uncle Willie was making his way down the long shadowed aisle between the shelves and the counter—hand over hand, like a man climbing out of a dream. I stayed quiet and watched him lurch from one side, bumping to the other, until he reached the coal-oil tank. He put his hand behind that dark recess and took his cane in the strong fist and shifted his weight on the wooden support. He thought he had pulled it off.

I'll never know why it was important to him that the couple (he said later that he'd never seen them before) would take a picture of a whole Mr. Johnson back to Little Rock.

He must have tired of being crippled, as prisoners tire of penitentiary bars and the guilty tire of blame. The high-topped shoes and the cane, his uncontrollable muscles and thick tongue, and the looks he suffered of either contempt or pity had simply worn him out, and for one afternoon, one part of an afternoon, he wanted no part of them.

I understood and felt closer to him at that moment than ever before or since.

During these years in Stamps, I met and fell in love with William Shakespeare. He was my first white love. Although I enjoyed and respected Kipling, Poe, Butler, Thackeray and Henley, I saved my young and loyal passion for Paul Laurence Dunbar, Langston Hughes, James Weldon Johnson and W.E.B. Du Bois' "Litany at Atlanta." But it was Shakespeare who said, "When in disgrace with fortune and men's eyes." It was a state with which I felt myself most familiar. I pacified myself about his whiteness by saying that after all he had been dead so long it couldn't matter to anyone any more.

Bailey and I decided to memorize a scene from *The Merchant of Venice*, but we realized that Momma would question us about the author and that we'd have to tell her that Shakespeare was white, and it wouldn't matter to her whether he was dead or not. So we chose "The Creation" by James Weldon Johnson instead.

Chapter 29

Our house was a fourteen-room typical San Franciscan post-Earthquake affair. We had a succession of roomers, bringing and taking their different accents, and personalities and foods. Shipyard workers clanked up the stairs (we all slept on the second floor except Mother and Daddy Clidell) in their steel-tipped boots and metal hats, and gave way to much-powdered prostitutes, who giggled through their make-up and hung their wigs on the doorknobs. One couple (they were college graduates) held long adult conversations with me in the big kitchen downstairs, until the husband went off to war. Then the wife who had been so charming and ready to smile changed into a silent shadow that played infrequently along the walls. An older couple lived with us for a year or so. They owned a restaurant and had no personality to enchant or interest a teenager, except that the husband was called Uncle Jim, and the wife Aunt Boy. I never figured that out.

The quality of strength lined with tenderness is an unbeatable combination, as are intelligence and necessity when unblunted by formal education. I was prepared to accept Daddy Clidell as one more faceless name added to Mother's roster of conquests. I had trained myself so successfully through the years to display interest, or at least attention, while my mind skipped free on other subjects that I could have lived in his house without ever seeing him and without his becoming the wiser. But his character beckoned and elicited admiration. He was a simple man who had no inferiority complex about his lack of education and, even more amazing, no superiority complex because he had succeeded despite that lack. He would say often, "I been to school three years in my life. In Slaten, Texas, times was hard, and I had to help my daddy on the farm."

No recriminations lay hidden under the plain statement, nor was there boasting when he said, "If I'm living a little better now, it's because I treats everybody right."

He owned apartment buildings and, later, pool halls, and was famous for being that rarity "a man of honor." He didn't suffer, as many "honest men" do, from the detestable righteousness that diminishes their virtue. He knew cards and men's hearts. So during the age when Mother was exposing us to certain facts of life, like personal hygiene, proper posture, table manners, good restaurants and tipping practices, Daddy Clidell taught me to play poker, blackjack, tonk and high, low, Jick, Jack and the

Game. He wore expensively tailored suits and a large yellow diamond stickpin. Except for the jewelry, he was a conservative dresser and carried himself with the unconscious pomp of a man of secure means. Unexpectedly, I resembled him, and when he, Mother and I walked down the street his friends often said, "Clidell, that's sure your daughter. Ain't no way you can deny her."

Proud laughter followed those declarations, for he had never had children. Because of his late-arriving but intense paternal sense, I was introduced to the most colorful characters in the Black underground. One afternoon, I was invited into our smoke-filled dining room to make the acquaintance of Stonewall Jimmy, Just Black, Cool Clyde, Tight Coat and Red Leg. Daddy Clidell explained to me that they were the most successful con men in the world, and they were going to tell me about some games so that I would never be "anybody's mark."

To begin, one man warned me, "There ain't never been a mark yet that didn't want something for nothing." Then they took turns showing me their tricks, how they chose their victims (marks) from the wealthy bigoted whites and in every case how they used the victims' prejudice against them.

Some of the tales were funny, a few were pathetic, but all were amusing or gratifying to me, for the Black man, the con man who could act the most stupid, won out every time over the powerful, arrogant white.

I remember Mr. Red Leg's story like a favorite melody.

"Anything that works against you can also work for you once you understand the Principle of Reverse.

"There was a cracker in Tulsa who bilked so many Negroes he could set up a Negro Bilking Company. Naturally he got to thinking, Black Skin means Damn Fool. Just Black and I went to Tulsa to check him out. Come to find out, he's a perfect mark. His momma must have been scared in an Indian massacre in Africa. He hated Negroes only a little more than he despised Indians. And he was greedy.

"Black and I studied him and decided he was worth setting up against the store. That means we were ready to put out a few thousand dollars in preparation. We pulled in a white boy from New York, a good con artist, and had him open an office in Tulsa. He was supposed to be a Northern real estate agent trying to buy up valuable land in Oklahoma. We investigated a piece of land near Tulsa that had a toll bridge crossing it. It used to be part of an Indian reservation but had been taken over by the state.

"Just Black was laid out as the decoy, and I was going to be the fool. After our friend from New York hired a secretary and had his cards printed, Black approached the mark with a proposition. He told him that he had heard that our mark was the only white man colored people could trust. He named some of the poor fools that had been taken by that crook.

It just goes to show you how white folks can be deceived by their own deception. The mark believed Black.

"Black told him about his friend who was half Indian and half colored and how some Northern white estate agent had found out that he was the sole owner of a piece of valuable land and the Northerner wanted to buy it. At first the man acted like he smelled a rat, but from the way he gobbled up the proposition, turns out what he thought he smelled was some nigger money on his top lip.

"He asked the whereabouts of the land but Black put him off. He told his cracker that he just wanted to make sure that he would be interested. The mark allowed how he was being interested, so Black said he would tell his friend and they'd get in touch with him. Black met the mark for about three weeks in cars and in alleys and kept putting him off until the white man was almost crazy with anxiety and greed and then accidentally it seemed Black let drop the name of the Northern real estate agent who wanted the property. From that moment on we knew we had the big fish on the line and all we had to do was to pull him in.

"We expected him to try to contact our store, which he did. That cracker went to our setup and counted on his whiteness to ally him with Spots, our white boy, but Spots refused to talk about the deal except to say the land had been thoroughly investigated by the biggest real estate concern in the South and that if our mark did not go around raising dust he would make sure that there would be a nice piece of money in it for him. Any obvious inquiries as to the rightful ownership of the land could alert the state and they would surely push through a law prohibiting the sale. Spots told the mark he would keep in touch with him. The mark went back to the store three or four times but to no avail, then just before we knew he would crack, Black brought me to see him. That fool was a happy as a sissy in a C.C.C. camp. You would have thought my neck was in a noose and he was about to light the fire under my feet. I never enjoyed taking anybody so much.

"Anyhow, I played scary at first but Just Black told me that this was one white man that our people could trust. I said I did not trust no white man because all they wanted was to get a chance to kill a Black man legally and get his wife in the bed. (I'm sorry, Clidell.) The mark assured me that he was the only white man who did not feel like that. Some of his best friends were colored people. In fact, if I didn't know it, the woman who raised him was a colored woman and he still sees her to this day. I let myself be convinced and then the mark began to drag the Northern whites. He told me that they made Negroes sleep in the street in the North and that they had to clean out toilets with their hands in the North and even things worse than that. I was shocked and said, 'Then I don't want to sell my land to that white man who offered seventy-five thousand dollars for it.' Just Black said, 'I wouldn't know what to do with that kind of money,' and I said that all I wanted was to have enough money to buy a home for my old mom, to buy a business and to make one trip to Harlem. The mark asked how much would that cost and I said I reckoned I could do it on fifty thousand dollars.

"The mark told me no Negro was safe with that kind of money. That white folks would take it from him. I said I knew it but I had to have at least forty thousand dollars. He agreed. We shook hands. I said it would do my heart good to see the mean Yankee go down on some of 'our land.' We met the next morning and I signed the deed in his car and he gave me the cash.

"Black and I had kept most of our things in a hotel over in Hot Springs, Arkansas. When the deal was closed we walked to our car, drove across the state line and on to Hot Springs.

"That's all there was to it."

When he finished, more triumphant stories rainbowed around the room riding the shoulders of laughter. By all accounts those storytellers, born Black and male before the turn of the twentieth century, should have been ground into useless dust. Instead they used their intelligence to pry open the door of rejection and not only became wealthy but got some revenge in the bargain.

It wasn't possible for me to regard them as criminals or be anything but proud of their achievements.

The needs of a society determine its ethics, and in the Black American ghettos the hero is that man who is offered only the crumbs from his country's table but by ingenuity and courage is able to take for himself a Lucullan feast. Hence the janitor who lives in one room but sports a robin's-egg-blue Cadillac is not laughed at but admired, and the domestic who buys forty-dollar shoes is not criticized but is appreciated. We know that they have put to use their full mental and physical powers. Each single gain feeds into the gains of the body collective.

Stories of law violations are weighed on a different set of scales in the Black mind than in the white. Petty crimes embarrass the community and many people wistfully wonder why Negroes don't rob more banks, embezzle more funds and employ graft in the unions. "We are the victims of the world's most comprehensive robbery. Life demands a balance. It's all right if we do a little robbing now." This belief appeals particularly to one who is unable to compete legally with his fellow citizens.

My education and that of my Black associates were quite different from the education of our white schoolmates. In the classroom we all learned past participles, but in the streets and in our homes the Blacks leared to drop *s*'s from plurals and suffixes from past-tense verbs. We were alert to the gap separating the written word from the colloquial. We learned to slide out of one language and into another without being conscious of the effort. At school, in a given situation, we might respond with "That's not unusual." But in the street, meeting the same situation, we easily said, "It be's like that sometimes."

CRY FOR ME

William Melvin Kelley (1937-)

This is about my Uncle Wallace, who most of you know by his last name—Bedlow—because that's all they ever put on his records. I only got one of his albums myself. It has a picture of him on it, sitting, holding his two guitars, wearing his white dinner jacket, his mouth wide open and his eyes squinted shut. The name of the album is: "Bedlow—Big Voice Crying in the Wilderness" and I got it in particular because it has the only two songs he sang that I really like: "Cotton Field Blues" and "John Henry." Besides that, I don't much like folk songs or folk singers. But I liked Uncle Wallace all right.

I guess I should tell you about the first time I met Uncle Wallace; this was even before he was folk singing, or maybe before any of us *knew* it. We just knew he was a relative, my old man's brother, come North from the South.

That was in June of 1957. We went to Pennsylvania Station to meet him. He sent us a telegram; there wasn't enough time for him to write a letter because, he told us later, he only decided to come two days before he showed up.

So we went to the station, and the loud-speaker called out his train from down South. A *whole* bunch of colored people got off the train, all looking like somebody been keeping it a secret from them they been free for a hundred years, bulgy-eyed and confused, carrying suitcases and shopping bags and boxes and little kids.

My old man was craning his neck, looking to find Uncle Wallace. None of us would-a recognized him because when my old man come North twenty years ago he didn't bring but one picture of Uncle Wallace and that was of him when he was about seven. But my old man been back South once and saw Uncle Wallace a man. He would recognize him all right.

But I heard my old man say to my mother, "Don't see him yet."

And then we did see him; we could not-a missed him because he come rumbling out the crowd—the size of a black Grant's Tomb with a white dinner jacket draped over it (he had the jacket even then, having won it in some kind-a contest driving piles, or cutting wood)—and

---

punched my old man square in the chops so he flew back about twenty feet, knocking over this little redcap, and springing all the locks on the four suitcases he was carrying, scattering clothes in all directions like a flock of pigeons in Central Park you tossed a rock at.

My old man is about six-five and two-fifty and works in heavy construction and I ain't never seen anyone hit him, let alone knock him off his feet, and I thought sure he'd go nuts and get mad, but he didn't; he started to laugh, and Uncle Wallace stood over him and said: "How you doing, Little Brother? I see you ain't been keeping up your strength. Use to have more trouble with you when I was six." And he reached out his hand to my old man, who got up, and even though he was on his feet still looked like he was lying down because Uncle Wallace was at least a head taller.

My old man said, "Never could beat you, Wallace. Pa's the only man could." And I remember figuring how to be able to do that, my Grandpa Mance Bedlow must-a been close to eight feet tall and made of some kind of fireproof metal.

Then my old man turned to us and said: "I'd like you to meet my family. This is my wife, Irene." He pointed at my mother. "And this is Mance; we call him Little Brother." He pointed at my brother. "And this is my first-born, Carlyle junior." And he pointed at me and I reached up my hand to Uncle Wallace before I realized he'd probably crush it. He took it, but didn't crush it at all, just squeezed it a little and smiled, looking down at me out tiny, red eyes in his black-moon face.

So we took Uncle Wallace home to the Bronx.

My old man got him a job with the same construction company he worked for, and the foreman, he'd send them both up on the girders and give them enough work for eight men and they'd get it done, and then they'd come home and Uncle Wallace'd watch television until one and then go to sleep. He never seen it before and it knocked him out.

He hadn't seen anything of New York but our house and the building he and my old man was practically putting up single-handed. That's why one Friday night, my old man said: "Carlyle, why don't you take old Wallace downtown and show him the city?"

I really didn't want to go; I mean, that's *nowhere*, getting stuck with a man could be your father, but I went.

First I took him to Harlem near where we used to live and we said hello to some of my old friends who was standing in front of a bar, watching the girls swishing by in dresses where you could see everything, either because the dresses was so tight over what they should-a been covering, or because there wasn't no dress covering the other parts. I guess Uncle Wallace liked that pretty much because everybody was colored and where we live in the Bronx, everybody is Italian. So in Harlem, he must-a felt at home.

Then we went to Times Square. I don't think he liked that too much, too big and noisy for him, him being right out of a cotton field. I was about to take him home, but then I said: "Hey, Uncle Wallace, you ever seen a queer?"

He looked down at me. "What's that, Carlyle?"

I was about to laugh because I figure maybe he ain't seen a queer, but I would-a thought *everybody* knew what they was. But then I decided just to explain—I knew how strong he was, but hadn't been knowing him long enough to know how fast he got mad. So I just told him what a queer was.

He looked down at me blank and sort of stupid. "No stuff?"

"I wouldn't lie to you, Uncle Wallace." I took him by the arm. "Come on, I'll show you some queers."

That's why we went to Greenwich Village.

It was comical to see him looking at his first queer, who was as queer as a giraffe sitting on a bird's nest. Uncle Wallace just gaped like he seen a farmer hitch a chipmunk to a plow, then turned to me. "Well, I'll be lynched, Carlyle!"

After that we walked around past the handbag and sandal shops and the coffee houses and dug the queers and some girls in sort of black underwear, and then all of a sudden, he wasn't with me no more. I turned all the way around, a little scared because if he would-a got his-self lost, I'd never see him again. He was halfway back up the block, his head way above everybody else's like he was standing on a box, and a look on his face like he been knocked up side his head with a cast-iron Cadillac. I ran back up to him, but by the time I got to where he been standing, he was most down some steps leading into a cellar coffee shop called The Lantern. I called to him but he must-a not heard me over the singing that was coming from inside. He was already at the door and a cross-eyed little blond girl was telling him to put a dollar in the basket she was tending. So I followed him down, paid my dollar, and caught up to him. "Hey, Uncle Wallace, what's the matter?"

He put his hand on my shoulder, grabbing it tight so I could hear the bones shift around. "Hush, boy." And then he turned to this little lit-up stage and there was this scrawny yellow Negro sitting on a stool playing the guitar and singing some folk song. He was wearing a green shirt open to his belly button, and a pair of tight black pants. What a queer!

The song he was singing was all about how life is tough—he looked like the toughest day he ever spent was when his boy friend didn't serve him breakfast in bed—and how when you're picking cotton, the sun seems to be as big as the whole sky. The last line was about how he'd pick all the cotton in the world and not plant no more and wouldn't have to work again and how he'd finally win out over the sun. When he finished, everybody snapped their fingers, which is what they do in the Village instead of clap.

Then he said: "And now, ladies and gentlemen, this next piece is another from the collection of Francis Mazer, a song he found during his 1948 trip through the South. A blues called "Wasn't That a Man." He struck a chord and started to sing: something about a Negro who swum a flooded, raging river with his two sons and his wife tied on his back. He sang it very fast so all the words ran together.

Uncle Wallace listened through one chorus, his eyes narrowing all the time until they about disappeared, and then he was moving, like a black battleship, and I grabbed his coat so he wouldn't make a fool of his-self in front of all them white folks, but then I just let him go. It was his business if he wanted to act like a nigger, and I couldn't stop him anyway. So I just stood there watching him walk in the dark between the little tables and looming out in the spotlight, burying the yellow Negro in his shadow.

Uncle Wallace reached out and put his hand around the neck of the guitar and the notes choked off. His hand must-a gone around the neck about three times.

The yellow Negro looked up at him, sort of shook. "I beg your pardon?"

"Brother, you better start begging somebody's pardon for what you doing to that song. You sings it all wrong."

Then a bald man in a shirt with the points of the collar all twisted and bent come up and patted Uncle Wallace on the back, hard. "Come on, buddy. Let's move out."

Uncle Wallace about-faced and looked way down at him. "Brother, next time you come up behind me and touch me, you'll find yourself peeping at me out of that guitar."

The bald man took a step back. Uncle Wallace looked at the yellow Negro again. "Now, look-a-here, colored brother, you can't sing my songs that way. You sing them like I made them up or don't sing them at all. And if you *do* sing them your way, then you may just never sing again, ever." He was still holding the neck of the guitar.

"Your songs? You didn't write these songs," the yellow Negro said. "They grew up out of the Rural Southern Negro Culture."

"Go on, nigger! They grew up out-a me. That song you was singing now, about the man and the river, I wrote that song about my very own Daddy."

A couple people in the audience started to sit up and listen. But that little yellow flit of a Negro didn't believe it. "I tell you, these songs were collected in 1948 by Francis Mazer, and there's no telling how long they've been sung. I heard the original tapes myself."

Uncle Wallace's eyes went blank for a second. Then he said: "What this Francis Mazer look like? He a little old gray-haired man with a game leg?"

That stopped the yellow Negro for a while. "Yessss." He held onto the word like he didn't want to let it out.

"Sure enough, I remember him. He was a mighty sweet old gentleman, told me all he wanted to do was put my songs on a little strip of plastic. I asked him if he meant to write *all* my songs on that small space. He said I got him wrong, that the machine he had with him would make a record of them. And I said for him to go on. I was playing a dance and the folks was happy and I sang from Friday night until the next afternoon, and that little gentleman stood by just putting them spools in his machine and smiling. And when I got done he give me thirty dollars, U.S. currency, and I went out and bought me some new strings and a plow too." Uncle Wallace stopped and shook his head. "Mighty sweet old gentleman. And you say his name was Mazer?"

"This has gone far enough!" The yellow Negro was real ticked off now, sort of cross like a chick. "Arthur, get him out of here." He was talking to the bald man.

Uncle Wallace looked at the bald man too, sort of menacing. Then he looked at the yellow Negro. "I don't want you singing my songs *at all*." Then he just walked away, out of the lights and it was like the sun come up on the yellow Negro all at once.

But the bald man wouldn't let it stop there and said: "Hey, you, mister, wait!" He was talking to Uncle Wallace, who didn't stop because (he told me later) he never in his life got called *Mister* by no white man, so he thought the bald man was talking to someone else.

The bald man run after him and was about to put his hand on his shoulder, but remembered what Uncle Wallace said before and hot-footed it around in front of him and started to talk, backing up. "I'm Arthur Friedlander. I own this place. If you're what you say you are, then I'd like you to sing some songs."

That stopped Uncle Wallace, who told me once he'd sing for anybody, even a president of a White Citizen's Council, if he got asked. So he came to a halt like a coal truck at a sudden red light and looked down at Mister Friedlander and said: "You want me to sing?"

And Mister Friedlander said: "If you can. Sure, go on."

"But I ain't brung my guitars."

"He'll let you use his. Go on." He reached out sort of timid, like at a real mean dog, and took Uncle Wallace's arm and started to lead him back to the lights.

The yellow Negro, he didn't really want to give up his guitar, but I guess he figured Mister Friedlander would fire him if he didn't, so he left it resting against the stool and stormed off the stage.

Uncle Wallace and Mister Friedlander went up there and Uncle Wallace picked up the guitar and ran his fingers over the strings. It looked like he was holding a ukulele.

Mister Friedlander looked at the audience and said: "The Lantern takes pleasure in presenting a new folk singer." He realized he didn't know Uncle Wallace's name and turned around.

"Bedlow," Uncle Wallace said, sort-a shy.

"Bedlow," said Mister Friedlander to the audience.

A couple people giggled and a couple others snapped their fingers, but they was joking. Uncle Wallace whacked the guitar again, and all of a sudden music come out of it. I was surprised because way down deep I thought sure Uncle Wallace was just a fool. He didn't play right off, though, just hit it a couple times and started to talk:

"That song the other fellow was playing. I wrote that when my Daddy died, for his funeral. That was 1947. It's all about how when I was a boy we had a flood down home and where we was living got filled up with water. There was only one safe, high spot in that country—an island in mid-river. But none of us could swim but my Daddy, so he tied me and my brother on his back and my Mama, she hung on and he swum the whole parcel of us over. So everybody remembered that and when he was taken I made a song about it to sing over his trench . . ." He hit another chord, but still didn't sing yet, just stopped.

"Say," he said, "anybody got another guitar?"

Some folks started mumbling about him being a fake and stalling and a couple of them laughed. I was thinking maybe they was right.

A white boy with a beard come up with a guitar case and opened it and reached over a guitar to Uncle Wallace and so now he had two guitars. I thought he didn't like the yellow Negro's guitar, but he started to get them in the same tune—hitting one and then the other. And when he judged they was all right, he put one on his left knee, with his left hand around the neck like anybody would hold a guitar, and then put the other one on his right knee and grabbed the neck of that one with his right hand. His arms was way out and he looked like he was about to fly away. Then he clamped his fingers down on the strings of them both so hard and so fast they both sounded, not just a little noise, but a loud chord like an organ in church, or two men playing guitars. Then he started to stamp his feet and clamp his fingers and you could hear the blues get going and then he was singing . . .

Well, not really, because the most you could say about his voice was that it was on key, and it was sure loud! It wasn't deep and hollow, or high and sweet. It didn't even sound like singing. In fact, I don't think anybody ever heard him sing or really listened to him. It wasn't a voice you heard or listened to; it was a voice you swallowed, because it always seemed to upset your stomach. I heard him sing lots of times and it was always the same: not hearing anything, but feeling kind of sick, like you been drinking a gallon of wine, and the wine was fighting you inside, grabbing at your belly and twisting it around so you wanted to yell out, but didn't because you was scared the wine might take offense and tear you to pieces. And when he stopped and the grabbing stopped, you'd feel all weak and terrible, like maybe you would feel if you gotten a date with a girl you thought might give you some tail and you been thinking about it all day in school and then you went out with her and when you took her home, her folks was out, and so she took you inside and you *did* get some tail and now that it was all over, you wished she'd run inside and not given you anything because then it wouldn't be all over now and you'd still have it to look forward to. But pretty soon he'd start singing again and everything would be like it was before, feeling sick, and wishing you was *still* sick when you didn't feel sick no more.

So that's the way it was that Friday in the Village; that's the way it always was. And the people was always the same. When he got through grabbing at them, no one snapped their fingers; no one ordered anything. The cooks come out the kitchen and the waitresses sat down with the customers. People came down the steps and paid their money and managed to get into a seat before he reached out and caught them, and when the seats was all gone—because nobody left—people kept coming until they was standing and sitting in the aisles, packed right to the doors, and even on the stage with him, nobody moving or making a sound, just getting sick in the stomach and hating it and loving it all at the same time.

So Uncle Wallace sang right until Saturday morning at four. And then we went home and I slept all day.

That was how we found out what Uncle Wallace was, or did. But for a while after he sang that Friday, he didn't sing no more. It was like before Uncle Wallace going to work, him and my old man building their building, coming home, and Uncle Wallace gassing himself on TV until one, then going to sleep.

But then the phone call came from Mister Friedlander and I answered it. He sounded real tired and said: "Hello? Is this the Bedlow residence? Do you have someone living with you or know of someone named Bedlow who sings folk songs?"

And when I answered the questions Yes, there was a silence and then I could hear sobbing on the other end of the line and through all the sobbing, him saying, "Thank God; Thank God," for about five minutes.

So at first I was about to hang up because I heard of guys calling up and cursing at women and all that mess, but then he said: "Who am I talking to?" I told him. "You were with that man who sang in my place four weeks ago? The Lantern? I'm Arthur Friedlander." So I said Hello, because I remembered him. He asked me what Uncle Wallace was to me and I told him.

"Carlyle," he said. "I've been trying to find your uncle for three weeks. I called Bedfords and Bradfords for the first two. It's like this, kid, every night a hundred people come into the place and ask for him and I have to say he isn't here and they get so mad they go away. He's ruining me! Where's your uncle now?"

I told him Uncle Wallace was at work.

"Listen, kid, there's a five in it for you if you can get him down here tonight by seven-thirty. And tell him I'll pay him thirty—no, make that fifty a week."

I said I could only *try* like I figured it might be hard to get Uncle Wallace to sing. Mister Friedlander gave me his number and told me to call him back when I had an answer and hung up.

When Uncle Wallace come home, I said: "That man you sang for a month ago?—he wants you to come again . . . for money." I didn't have to add the money part because I could tell by his face, he was ready to go.

So I called back Mister Friedlander and told him we was coming. I said that to get Uncle Wallace to sing, which he hadn't wanted to do, I had to say Mister Friedlander was paying him seventy-five dollars a week.

Mister Friedlander didn't even seem surprised. He just said, "But you got him to come?"

"Yes, sir," I said.

"Good boy! I'm giving you ten dollars instead of five." Which is what I figured he'd do if I told him I had trouble.

When we turned the corner into The Lantern's block there was a riot going on, with a hundred people, maybe even a thousand there, not all Village people neither. A whole bunch of them was in suits, and fur coats, and jewels. Man, if I been a pickpocket I could-a retired on what I could-a got there that night. And there was cops in their green cars with flashing lights going off and on, and on horses. Folks was pushing each other into the gutter and throwing punches. I looked up at Uncle Wallace and said: "Hey, we better split. We ain't got nothing to do with this, and you know how cops pick on colored folks."

"But I promised the man I'd sing, Carlyle," he said. But I could tell it wasn't that: he just wanted to sing, promise or no promise.

So we tried to sneak around behind all the rioting to get into The Lantern. And we most made it, but someone said: "Is that him?"

And someone answered: "Got to be."

I poked Uncle Wallace and said: "Now we really better get out-a here. These white folks think you done something."

"What?" he asked.

"I don't know, but we better get out-a here, *now*." And I grabbed his arm and started to pull him away, out-a there. I could tell he didn't want to go; he wanted to sing, but I figured I had to keep him out-a jail if I could.

Then someone started to yell at us to stop and I turned around to see how big they was and if there was more than we could handle, because either Uncle Wallace could flatten them or we could outrun them. But it was Mister Friedlander, chugging up the stairs, yelling.

We stopped.

He got to us and said, "What's wrong?"

"They think Uncle Wallace did something. He didn't do nothing. We just got here. We don't know nothing about this riot."

"Come inside. I'll explain," Mister Friedlander said. So we went down the stairs and inside, and he locked the door.

The place was jammed! There was more people there than that first Friday night.

Mister Friedlander said: "After you called, I put a sign in the window saying: *Bedlow here tonight.* Those people, they're here to see him. That's what the riot is." Then he asked me if I read that New York Sunday paper which weighs so much and ain't got no funnies. I told him No.

"Well, that Friday night your Uncle Wallace was here, there was a guy here from that paper. And the next Sunday he wrote an article—wait, I'll show you." So he ran behind the counter and come out with this page of a newspaper that he got magnified around forty times and pasted on cardboard. At the top of the page was this title: "Big Voice Crying in the Wilderness."

The article under it was about Uncle Wallace. It told all about that other Friday night and said that Uncle Wallace was a voice speaking for all the colored folks and that to hear him was to understand the pain of discrimination and segregation and all that kind of stuff, which seemed like a lot of B-S to me because I didn't understand Uncle Wallace hardly myself; I didn't understand why he sang folk songs when he could sing rock-and-roll or jazz. So how the hell could he be *my* voice or the voice of anybody like me? But that's what this writer said anyway.

When I looked up from the story I must-a been frowning, or maybe looked like I didn't get it, because Mister Friedlander grabbed me by the shoulders and shook me. "Don't you see? Your uncle is the hottest thing to hit New York since the Chicago Fire. He's a fad!"

And all the time he was telling me this, Uncle Wallace was standing by the window looking out at the people, not realizing this was all about him. That was when I started to dig something about him I never had before, and when I started to really like him and decided I'd have to look after him, even though he was old enough and big enough and smart enough to look after his-self: Uncle Wallace was innocent. To him you didn't sing for money, or for people even, but because you wanted to. And I guess the most important thing was that he wasn't some guy singing about love who never loved, or hard work who never worked hard, because he done all that, loved women and picked cotton and plowed and chopped trees. And even though he was in show business, he wasn't at all like anybody else in it. He was more real somehow.

Anyway, I could say he was better that night than he was before, but that wouldn't be really honest because I didn't dig his music so I don't know if he was better or not. I think the people liked him better, but I can't be sure of *that* either because when he finished, they was in so much pain, they never snapped their fingers for him, just sat staring, sad and hurting like before.

After he sung three sets and was sitting back in the kitchen drinking gin and fruit juice, this man come in with Mister Friedlander. "Bedlow, this is A. V. Berger. He wants to speak to you a minute."

This Mister Berger was five feet tall—tops—but weighed close to three hundred pounds, with black hair, straight and greasy. He was wearing a black wool suit—this was in mid-summer now—with a vest and scarf, which was black wool too. And the English this man spoke was fantabulous! I can only *try* to copy it. He hemmed and hawed a lot too so it sounded like: "Mister Below, (hem) I'm a concert producer. And (hem) I have been watching you perform. It seems quite likely that (hem) I can use you in a concert (hem) I'm staging at Carnegie Hall." He stopped there. I could see he was looking for Uncle Wallace to jump in the air and clap his hands. I knew what Carnegie Hall was, but I bet Uncle Wallace didn't. Mister Berger thought Uncle Wallace was playing it cagey.

"Mr. Bedlow, (hem) I'm prepared to offer you a good price to appear in the show."

"What's it to be? A dance?" Uncle Wallace said. "Sure, I'll play for a dance. That's what I done down home."

"No, Mister Bedlow. You (hem) misunderstand. This will be a concert."

"Like what?" He turned to me. "Like what, Carlyle?"

"A concert, Uncle Wallace. That's when a whole lot of folks come and just sit and listen to you sing."

"You mean just like here?"

"No, Uncle Wallace. It's like a church." I was thinking about how the seats was arranged, but he didn't get me.

"But I don't sing church music, Carlyle. My songs is too dirty for church. They never let me sing in no church." He looked back at Mister Berger. "What kind-a church you running, mister, that they sing my kind-a songs in there?"

"(hem) I don't run a church, Mister Bedlow." Mister Berger looked sort-a bleak and confused.

"No, Uncle Wallace, it ain't in no church," I said. "It's in a big hall and they want you to sing for a couple thousand people."

"No stuff?"

"Yeah, sure," I said.

"That's (hem) right," said Mister Berger.

"Go on, Bedlow," chimed in Mister Friedlander.

So he did.

But that concert wasn't until October and Mister Berger asked him to appear in early July, so there was a lot of time in between, when Uncle Wallace was making all his records.

And there was that damn movie. It was about this plantation family and all their problems in the Civil War. It wasn't really such a bad movie, but Uncle Wallace made it worse. I mean, he was the best thing in it, but after he was on the screen you couldn't look at the movie no more.

The movie would be going on all right and then would come Uncle Wallace's scene. He be sitting on this log in raggedy clothes and they *even* had a bandana around his head. You know how they make movies about colored people in Hollywood; the slaves act like slavery was the best God-damn thing ever happened to them and all they did all day was sit around on logs and sing and love Old Master, instead of breaking their asses in his cotton field and waiting for the chance to run away or slit Old Master's throat wide open. But that wasn't the worst. Dig this! They made him sing "John Henry." But it didn't matter. They didn't know Uncle Wallace. He started playing and singing, and when he got through, you had the feeling old John Henry wasn't no idiot after all. I mean, I heard some guy sing that song once and I said to myself: what an idiot this John Henry must-a been, killing his-self to beat a machine when he could-a joined a union, like my old man's, and made twice the money and kept the machine out.

But when Uncle Wallace sang "John Henry" you didn't feel that way. You felt like old John Henry was trapped and he had to do what he did, like when a fellow says your Mama screws for syphilitic blind men, you got to hit him; you don't think about it; it doesn't even matter if he joking or not, you just got to hit him even if he beats all hell out-a you. Well, that's what Uncle Wallace did to you.

So when them white folks come back on the screen with their dumb problems, and started kissing it up, you could see they was cardboard; you could see they was acting, and you got up and left out of there because you had to see real people again, and even when you got out in the street you sort-a felt like the people *out there* wasn't real neither, so what you did was go back in and stand in the lobby until the next showing, when Uncle Wallace come on again for his two minutes and you'd go in and see him. Then you'd walk out again to the lobby. There was always a whole lot of folks out there, waiting like you and not looking at you because you was as cardboardy to them as they was to you, and you'd wait for his two minutes again, and like that all day until you got too hungry to see.

After he made the movie he come back East and it was October and it was time for the concert at Carnegie Hall. And I guess you know what happened at the concert, but I'll tell it again and also some things I felt about it.

Mister Berger had-a told Uncle Wallace to play it cool and save his best until last, which meant that Uncle Wallace was to come out and sing a couple songs with only one guitar and then—bingo!—lay the two guitars on them. So they fixed me up in a tux and when the time come, I paraded out and give him the other guitar.

Uncle Wallace was tuning the second guitar when a voice come whispering up from the dark in the front row. "Hey, nigger, you the same one, ain't you."

Uncle Wallace squinted down, and there in the front row with all them rich white folks was this dark little Negro. There was a woman with him and a whole bunch of little kids, all shabby-looking, all their eyes shining like a row of white marbles.

"The same as what?" Uncle Wallace said.

And the voice come back. "The same fellow what played at a East Willson café in 1948."

"Yeah, I played there that year."

"There was one night in particular, when a cripple white man was taping you, and we all danced until the next day."

"Sure, it was!" Uncle Wallace snapped his fingers. "I remember you. You was with a *pretty* girl."

"You right, man. Here she is; my wife." He turned to the woman. "Honey, get up and meet Mister Bedlow." She did, and Uncle Wallace leaned over the edge of the stage and shook her hand. "Say, you know, I bought these big money seats because I wanted my kids to see you up close. Them is them." He pointed at the row of kids. "The oldest one, he's Bedlow. I named him after you because me and the wife wasn't getting on so good until that night." It was like they was all alone in that great big place, just those two down-home Negroes talking over old times. "And them others is Booker, Carver, Robeson, Robinson, and Bunche."

"Man, you do me proud. Pleased to meet you all. Say, you want to come up here and sit with me?"

"Now, you do *me* proud." So they all come up on stage like a row of ducks.

Then Uncle Wallace started to play and the littlest kid, that was Bunche—he was about three—he sat there for about one minute and then I saw him jump on his feet and start to do these wild little steps, just his feet moving like little pistons. Then the man got up and asked his wife to dance and the next thing I knew, everybody was dancing—even me; I danced right out on stage—and all the rich white folks was on their feet in the aisles and their wives was hugging strangers, black and white, and taking off their jewelry and tossing it in the air and all the poor people was ignoring the jewelry, was dancing instead, and you could see everybody laughing like crazy and having the best old time ever. Colored folks was teaching white folks to dance, and white folks was dancing with colored folks, and all the seats was empty and people was coming on stage to dance. Then the other singers backstage come out and started to back up Uncle Wallace and we was all dancing, all of us, and over all the noise and laughing you could hear Uncle Wallace with his two guitars. You could hear him over the whole thing.

Then the air changed; you could feel it. It wasn't just air any more, it started to get sweet-tasting to breathe, like perfume, and the people started to run down the aisles toward the stage, and everybody on the stage started to dance in toward Uncle Wallace, and everybody, *everybody* in the whole place was sobbing and crying and tears was pouring down their cheeks and smearing their make-up and making their eyes red and big. I could hear Uncle Wallace singing louder than ever. The people was rushing toward him. They was all crying and smiling too like people busting into a trance in church and it seemed like everybody in the place was on stage, trying to get near enough to touch him, grab his hand and shake it and hug him and kiss him even. And then the singing stopped.

I pushed my way through the crowd up to his chair. The first thing I seen was his two guitars all tore up and smashed and the strings busted. Uncle Wallce was sitting in his chair, slumped over, his face in his lap. And this was real strange; he looked like an old, punctured black balloon, deflated and all. There wasn't a mark on him, but he was dead all right.

Mister Berger called in a whole bunch of doctors, but they just stood around shaking their heads. They couldn't figure out how he'd died. One of them said, "There isn't nothing wrong with him, except he's dead."

Now I know this'll sound lame to you, but I don't think anything killed him except maybe at that second, he'd done everything that he ever wanted to do; he'd taken all them people, and sung to them, and made them forget who they was, and what they come from, and remember only that they was people. So he'd seen all he wanted to see and there was no use going on with it. I mean he'd made it. He got over.

It's kind of like that girl I was telling you about—the one who'd promised you some tail, and when you got it, you was sorry, because then you'd still have it to look forward to? Well, I think it's like that: getting tail and coming out of her house and there ain't nothing but pussycats and garbage cans in the street, and it's lonely and late and you wished you hadn't done it, but then you shrug and say to yourself: "Hell, man, you did, and that's it." And there ain't nothing to do but leave, because it's finished. But then there's something else. You're walking along and all at once you smile, and maybe even laugh, and you say: "Man, that was some *good* tail!" And it's a nice memory to walk home with.

THE IDIOT

Dudley Randall (1914-   )

"That cop was powerful mean.
First he called me, 'Black boy.'
Then he punched me in the face
and drug me by the collar to a wall
and made me lean against it with my hands spread
while he searched me,
and all the time he searched me
he kicked me and cuffed me and cussed me.

I was mad enough
to lay him out,
and would've did it, only
I didn't want to hurt his feelings,
and lose the good will
of the good white folks downtown,
who hired him."

MINSTREL MAN

Langston Hughes (1902-1967)

Because my mouth
Is wide with laughter
And my throat
Is deep with song,
You do not think
I suffer after
I have held my pain
So long.

Because my mouth
Is wide with laughter
You do not hear
My inner cry;

Because my feet
Are gay with dancing
You do not know
I die.

° ° °

OTHER SUGGESTED WORKS

Ray Bradbury, "Way In the Middle of the Air" from *Martian Chronicles*
Stephen Crane, "The Monster"
Ralph Ellison, *Shadow and Act*
William Faulkner, "Dry September"
LeRoi Jones, *Dutchman*
Malcolm X, *Autobiography*
Flanner O'Connor, "Artificial Nigger"

QUESTIONS

1. For whom is the poet speaking in "We Wear the Mask"? Why do they wear masks? What are the masks hiding? Do they serve as disguises? How do masks affect those who wear them? In what ways are masks useful tools? Why would the mask wearers "let the world dream otherwise" about their feelings?

2. The speaker in "Outcast" claims that he is held "in fee" by the "great western world." What does he mean? Why can't he return to his "native clime." What does the phrase "out of time" suggest about the black experience in America? What mask is being worn here? Who fashioned it? Why must it be worn?

3. In "The White House" (which McKay said is a symbolic title having no reference to the residence of the President) the poet speaks of bearing anger "proudly and unbent." What sort of mask is this? Do you think that the struggle against hatred, anger, and closed doors is worth this superhuman effort? Why or why not?

4a. In "The Knife" the relationship between a black man, Peter Washington, and a white man, Si Bryant, allows them to joke about the stereotypical Negro's love of watermelon. Does Stephen Crane convince you that such a relationship is possible? Why or why not?

b. Describe the interaction of the black and white communities in the story. Do individuals encounter each other as equals? Why or why not?

c. What black stereotypes appear in the story? White writers are sometimes accused of portraying black people as exotic primitives. What evidence is there of this in "The Knife"?

d. Compare Si Bryant's conversation with Peter Washington to that with Alek Williams. Is the mask wearing successful? In what way? Why is the mask being worn?

e. What bearing, if any, does the time it was written have on the relationships revealed in this story? Why do you think Crane wrote the story?

5*a.* Give examples of black figures who appear in Sherwood Anderson's "Notes." What characteristics do these people have in common? How do they differ from whites?

b. How do you account for the air of mystery that Anderson attributes to blacks? Why does Anderson say that white writers can't go among blacks without self-consciousness? Would you expect the same caution among white writers today? Why or why not?

c. What does Anderson envy in black people? How real are those characteristics? Would the blacks he describes identify themselves in the same way? Why or why not?

6*a.* What has occurred at the opening of "Pantaloon in Black?" What does Rider find when he goes home? Why can't he stay there? What do you know of the relationship between Rider and his wife?

b. Rider's behavior the next day seems unusual. What risks does he take? What happens at the nightly crap game? Why does Rider act?

c. The sheriff's deputy's account of the events leading to Rider's lynching is different from the description offered in Part One. What things about Rider does the deputy not know, or not understand, or ignore? Why does Faulkner choose to end the story with the deputy's account of the incident as told to his indifferent wife?

d. Rider is reported to have said, "Ah ain't trying to get away." What do you think he meant? What was he trying to do?

e. A pantaloon is a kind of straight man in classic Italian comedy. He is the butt of the clown's jokes, the fool who assists in playing tricks, even on himself. How do you explain Faulkner's title? How does Rider fit the pantaloon stereotype? What is the irony in suggesting that such pain might be seen as ridiculous?

f. What is Faulkner's opinion of Rider? of the sheriff? of the story? Where do his sympathies lie? How do you know?

g. What sort of mask does Rider wear? Is he hiding? Is he disguising himself? Why? Why does he decide to achieve his ends in this way?

7. In "Black Tambourine" Hart Crane offers an image of blacks wandering forlorn in dark cellars. Where is the dark "mid-kingdom"? Why is the black man there? Has he any alternatives? If so, what are they? If not, why not?

8a. Compare the condition of Uncle Willie in *I Know Why the Caged Bird Sings* to that of an able-bodied black man. Why does Maya Angelou say that "Fate not only disabled him but laid a double-tiered barrier in his path."

b. Why did Uncle Willie stand erect? Why does he want the strangers to remember him as whole? Is this a form of mask wearing? Does Uncle Willie have any other moments of pretense? What does the phrase of Shakespeare, "When in disgrace with fortune and men's eyes," tell you about Uncle Willie?

9a. What is a mark? Do you think that victims are in any way responsible for what happens to them? Why or why not? Why does "the con man who could act the most stupid win out every time"? What mask is being worn? Compare the con men in this story to Babo as first seen by Captain Delano in "Benito Cereno." Was Babo "playing the fool"?

b. Discuss the con game as a response to rejection. Do you think that using one's intelligence to pry open doors and to get revenge at the same time is appropriate? Why or why not?

c. "The needs of a society determine its ethics." Discuss. Do you agree? What do you think of the author's explanation for the cars and expensive tastes?

d. Maya Angelou suggests that even when they are learning in the same classroom, black and white children receive a different education, for blacks must learn two languages. Are children who do this wearing masks when they speak school language? when they speak street language? Explain.

4a. In "Cry for Me" William Kelley offers a fable of the impact of a Southern black man on a Northern city. Rather than wear a mask, Uncle Wallace Bedlow reveals more of himself than most people are willing to show. Compare his honesty to that of a mask wearer.

b. What is Carlyle's explanation of Bedlow's death? Does it "explain" anything to you? Why or why not?

10. How do you account for the tone of bravado in "The Idiot"? Explain the title of the poem.

11. The minstrel is a familiar black stereotype, but Langston Hughes offers a new perspective on his antics. How does the minstrel's mask affect him? Compare the tone of this poem to that of "We Wear the Mask." How do these poems differ in their advocacy of mask wearing?

12a. What are some of the reasons that people wear masks? How are masks useful? How are they hindrances? What are the advantages of mask wearing? What are the dangers? Does anyone other than a black person wear a mask? Who, and when?

b. Do people ever wear masks unknowingly? When might people wear masks that others have placed on them? Give examples.

PART III

The Lamp

Without light I am not only invisible, but formless as well; and to be unaware of one's form is to live a death.

Ralph Ellison, from "Invisible Man"

The Lamp

Babo's voice is never heard, his true face never seen. His opinions, his purposes, his perception of reality are not revealed directly. Indeed, we know him only through the eyes of the whites who have enslaved him. Yet, we need to hear from him if we want to understand the events that have taken place, to appreciate their significance, to know why they occurred. We need his viewpoint, finally, if we are to understand the nature of good and evil. The ambiguities of the story suggest that Melville realized that the stereotypes of blacks were, at best, inadequate, at worst, lies, and that until the black voice was heard, truth would continue to elude us.

This final section includes attempts by black and white writers to give voice to the black experience, to shed light so that we might better see what our collective experience has been, understand how we, black and white, affect each other and reveal at last what has long been shrouded in mystery.

° ° °

Unity of Self and Name

In the first selection that follows, Ralph Ellison speaks of the need to give meaning to "our true names," which must "become our masks and our shields and the containers of all those values and traditions which we learn and/or imagine as being the meaning of our familial past." Our knowledge of ourselves and of others begins with learning the names by which we are called and ascribing significance to them. Ellison's essay explores the consequences of the meaning attached to his name. Claude McKay, in probably his best known poem, calls for a black image of courage and nobility. The three poems by Bontemps, Cullen, and Toomer use the metaphor of reaping to describe particular aspects of the black experience in America. Cullen's poem serves as a reminder that the assertion that "black is beautiful" did not originate in the 1960s. He was active during the Harlem Renaissance, and his first collection of poems, *Color*, was published when he was an undergraduate at New York University. Bontemps wrote novels, short stories, children's fiction, and biographies in addition to his poetry. Jean Toomer's *Cane* is a remarkable collection of sketches, stories, and poems about Southern blacks in the country and in the city.

HIDDEN NAME AND COMPLEX FATE

Ralph Ellison (1914-   )

A WRITER'S EXPERIENCE IN THE UNITED STATES°

In *Green Hills of Africa*, Ernest Hemingway reminds us that both Tolstoy and Stendhal had seen war, that Flaubert had seen a revolution and the Commune, that Dostoievsky had been sent to Siberia and that such experiences were important in shaping the art of these great masters. And he goes on to observe that "writers are forged in injustice as a sword is forged." He declined to describe the many personal forms which injustice may take in this chaotic world—who would be so mad as to try?—nor does he go into the personal wounds which each of these writers sustained. Now, however, thanks to his brother and sister, we do know something of the injustice in which he himself was forged, and this knowledge has been added to what we have long known of Hemingway's artistic temper.

In the end, however, it is the quality of his art which is primary. It is the art which allows the wars and revolutions which he knew, and the personal and social injustice which he suffered, to lay claims upon our attention; for it was through his art that they achieved their most enduring meaning. It is a matter of outrageous irony, perhaps, but in literature the great social clashes of history no less than the painful experience of the individual are secondary to the meaning which they take on through the skill, the talent, the imagination and personal vision of the writer who transforms them into art. Here they are reduced to more manageable proportions; here they are imbued with humane values; here, injustice and catastrophe become less important in themselves than what the writer makes of them. This is *not* true, however, of the writer's struggle with that recalcitrant angel called Art; and it was through *this* specific struggle that Ernest Hemingway became *Hemingway* (now refined to a total body of transcendent work, after forty years of being endlessly dismembered and resurrected, as it continues to be, in the styles, the themes, the sense of life and literature of countless other writers). And it was through this struggle with form that he became the master, the culture hero, whom we have come to know and admire.

It was suggested that it might be of interest if I discussed here this evening some of my notions of the writer's experience in the United States, hence I have evoked the name of Hemingway, not by way of inviting farfetched comparisons but in order to establish a perspective, a set of as-

°Address sponsored by the Gertrude Clarke Whittall Foundation, Library of Congress, January 6, 1964.

sumptions from which I may speak, and in an attempt to avoid boring you by emphasizing those details of racial hardship which for some forty years now have been evoked whenever writers of my own cultural background have essayed their experience in public.

I do this *not* by way of denying totally the validity of these by now stylized recitals, for I have shared and still share many of their detailed injustices—what Negro can escape them?—but by way of suggesting that they are, at least in a discussion of a writer's experience, as *writer*, as artist, somewhat beside the point.

For we select neither our parents, our race nor our nation; these occur to us out of the love, the hate, the circumstances, the fate, of others. But we *do* become writers out of an act of will, out of an act of choice; a dim, confused and ofttimes regrettable choice, perhaps, but choice nevertheless. And what happens thereafter causes all those experiences which occurred before we began to function as writers to take on a special quality of uniqueness. If this does not happen then as far as writing goes, the experiences have been misused. If we do not make of them a value, if we do not transform them into forms and images of meaning which they did not possess before, then we have failed as artists.

Thus for a writer to insist that his personal suffering is of special interest in itself, or simply because he belongs to a particular racial or religious group, is to advance a claim for special privileges which members of his group who are not writers would be ashamed to demand. The kindest judgment one can make of this point of view is that it reveals a sad misunderstanding of the relationship between suffering and art. Thomas Mann and André Gide have told us much of this and there are critics, like Edmund Wilson, who have told of the connection between the wound and the bow.

As I see it, it is through the process of making artistic forms—plays, poems, novels—out of one's experience that one becomes a writer, and it is through this process, this struggle, that the writer helps give meaning to the experience of the group. And it is the process of mastering the discipline, the techniques, the fortitude, the culture, through which this is made possible that constitutes the writer's real experience as *writer*, as artist. If this sounds like an argument for the artist's withdrawal from social struggles, I would recall to you W. H. Auden's comment to the effect that:

> In our age, the mere making of a work of art is itself a political act. So long as artists exist, making what they please, and think they ought to make, even if it is not terribly good, even if it appeals to only a handful of people, they remind the Management of something managers need to be reminded of, namely, that the managed are people with faces, not anonymous members, that *Homo Laborans* is also *Homo Ludens*. . . .

Without doubt, even the most *engagé* writer—and I refer to true artists, not to artists *manqués*—begin their careers in play and puzzlement, in dreaming over the details of the world in which they become conscious of themselves.

Let Tar Baby, that enigmatic figure from Negro folklore, stand for the world. He leans, black and gleaming, against the wall of life utterly noncommittal under our scrutiny, our questioning, starkly unmoving before our naive attempts at intimidation. Then we touch him playfully and before we can say *Sonny Liston!* we find ourselves stuck. Our playful investigations become a labor, a fearful struggle, an *agon*. Slowly we perceive that our task is to learn the proper way of freeing ourselves to develop, in other words, technique.

Sensing this, we give him our sharpest attention, we question him carefully, we struggle with more subtlety; while he, in his silent way, holds on, demanding that we perceive the necessity of calling him by his true name as the price of our freedom. It is unfortunate that he has so many, many "true names"—all spelling chaos; and in order to discover even one of these we must first come into the possession of our own names. For it is through our names that we first place ourselves in the world. Our names, being the gift of others, must be made our own.

Once while listening to the play of a two-year-old girl who did not know she was under observation, I heard her saying over and over again, at first with questioning and then with sounds of growing satisfaction, "I am Mimi Livisay? . . . *I* am Mimi Livisay. I *am* Mimi Livisay . . . I am *Mimi* Li-vi-say! I am Mimi . . ."

And in deed and in fact she was—or became so soon thereafter, by working playfully to establish the unity between herself and her name.

For many of us this is far from easy. We must learn to wear our names within all the noise and confusion of the environment in which we find ourselves; make them the center of all of our associations with the world, with man and with nature. We must charge them with all our emotions, our hopes, hates, loves, aspirations. They must become our masks and our shields and the containers of all those values and traditions which we learn and/or imagine as being the meaning of our familial past.

And when we are reminded so constantly that we bear, as Negroes, names originally possessed by those who owned our enslaved grandparents, we are apt, especially if we are potential writers, to be more than ordinarily concerned with the veiled and mysterious events, the fusions of blood, the furtive couplings, the business transactions, the violations of faith and loyalty, the assaults; yes, and the unrecognized and unrecognizable loves through which our names were handed down unto us.

So charged with emotion does this concern become for some of us, that we have, earlier, the example of the followers of Father Divine and, now, the Black Muslims, discarding their original names in rejection of the bloodstained, the brutal, the sinful images of the past. Thus they would declare new identities, would clarify a new program of intention and destroy the verbal evidence of a willed and ritualized discontinuity of blood and human intercourse.

Not all of us, actually only a few, seek to deal with our names in this manner. We take what we have and make of them what we can. And there are even those who know where the old broken connections lie, who recognize their relatives across the chasm of historical denial and the artificial barriers of society, and who see themselves as bearers of many of the qualities which were admirable in the original sources of their common line (Faulkner has made much of this); and I speak here not of mere forgiveness, nor of obsequious insensitivity to the outrages symbolized by the denial and the division, but of the conscious acceptance of the harsh realities of the human condition, of the ambiguities and hypocrisies of human history as they have played themselves out in the United States.

Perhaps, taken in aggregate, these European names which (sometimes with irony, sometimes with pride, but always with personal investment) represent a certain triumph of the spirit, speaking to us of those who rallied, reassembled and transformed themselves and who under dismembering pressures refused to die. "Brothers and sisters," I once heard a Negro preacher exhort, "let us make up our faces before the world, and our names shall sound throughout the land with honor! For we ourselves are our *true* names, not their epithets! So let us, I say, Make Up Our Faces and Our Minds!"

Perhaps my preacher had read T. S. Eliot, although I doubt it. And in actuality, it was unnecessary that he do so, for a concern with names and naming was very much a part of that special area of American culture from which I come, and it is precisely for this reason that this example should come to mind in a discussion of my own experience as a writer.

Undoubtedly, writers begin their *conditioning* as manipulators of words long before they become aware of literature—certain Freudians would say at the breast. Perhaps. But if so, that is far too early to be of use at this moment. Of this, though, I am certain: that despite the misconceptions of those educators who trace the reading difficulties experienced by large numbers of Negro children in Northern schools to their Southern background, these children are, in *their* familiar South, facile manipulators of words. I know, too, that the Negro community is deadly in its ability to create nicknames and to spot all that is ludicrous in an unlikely name or that which is incongruous in conduct. Names are not qualities; nor are words, in this particular sense, actions. To assume that they are could cost one his life many times a day. Language skills depend to a large extent upon a knowledge of the details, the manners, the objects, the folkways, the psychological patterns, of a given environment. Humor and wit depend upon much the same awareness, and so does the suggestive power of names.

"A small brown bowlegged Negro with the name 'Franklin D. Roosevelt Jones' might sound like a clown to someone who looks at him from the outside," said my friend Albert Murray, "but on the other hand he just might turn out to be a hell of a fireside operator. He might just lie back in all of that comic juxtaposition of names and manipulate you deaf, dumb and blind—and you not even suspecting it, because you're thrown out of stance by his name! There you are, so dazzled by the F.D.R. image—which you *know* you can't see—and so delighted with your own superior position that you don't realize that its *Jones* who must be confronted."

Well, as you must suspect, all of this speculation on the matter of names has a purpose, and now, because it is tied up so ironically with my own experience as a writer, I must turn to my own name.

For in the dim beginnings, before I ever thought consciously of writing, there was my own name, and there was, doubtless, a certain magic in it. From the start I was uncomfortable with it, and in my earliest years it caused me much puzzlement. Neither could I understand what a poet was, nor why, exactly, my father had chosen to name me after one. Perhaps I could have understood it perfectly well had he named me after his own father, but that name had been given to an older brother who died and thus was out of the question. But why hadn't he named me after a hero, such as Jack Johnson, or a soldier like Colonel Charles Young, or a great seaman like Admiral Dewey, or an educator like Booker T. Washington, or a great orator and abolitionist like Frederick Douglass? Or again, why hadn't he named me (as so many Negro parents had done) after President Teddy Roosevelt?

Instead, he named me after someone called Ralph Waldo Emerson, and then, when I was three, he died. It was too early for me to have understood his choice, although I'm sure he must have explained it many times, and it was also too soon for me to have made the connection between my name and my father's love for reading. Much later, after I began to write and work with words, I came to suspect that he was aware of the suggestive powers of names and of the magic involved in naming.

I recall an odd conversation with my mother during my early teens in which she mentioned their interest in, of all things, prenatal culture! But for a long time I actually knew only that my father read a lot, and that he admired this remote Mr. Emerson, who was something called a "poet and philosopher"—so much so that he named his second son after him.

I knew, also, that whatever his motives, the combination of names he'd given me caused me no end of trouble from the moment when I could talk well enough to respond to the ritualized question which grownups put to very young children. Emerson's name was quite familiar to Negroes in

Oklahoma during those days when World War I was brewing, and adults, eager to show off their knowledge of literary figures, and obviously amused by the joke implicit in such a small brown nubbin of a boy carrying around such a heavy moniker, would invariably repeat my first two names and then to my great annoyance, they'd add "Emerson."

And I, in my confusion, would reply, "No, *no*, *I'm* not Emerson; he's the little boy who lives next door." Which only made them laugh all the louder. "Oh no," they'd say, "*you're* Ralph Waldo Emerson," while I had fantasies of blue murder.

For a while the presence next door of my little friend, Emerson, made it unnecessary for me to puzzle too often over this peculiar adult confusion. And since there were other Negro boys named Ralph in the city, I came to suspect that there was something about the combination of names which produced their laughter. Even today I know of only one other Ralph who had as much comedy made out of his name, a campus politician and deep-voiced orator whom I knew at Tuskegee, who was called in friendly ribbing, *Ralph Waldo Emerson Edgar Allan Poe*, spelled Powe. This must have been quite a trial for him, but I had been initiated much earlier.

During my early school years the name continued to puzzle me, for it constantly evoked in the faces of others some secret. It was as though I possessed some treasure or some defect, which was invisible to my own eyes and ears; something which I had but did not *possess*, like a piece of property in South Carolina, which was mine but which I could not have until some future time. I recall finding, about this time, while seeking adventure in back alleys—which possess for boys a superiority over playgrounds like that which kitchen utensils possess over toys designed for infants—a large photographic lens. I remember nothing of its optical qualities, of its speed or color correction, but it gleamed with crystal mystery and it was beautiful.

Mounted handsomely in a tube of shiny brass, it spoke to me of distant worlds of possibility. I played with it, looking through it with squinted eyes, holding it in shafts of sunlight, and tried to use it for a magic lantern. But most of this was as unrewarding as my attempts to make the music come from a phonograph record by holding the needle in my fingers.

I could burn holes through newspapers with it, or I could pretend that it was a telescope, the barrel of a cannon, or the third eye of a monster—*I* being the monster—but I could do nothing at all about its proper function of making images; nothing to make it yield its secret. But I could not discard it.

Older boys sought to get it away from me by offering knives or tops, agate marbles or whole zoos of grass snakes and horned toads in trade, but I held on to it. No one, not even the white boys I knew, had such a lens, and it was my own good luck to have found it. Thus I would hold on to it until such time as I could acquire the part needed to make it function. Finally I put it aside and it remained buried in my box of treasures, dusty and dull, to be lost and forgotten as I grew older and became interested in music.

I had reached by now the grades where it was necessary to learn something about Mr. Emerson and what he had written, such as the "Concord Hymn" and the essay "Self-Reliance," and in following his advice, I reduced the "Waldo" to a simple and, I hoped, mysterious "W," and in my own reading I avoided his works like the plague. I could no more deal with my name—I shall never really master it—than I could find a creative use for my lens. Fortunately there were other problems to occupy my mind. Not that I forgot my fascination with names, but more about that later.

Negro Oklahoma City was starkly lacking in writers. In fact, there was only Roscoe Dungee, the editor of the local Negro newspaper and a very fine editorialist in that valuable tradition of personal journalism which is now rapidly disappearing; a writer who in his emphasis upon the possibilities for justice offered by the Constitution anticipated the anti-segregation struggle by decades. There were also a few reporters who drifted in and out, but these were about all. On the level of *conscious* culture the Negro community was biased in the direction of music.

These were the middle and late twenties, remember, and the state was still a new frontier state. The capital city was one of the great centers for southwestern jazz, along with Dallas and Kansas City. Orchestras which were to become famous within a few years were constantly coming and going. As were the blues singers—Ma Rainey and Ida Cox, and the old bands like that of King Oliver. But best of all, thanks to Mrs. Zelia N. Breaux, there was an active and enthusiastic school music program through which any child who had the interest and the talent could learn to play an instrument and take part in the band, the orchestra, the brass quartet. And there was a yearly operetta and a chorus and a glee club. Harmony was taught throughout the Negro school system, and we we were also taught complicated patterns of military drill.

I tell you this to point out that although there were no incentives to write, there was ample opportunity to receive an artistic discipline. Indeed, once one picked up an instrument it was difficult to escape. If you chafed at the many rehearsals of the school band or orchestra and were drawn to the many small jazz groups, you were likely to discover that the jazzmen were apt to rehearse far more than the school band; it was only that they seemed to enjoy themselves better and to possess a freedom of imagination which we were denied at school. And one soon learned that the wild, transcendent moments which occurred at dances or "battles of music," moments in which memorable improvisations were ignited, depended upon a dedication to a discipline which was observed even when rehearsals had to take place in the crowded quarters of Halley Richardson's shoeshine parlor.

It was not the place which counted, although a large hall with good acoustics was preferred, but what one did to perfect one's performance.

If this talk of musical discipline gives the impression that there were no forces working to nourish one who would one day blunder, after many a twist and turn, into writing, I am misleading you. And here I might give you a longish lecture on the Ironies and Uses of Segregation. When I was a small child there was no library for Negroes in our city; and not until a Negro minister invaded the main library did we get one. For it was discovered that there was no law, only custom, which held that we could not use these public facilities. The results were the quick renting of two large rooms in a Negro office building (the recent site of a pool hall), the hiring of a young Negro librarian, the installation of shelves and a hurried stocking of the walls with any and every book possible. It was, in those first days, something of a literary chaos.

But how fortunate for a boy who loved to read! I started with the fairy tales and quickly went through the junior fiction; then through the Westerns and the detective novels, and very soon I was reading the classics—only I didn't know it. There were also the Haldeman Julius Blue Books, which seem to have floated on the air down from Girard, Kansas; the syndicated columns of O. O. McIntyre, and the copies of *Vanity Fair* and the *Literary Digest* which my mother brought home from work—how could I ever join uncritically in the heavy handed attacks on the so-called Big Media which have become so common today?

There were also the pulp magazines and, more important, that other library which I visited when I went to help my adopted grandfather, J. D. Randolph (my parents had been living in his rooming house when I was born), at his work as custodian of the law library of the Oklahoma State Capitol. Mr. Randolph had been one of the first teachers in what became Oklahoma City; and he'd also been one of the leaders of a group who walked from Gallatin, Tennessee, to the Oklahoma Territory. He was a tall man, as brown as smoked leather, who looked like the Indians with whom he'd herded horses in the early days.

And while his status was merely the custodian of the law library, I was to see the white legislators come down on many occasions to question him on points of law, and often I was to hear him answer without recourse to the uniform rows of books on the shelves. This was a thing to marvel at in itself, and the white lawmakers did so, but even more marvelous, ironic, intriguing, haunting—call it what you will—is the fact that the Negro who knew the answers was named after Jefferson Davis. What Tennessee lost, Oklahoma was to gain, and after gaining it (a gift of courage, intelligence, fortitude and grace), used it only in concealment and, one hopes, with embarrassment.

So, let us, I say, make up our faces and our minds!

In the loosely structured community of that time, knowledge, news of other ways of living, ancient wisdom, the latest literary fads, hate literature—for years I kept a card warning Negroes away from the polls, which had been dropped by the thousands from a plane which circled over the Negro community—information of all kinds, found its level, catch-as-catch can, in the minds of those who were receptive to it. Not that there was no conscious structuring—I read my first Shaw and Maupassant, my first Harvard Classics in the home of a friend whose parents were products of that stream of New England education which had been brought to Negroes by the young and enthusiastic white teachers who staffed the schools set up for the freedmen after the Civil War. These parents were both teachers and there were others like them in our town.

But the places where a rich oral literature was truly functional were the churches, the schoolyards, the barbershops, the cotton-picking camps; places where folklore and gossip thrived. The drug store where I worked was such a place, where on days of bad weather the older men would sit with their pipes and tell tall tales, hunting yarns and homely versions of the classics. It was here that I heard stories of searching for buried treasure and of headless horsemen, which I was told were my own father's versions told long before. There were even recitals of popular verse, "The Shooting of Dan McGrew," and, along with these, stories of Jesse James, of Negro outlaws and black United States marshals, of slaves who became the chiefs of Indian tribes and of the exploits of Negro cowboys. There was both truth and fantasy in this, intermingled in the mysterious fashion of literature.

Writers, in their formative period, absorb into their consciousness much that has no special value until much later, and often much which is of no special value even then—perhaps, beyond the fact that it throbs with affect and mystery and in it "time and pain and royalty in the blood" are suspended in imagery. So, long before I thought of writing, I was claimed by weather, by speech rhythms, by Negro voices and their different idioms, by husky male voices and by the high shrill singing voices of certain Negro women, by music; by tight spaces and by wide spaces in which the eyes could wander; by death, by newly born babies, by manners of various kinds, company manners and street manners; the manners of white society and those of our own high society; and by interracial manners; by street fights, circuses and minstrel shows; by vaudeville and moving pictures, by prize fights and foot races, baseball games and football matches. By spring floods and blizzards, catalpa worms and jack rabbits; honeysuckle and snapdragons (which smelled like old cigar butts); by sunflowers and hollyhocks, raw sugar cane and baked yams; pigs' feet, chili and blue haw ice cream. By parades, public dances and jam sessions, Easter sunrise ceremonies and large funerals. By contests between fire-and-brimstone preachers and by presiding elders who got "laughing-happy" when moved by the spirit of God.

I was impressed by expert players of the "dozens" and certain notorious bootleggers of corn whiskey. By jazz musicians and fortunetellers and by men who did anything well, by strange sickness and by interesting brick or razor scars; by expert cursing vocabularies as well as by exalted praying and terrifying shouting, and by transcendent playing or singing of the blues. I was fascinated by old ladies, those who had seen slavery and those who were defiant of white folk and black alike; by the enticing walks of prostitutes and by the limping walks affected by Negro hustlers, especially those who wore Stetson hats, expensive shoes with well-starched overalls, usually with a diamond stickpin (when not in hock) in their tieless collars as their gambling uniforms.

And there were the blind men who preached on corners, and the blind men who sang the blues to the accompaniment of washboard and guitar; and the white junkmen who sang mountain music and the famous huckster of fruit and vegetables.

And there was the Indian-Negro confusion. There were Negroes who were part Indian and who lived on reservations, and Indians who had children who lived in towns as Negroes, and Negroes who were Indians and traveled back and forth between the groups with no trouble. And Indians who were as wild as wild Negroes and others who were as solid and as steady as bankers. There were the teachers, too, inspiring teachers and villainous teachers who chased after the girl students, and certain female teachers who one wished would chase after young male students. And a handsome old principal of military bearing who had been blemished by his classmates at West Point when they discovered on the eve of graduation that he was a Negro. There were certain Jews, Mexicans, Chinese cooks, a German orchestra conductor and an English grocer who owned a Franklin touring car. And certain Negro mechanics—"Cadillac Slim," "Sticks" Walker, Buddy Bunn and Oscar Pitman—who had so assimilated the automobile that they seemed to be behind a steering wheel even as they walked the streets or danced with girls. And there were the whites who despised us and the others who shared our hardships and our joys.

There is much more, but this is sufficient to indicate some of what was present even in a segregated community to form the background of my work, my sense of life.

And now comes the next step. I went to Tuskegee to study music, hoping to become a composer of symphonies and there, during my second year, I read *The Waste Land* and that, although I was then unaware of it, was the real transition to writing.

Mrs. L. C. McFarland had taught us much of Negro history in grade school and from her I'd learned of the New Negro Movement of the twenties, of Langston Hughes, Countee Cullen, Claude McKay, James Weldon Johnson and the others. They had inspired pride and had given me a closer identification with poetry (by now, oddly enough, I seldom thought of my hidden name), but with music so much on my mind it never occurred to me to try to imitate them. Still I read their work and was excited by the glamour of the Harlem which emerged from their poems and it was good to know that there were Negro writers. —Then came *The Waste Land.*

I was much more under the spell of literature than I realized at the time. *Wuthering Heights* had caused me an agony of unexpressible emotion and the same was true of *Jude the Obscure*, but *The Waste Land* seized my mind. I was intrigued by its power to move me while eluding my understanding. Somehow its rhythms were often closer to those of jazz than were those of the Negro poets, and even though I could not understand then, its range of allusion was as mixed and as varied as that of Louis Armstrong. Yet there were its discontinuities, its changes of pace and its hidden system of organization which escaped me.

There was nothing to do but look up the references in the footnotes to the poem, and thus began my conscious education in literature.

For this, the library at Tuskegee was quite adequate and I used it. Soon I was reading a whole range of subjects drawn upon by the poet, and this led, in turn, to criticism and to Pound and Ford Madox Ford, Sherwood Anderson and Gertrude Stein, Hemingway and Fitzgerald and "round about 'til I was come" back to Melville and Twain—the writers who are taught and doubtedlessly overtaught today. Perhaps it was my good luck that they were not taught at Tuskegee, I wouldn't know. But at the time I was playing, having an intellectually interesting good time.

Having given so much attention to the techniques of music, the process of learning something of the craft and intention of modern poetry and fiction seemed quite familiar. Besides, it was absolutely painless because it involved no deadlines or credits. Even then, however, a process which I described earlier had begun to operate. The more I learned of literature in this conscious way, the more the details of my background became transformed. I heard undertones in remembered conversations which had escaped me before, local customs took on a more universal meaning, values which I hadn't understood were revealed; some of the people whom I had known were diminished while others were elevated in stature. More important, I began to see my own possibilities with more objective, and in some ways, more hopeful eyes.

The following summer I went to New York seeking work, which I did not find, and remained there, but the personal transformation continued. Reading had become a conscious process of growth and discovery, a method of reordering the world. And that world had widened considerably.

At Tuskegee I had handled manuscripts which Prokofiev had given to Hazel Harrison, a Negro concert pianist who taught there and who had known him in Europe, and through Miss Harrison I had become aware of Prokofiev's symphonies. I had also become aware of the radical movement in politics and art, and in New York had begun reading the work of André

Malraux, not only the fiction but chapters published from his *Psychology of Art*. And in my search for an expression of modern sensibility in the works of Negro writers I discovered Richard Wright. Shortly thereafter I was to meet Wright, and it was at his suggestion that I wrote both my first book review and my first short story. These were fatal suggestions.

For although I had tried my hand at poetry while at Tuskegee, it hadn't occurred to me that I might write fiction, but once he suggested it, it seemed the most natural thing to try. Fortunately for me, Wright, then on the verge of his first success, was eager to talk with a beginner and I was able to save valuable time in searching out those works in which writing was discussed as a craft. He guided me to Henry James' prefaces, to Conrad, to Joseph Warren Beach and to the letters of Dostoievsky. There were other advisers and other books involved, of course, but what is important here is that I was consciously concerned with the art of fiction, that almost from the beginning I was grappling quite consciously with the art through which I wished to realize myself. And this was not done in isolation; the Spanish Civil War was now in progress and the Depression was still on. The world was being shaken up, and through one of those odd instances which occur to young provincials in New York, I was to hear Malraux make an appeal for the Spanish Loyalists at the same party where I first heard the folk singer Leadbelly perform. Wright and I were there seeking money for the magazine which he had come to New York to edit.

Art and politics; a great French novelist and a Negro folk singer; a young writer who was soon to publish *Uncle's Tom's Children*; and I who had barely begun to study his craft. It is such accidents, such fortuitous meetings, which count for so much in our lives. I had never dreamed that I would be in the presence of Malraux, of whose work I became aware on my second day in Harlem when Langston Hughes suggested that I read *Man's Fate* and *Days of Wrath* before returning them to a friend of his. And it is this fortuitous circumstance which led to my selecting Malraux as a literary "ancestor," whom, unlike a relative, the artist is permitted to choose. There was in progress at the time all the agitation over the Scottsboro boys and the Herndon Case, and I was aware of both. I had to be; I myself had been taken off a freight train at Decatur, Alabama, only three years before while on my way to Tuskegee. But while I joined in the agitation for their release, my main energies went into learning to write.

I began to publish enough, and not too slowly, to justify my hopes for success, and as I continued, I made a most perplexing discovery; namely, that for all his conscious concern with technique, a writer did not so much create the novel as he was created *by* the novel. That is, one did not make an arbitrary gesture when one sought to write. And when I say that the novelist is created by the novel, I mean to remind you that fictional techniques are not a mere set of objective tools, but something much more intimate: a way of feeling, of seeing and of expressing one's sense of life.

And the process of *acquiring* technique is a process of modifying one's responses, of learning to see and feel, to hear and observe, to evoke and evaluate the images of memory and of summoning up and directing the imagination; of learning to conceive of human values in the ways which have been established by the great writers who have developed and extended the art. And perhaps the writer's greatest freedom, as artist, lies precisely in his possession of technique; for it is through technique that he comes to possess and express the meaning of his life.

Perhaps at this point it would be useful to recapitulate the route—perhaps as mazelike as that of *Finnegan's Wake*—which I have been trying to describe; that which leads from the writer's discovery of a sense of purpose, which is that of becoming a writer, and then the involvement in the passionate struggle required to master a bit of technique, and then, as this begins to take shape, the disconcerting discovery that it is *technique* which transforms the individual before he is able in turn to transform it. And in that personal transformation he discovers somethings else: he discovers that he has taken on certain obligations, that he must not embarrass his chosen form, and that in order to avoid this he must develop taste. He learns—and this is most discouraging—that he is involved with values which turn in their *own* way, and not in the ways of politics, upon the central issues affecting his nation and his time. He learns that the American novel, from its first consciousness of itself as a literary form, has grappled with the meaning of the American experience; that it has been aware and has sought to define the nature of that experience by addressing itself to the specific details, the moods, the landscapes, the cityscapes, the tempo of American change. And that it has borne, at its best, the full weight of that burden of conscience and consciousness which Americans inherit as one of the results of the revolutionary circumstances of our national beginnings.

We began as a nation not through the accidents of race or religion or geography (Robert Penn Warren has dwelled on these circumstances) but when a group of men, *some* of them political philosophers, put down, upon what we now recognize as being quite sacred papers, their conception of the nation which they intended to establish on these shores. They described, as we know, the obligations of the state to the citizen, of the citizen to the state; they committed themselves to certain ideas of justice, just as they committed us to a system which would guarantee all of its citizens equality of opportunity.

I need not describe the problems which have arisen from these beginnings. I need only remind you that the contradiction between these noble ideals and the actualities of our conduct generated a guilt, an unease of spirit, from the very beginning, and that the American novel at its best has always been concerned with this basic moral predicament. During Melville's time and Twain's, it was an implicit aspect of their major themes; by the twentieth century and after the discouraging and traumatic effect of the Civil War and the Reconstruction it had gone underground, had become *understated*. Nevertheless it did not disappear completely and it is to be found operating in the work of Henry James as well as in that of Hemingway and Fitzgerald. And then (and as one who believes in the impelling moral function of the novel and who believes in the moral seriousness of the form) it pleases me no end that it comes into explicit statement again in the works of Richard Wright and William Faulkner, writers who lived close to moral and political problems which would not stay put underground.

I go into these details not to recapitulate the history of the American novel but to indicate the trend of thought which was set into motion when I began to discover the nature of that process with which I was actually involved. Whatever the opinions and decisions of critics, a novelist must arrive at his own conclusions as to the meaning and function of the form with which he is engaged, and these are, in all modesty, some of mine.

In order to orient myself I also began to learn that the American novel had long concerned itself with the puzzle of the one-and-the-many; the mystery of how each of us, despite his origin in diverse regions, with our diverse racial, cultural, religious backgrounds, speaking his own diverse idiom of the American in his own accent, is, nevertheless, American. And with this concern with the implicit pluralism of the country and with the composite nature of the ideal character called "the American," there goes a concern with gauging the health of the American promise, with depicting the extent to which it was being achieved, being made manifest in our daily conduct.

And with all of this there still remained the specific concerns of literature. Among these is the need to keep literary standards high, the necessity of exploring new possibilities of language which would allow it to retain that flexibility and fidelity to the common speech which has been its glory since Mark Twain. For me this meant learning to add to it the wonderful resources of Negro American speech and idiom and to bring into range as fully and eloquently as possible the complex reality of the American experience as it shaped and was shaped by the lives of my own people.

Notice that I stress as "fully" as possible, because I would no more strive to write great novels by leaving out the complexity of circumstances which go to make up the Negro experience and which alone go to make the obvious injustice bearable, than I would think of preparing myself to become President of the United States simply by studying Negro American history or confining myself to studying those laws affecting civil rights.

For it seems to me that one of the obligations I took on when I committed myself to the art and form of the novel was that of striving for the broadest range, the discovery and articulation of the most exalted values. And I must squeeze these from the life which I know best. (A highly truncated impression of that life I attempted to convey to you earlier.)

If all this sound a bit heady, remember that I did not destroy that troublesome middle name of mine, I only suppressed it. Sometimes it reminds me of my obligations to the man who named me.

It is our fate as human beings always to give up some good things for other good things, to throw off certain bad circumstances only to create others. Thus there is a value for the writer in trying to give as thorough a report of social reality as possible. Only by doing so may we grasp and convey the cost of change. Only by considering the broadest accumulation of data may we make choices that are based upon our own hard-earned sense of reality. Speaking from my own special area of American culture, I feel that to embrace uncritically values which are extended to us by others is to reject the validity, even the sacredness, of our own experience. It is also to forget that the small share of reality which each of our diverse groups is able to snatch from the whirling chaos of history belongs not to the group alone, but to all of us. It is a property and a witness which can be ignored only to the danger of the entire nation.

I could suppress the name of my namesake out of respect for the achievements of its original bearer but I cannot escape the obligation of attempting to achieve some of the things which he asked of the American writer. As Henry James suggested, being an American is an arduous task, and for most of us, I suspect, the difficulty begins with the name.

IF WE MUST DIE

Claude McKay (1891-1948)

If we must die—let it not be like hogs
Hunted and penned in an inglorious spot,
While round us bark the mad and hungry dogs,
Making their mock at our accursed lot.
If we must die—oh, let us nobly die,
So that our precious blood may not be shed
In vain; then even the monsters we defy
Shall be constrained to honor us though dead!
Oh, Kinsmen! We must meet the common foe;
Though far outnumbered, let us show us brave,
And for their thousand blows deal one deathblow!
What though before us lies the open grave?
Like men we'll face the murderous, cowardly pack,
Pressed to the wall, dying, but fighting back!

A BLACK MAN TALKS OF REAPING

Arna Bontemps (1902-1973)

I have sown beside all waters in my day.
I planted deep, within my heart the fear
that wind or fowl would take the grain away.
I planted safe against this stark, lean year.

I scattered seed enough to plant the land
in rows from Canada to Mexico,
but for my reaping only what the hand
can hold at once is all that I can show.

Yet what I sowed and what the orchard yields
my brother's sons are gathering stalk and root;
small wonder then my children glean in fields
they have not sown, and feed on bitter fruit.

FROM THE DARK TOWER

Countee Cullen (1903-1946)

(TO CHARLES S. JOHNSON)

We shall not always plant while others reap
The golden increment of bursting fruit,
Not always countenance, abject and mute,
That lesser men should hold their brothers cheap;
Not everlastingly while others sleep
Shall we beguile their limbs with mellow flute,
Not always bend to some more subtle brute;
We were not made eternally to weep.

The night whose sable breast relieves the stark,
White stars is no less lovely being dark,
And there are buds that cannot bloom at all
In light, but crumple, piteous, and fall;
So in the dark we hide the heart that bleeds,
And wait, and tend our agaonizing seeds.

REAPERS

Jean Toomer (1894-1967)

Black reapers with the sound of steel on stones
Are sharpening scythes. I see them place the hones
In their hip-pockets as a thing that's done,
And start their silent swinging, one by one.
Black horses drive a mower through the weeds,
And there, a field rat, startled, squealing bleeds,
His belly close to ground. I see the blade,
Blood-stained, continue cutting weeds and shade.

° ° °

Lifting the Veil

The selections in this section offer numerous examples of black experience and black-white experience from times of slavery to the present. Beginning with W. E. B. DuBois's prophesy that the problem of the 20th century is the problem of the color line, the selections show some of the ways in which race affects individuals, confuses them, distorts their sense of each other, and prevents love between them. "Of Our Spiritual Strivings" is the first chapter of DuBois's turn-of-the-century study of Negro life, *The Souls of Black Folk.* The most widely read of DuBois's work, this collection of essays explores certain phases of black history and culture, the philosophy of Booker T. Washington, and in this selection the issue of color consciousness.

Frederick Douglass escaped from slavery in Maryland in 1841. He became a leader in the abolitionist movement and traveled and spoke throughout the United States and Britain. The open letter to his master was published in the *Liberator* in 1848.

Both Eudora Welty and William Faulkner offer images of old women carrying out familial responsibilities. As Southern white writers Welty and Faulkner are known for their sensitive exploration of the impact of race consciousness on human experience. Bernard Malamud offers still another view of the ways in which racial issues complicate human relationships. His perspective is Northern and urban, however, and he adds the dimension of conflict and misunderstanding between minority groups, here Jewish and black.

From THE SOULS OF BLACK FOLK

W. E. B. DuBois (1868-1963)

OF OUR SPIRITUAL STRIVINGS

O water, voice of my heart, crying in the sand,
All night long crying with a mournful cry,
As I lie and listen, and cannot understand
The voice of my heart in my side or the voice of the sea,
O water, crying for rest, is it I, is it I?
All night long the water is crying to me.

Unresting water, there shall never be rest
Till the last moon droop and the last tide fail,
And the fire of the end begin to burn in the west;
And the heart shall be weary and wonder and cry like the sea,
All life long crying without avail,
As the water all night long is crying to me.

—ARTHUR SYMONS

Between me and the other world there is ever an unasked question: unasked by some through feelings of delicacy; by others through the difficulty of rightly framing it. All, nevertheless, flutter round it. They approach me in a half-hesitant sort of way, eye me curiously or compassionately, and then, instead of saying directly, How does it feel to be a problem? they say, I know an excellent colored man in my town; or, I fought at Mechanicsville; or, Do not these Southern outrages make your blood boil? At these I smile, or am interested, or reduce the boiling to a simmer, as the occasion may require. To the real question, How does it feel to be a problem? I answer seldom a word.

And yet, being a problem is a strange experience,—peculiar even for one who has never been anything else, save perhaps in babyhood and in Europe. It is in the early days of rollicking boyhood that the revelation first bursts upon one, all in a day, as it were. I remember well when the shadow swept across me. I was a little thing, away up in the hills of New England, where the dark Housatonic winds between Hoosac and Taghkanic to the sea. In a wee wooden schoolhouse, something put it into the boys' and girls' heads to buy gorgeous visiting-cards—ten cents a package—and exchange. The exchange was merry, till one girl, a tall newcomer, refused my card,—refused it peremptorily, with a glance. Then it dawned upon me with a certain suddenness that I was different from the others; or like, mayhap, in heart and life and longing, but shut out from their world by a vast veil. I had thereafter no desire to tear down that veil, to creep through; I held all beyond it in common contempt, and lived above it in a region of blue sky and great wandering shadows. That sky was bluest when I could beat my mates at examination-time, or beat them at a foot-race, or even beat their stringy heads. Alas, with the years all this fine contempt began to fade; for the worlds I longed for, and all their dazzling opportunities, were theirs, not mine. But they should not keep these prizes, I said; some, all, I would wrest from them. Just how I would do it I could never decide: by reading law, by healing the sick, by telling the wonderful tales that swam in my head,—some way. With other black boys the strife was not so fiercely sunny: their youth shrunk into tasteless sycophancy, or into silent hatred of the pale world about them and mocking distrust of everything white; or wasted itself in a bitter cry, Why did God make me an outcast and a stranger in mine own house? The shades of the prison-house closed round about us all: walls strait and stubborn to the whitest, but relentlessly narrow, tall, and unscalable to sons of night who must plod darkly on in resignation, or beat unavailing palms against the stone, or steadily, half hopelessly, watch the streak of blue above.

After the Egyptian and Indian, the Greek and Roman, the Teuton and Mongolian, the Negro is a sort of seventh son, born with a veil, and gifted with second-sight in this American world—a world which yields him no true self-consciousness, but only lets him see himself through the revelation of the other world. It is a peculiar sensation, this double-consciousness, this sense of always looking at one's self through the eyes of others, of measuring one's soul by the tape of a world that looks on in amused contempt and pity. One ever feels his twoness—an American, a Negro; two souls, two thoughts, two unreconciled strivings; two warring ideals in one dark body, whose dogged strength alone keeps it from being torn asunder.

The history of the American Negro is the history of this strife—this longing to attain self-conscious manhood, to merge his double self into a better and truer self. In this merging he wishes neither of the older selves to be lost. He would not Africanize America, for America has too much to teach the world and Africa. He would not bleach his Negro soul in a flood of white Americanism, for he knows that Negro blood has a message for the world. He simply wishes to make it possible for a man to be both a Negro and an American, without being cursed and spit upon by his fellows, without having the doors of Opportunity closed roughly in his face.

This, then, is the end of his striving; to be a co-worker in the kingdom of culture, to escape both death and isolation, to husband and use his best powers and his latent genius. These powers of body and mind have in the past been strangely wasted, dispersed, or forgotten. The shadow of a mighty Negro past flits through the tale of Ethiopia the Shadowy and of Egypt the Sphinx. Throughout history, the powers of single black men flash here and there like falling stars, and die sometimes before the world has rightly gauged their brightness. Here in America, in the few days since Emancipation, the black man's turning hither and thither in hesitant and doubtful striving has often made his very strength to lose effectiveness, to seem like absence of power, like weakness. And yet it is not weakness—it is the contradiction of double aims. The double-aimed struggle of the black artisan—on the one hand to escape white contempt for a nation of mere hewers of wood and drawers of water, and on the other hand to plough and nail and dig for a poverty-stricken horde—could only result in making him a poor craftsman, for he had but half a heart in either cause. By the poverty and ignorance of his people, the Negro minister or doctor was tempted toward quackery and demagogy; and by the criticism of the other world, toward ideals that made him ashamed of his lowly tasks. The would-be black *savant* was confronted by the paradox that the knowledge his people needed was a twice-told tale to his white neighbors, while the knowledge which would teach the white world was Greek to his own flesh and blood. The innate love of harmony and beauty that set the ruder souls of his people a-dancing and a-singing raised but confusion and doubt in the soul of the black artist; for the beauty revealed to him was the soul-beauty of a race which his larger audience despised, and he could not articulate the message of another people. This waste of double aims, this seeking to satisfy two unreconciled ideals, has wrought sad havoc with the courage and faith and deeds of ten thousand thousand people,—has sent them often wooing false gods and invoking false means of salvation, and at times has even seemed about to make them ashamed of themselves.

Away back in the days of bondage they thought to see in one divine event the end of all doubt and disappointment; few men ever worshipped Freedom with half such unquestioning faith as did the American Negro for two centuries. To him, so far as he thought and dreamed, slavery was indeed the sum of all villainies, the cause of all sorrow, the root of all prejudice; Emancipation was the key to a promised land of sweeter beauty than ever stretched before the eyes of wearied Israelites. In song and exhortation swelled one refrain—Liberty; in his tears and curses the God he implored had Freedom in his right hand. At last it came—suddenly, fearfully, like a dream. With one wild carnival of blood and passion came the message in his own plaintive cadences:

> "Shout, O children!
> Shout, you're free!
> For God has bought your liberty!"

Years have passed away since then—ten, twenty, forty; forty years of national life, forty years of renewal and development, and yet the swarthy spectre sits in its accustomed seat at the Nation's feast. In vain do we cry to this our vastest social problem:

> "Take any shape but that, and my firm nerves
> Shall never tremble!"

The Nation has not yet found peace from its sins; the freedman has not yet found in freedom his promised land. Whatever of good may have come in these years of change, the shadow of a deep disappointment rests upon the Negro people—a disappointment all the more bitter because the unattained ideal was unbounded save by the simple ignorance of a lowly people.

The first decade was merely a prolongation of the vain search for freedom, the boon that seemed ever barely to elude their grasp—like a tantalizing will-o'-the-wisp, maddening and misleading the headless host. The holocaust of war, the terrors of the Ku Klux Klan, the lies of carpet-baggers, the disorganization of industry, and the contradictory advice of friends and foes, left the bewildered serf with no new watchword beyond the old cry for freedom. As the time flew, however, he began to grasp a new idea. The ideal of liberty demanded for its attainment powerful means, and these the Fifteenth Amendment gave him. The ballot, which before he had looked upon as a visible sign of freedom, he now regarded as the chief means of gaining and perfecting the liberty with which war had partially endowed him. And why not? Had not votes made war and emancipated millions? Had not votes enfranchised the freedmen? Was anything impossible to a power that had done all this? A million black men started with renewed zeal to vote themselves into the kingdom. So the decade flew away, the revolution of 1876 came, and left the half-free serf weary, wondering but still inspired. Slowly but steadily, in the following years, a new vision began gradually to replace the dream of political power—a powerful movement, the rise of another ideal to guide the unguided, another pillar of fire by night after a clouded day. It was the ideal of "book-learning"; the curiosity, born of compulsory ignorance, to know and test the power of the cabalistic letters of the white man, the longing to know. Here at last seemed to have been discovered the mountain path to Canaan; longer than the highway of Emancipation and law, steep and rugged, but straight, leading to heights high enough to overlook life.

Up the new path the advance guard toiled, slowly, heavily, doggedly; only those who have watched and guided the faltering feet, the misty minds, the dull understandings, of the dark pupils of these schools know how faithfully, how piteously, this people strove to learn. It was weary work. The cold statistician wrote down the inches of progress here and there, noted also where here and there a foot had slipped or some one had fallen. To the tired climbers, the horizon was ever dark, the mists were often cold, the Canaan was always dim and far away. If, however, the vistas disclosed as yet no goal, no resting-place, little but flattery and criticism, the journey at least gave leisure for reflection and self-examination; it changed the child of Emancipation to the youth with dawning self-consciousness, self-realization, self-respect. In those sombre forests of his striving his own soul rose before him, and he saw himself—darkly as through a veil; and yet he saw in himself some faint revelation of his power, of his mission. He began to have a dim feeling that, to attain his place in the world, he must be himself, and not another. For the first time he sought to analyze the burden he bore upon his back, that deadweight of social degradation partially masked behind a half-named Negro problem. He felt his poverty; without a cent, without a home, without land, tools, or savings, he had entered into competition with rich, landed, skilled neighbors. To be a poor man is hard, but to be a poor race in a land of dollars is the very bottom of hardships. He felt the weight of his ignorance—not simply of letters, but of life, of business, of the humanities; the accumulated sloth and shirking and awkwardness of decades and centuries shackled his hands and feet. Nor was his burden all poverty and ignorance. The red stain of bastardy, which two centuries of systematic legal defilement of Negro women had stamped upon his race, meant not only the loss of ancient African chastity, but also the hereditary weight of a mass of corruption from white adulterers, threatening almost the obliteration of the Negro home.

A people thus handicapped ought not to be asked to race with the world, but rather allowed to give all its time and thought to its own social problems. But alas! while sociologists gleefully count his bastards and his prostitutes, the very soul of the toiling, sweating black man is darkened by the shadow of a vast despair. Men call the shadow prejudice, and learnedly explain it as the natural defense of culture against barbarism, learning against ignorance, purity against crime, the "higher" against the "lower" races. To which the Negro cries Amen! and swears that to so much of this strange prejudice as is founded on just homage to civilization, culture, righteousness, and progress, he humbly bows and meekly does obeisance. But before that nameless prejudice that leaps beyond all this he stands helpless, dismayed, and well-nigh speechless; before that personal disrespect and mockery, the ridicule and systematic humiliation, the distortion of fact and wanton license of fancy, the cynical ignoring of the better and the boisterous welcoming of the worse, the all-pervading desire to inculcate disdain for everything black, from Toussaint to the devil—before this there rises a sickening despair that would disarm and discourage any nation save that black host to whom "discouragement" is an unwritten word.

But the facing of so vast a prejudice could not but bring the inevitable self-questioning, self-disparagement, and lowering of ideals which ever accompany repression and breed in an atmosphere of contempt and hate. Whispering and portents came borne upon the four winds: Lo! we are diseased and dying, cried the dark hosts; we cannot write, our voting is vain; what need of education, since we must always cook and serve? And the Nation echoed and enforced this self-criticism, saying: Be content to be servants, and nothing more; what need of higher culture for half-men? Away with the black man's ballot, by force or fraud—and behold the suicide of a race! Nevertheless, out of the evil came something of good—

the more careful adjustment of education to real life, the clearer perception of the Negroes' social responsibilities, and the sobering realization of the meaning of progress.

So dawned the time of *Sturm and Drang:* storm and stress today rocks our little boat on the mad waters of the world-sea; there is within and without the sound of conflict, the burning of body and rending of soul; inspiration strives with doubt, and faith with vain questionings. The bright ideals of the past—physical freedom, political power, the training of brains and the training of hands—all these in turn have waxed and waned, until even the last grows dim and overcast. Are they all wrong—all false? No, not that, but each alone was over-simple and incomplete—the dreams of a credulous race-childhood or the fond imaginings of the other world which does not know and does not want to know our power. To be really true, all these ideals must be melted and welded into one. The training of the schools we need today more than ever—the training of deft hands, quick eyes and ears, and above all the broader, deeper, higher culture of gifted minds and pure hearts. The power of the ballot we need in sheer self-defense—else what shall save us from a second slavery? Freedom, too, the long-sought, we still seek—the freedom of life and limb, the freedom to work and think, the freedom to love and aspire. Work, culture, liberty—all these we need, not singly but together, not successively but together, each growing and aiding each, and all striving toward that vaster ideal that swims before the Negro people, the ideal of human brotherhood, gained through the unifying ideal of Race; the ideal of fostering and developing the traits and talents of the Negro, not in opposition to or contempt for other races, but rather in large conformity to the greater ideals of the American Republic, in order that some day on American soil two world-races may give each to each those characteristics both so sadly lack. We the darker ones come even now not altogether empty-handed: there are today no truer exponents of the pure human spirit of the Declaration of Independence than the American Negroes; there is no true American music but the wild sweet melodies of the Negro slave; the American fairy tales and folklore are Indian and African; and, all in all, we black men seem the sole oasis of simple faith and reverence in a dusty desert of dollars and smartness. Will America be poorer if she replace her brutal dyspeptic blundering with light-hearted but determined Negro humility? or her coarse and cruel wit with loving jovial good-humor? or her vulgar music with the soul of the Sorrow Songs?

Merely a concrete test of the underlying principles of the great republic is the Negro Problem, and the spiritual striving of the freedmen's sons is the travail of souls whose burden is almost beyond the measure of their strength, but who bear it in the name of an historic race, in the name of this the land of their fathers' fathers, and in the name of human opportunity.

And now what I have briefly sketched in large outline let me on coming pages tell again in many ways, with loving emphasis and deeper detail, that men may listen to the striving in the souls of black folk.

LETTER TO HIS MASTER

Frederick Douglass (1817?-1895)

THOMAS AULD:

Sir—The long and intimate, though by no means friendly relation which unhappily subsisted between you and myself, leads me to hope that you will easily account for the great liberty which I now take in addressing you in this open and public manner. The same fact may possibly remove any disagreeable surprise which you may experience on again finding your name coupled with mine, in any other way than in an advertisement, accurately describing my person, and offering a large sum for my arrest. In thus dragging you again before the public, I am aware that I shall subject myself to no inconsiderable amount of censure. I shall probably be charged with an unwarrantable, if not a wanton and reckless disregard of the rights and proprieties of private life. There are those North as well as South who entertain a much higher respect for rights which are merely conventional, than they do for rights which are personal and essential. Not a few there are in our country, who, while they have no scruples against robbing the laborer of the hard earned results of his patient industry, will be shocked by the extremely indelicate manner of bringing your name before the public. . . .

I have selected this day on which to address you, because it is the anniversary of my emancipation; and knowing of no better why. I am led to this as the best mode of celebrating that truly important event. Just ten years ago this beautiful September morning, yon bright sun beheld me a slave—a poor, degraded chattel—trembling at the sound of your voice, lamenting that I was a man, and wishing myself a brute. The hopes which I had treasured up for weeks of a safe and successful escape from your grasp, were powerfully confronted at this last hour by dark clouds of doubt and fear, making my person shake and my bosom to heave with the heavy contest between hope and fear. I have no words to describe to you the deep agony of soul which I experienced on that never to be forgotten morning—(for I left by daylight). I was making a leap in the dark. The probabilities, so far as I could by reason determine them, were stoutly against the undertaking. The preliminaries and precautions I had adopted previously, all worked badly. I was like one going to war without weapons—ten chances of defeat to one of victory. One in whom I had confided, and one who had promised me assistance, appalled by fear at the trial hour, deserted me, thus leaving the responsibility of success or failure solely with myself. You, sir, can never know my feelings. As I look back to them I can scarcely realize that I have passed through a scene so trying. Trying however as they were, and gloomy as was the prospect, thanks be to the Most High, who is ever the God of the oppressed, at the moment which was to determine my whole earthly career. His grace was sufficient, my mind was made up. I embraced the golden opportunity, took the morning tide at the flood, and a free man, young, active and strong, is the result. . . .

Since I left you, I have had a rich experience. I have occupied stations which I never dreamed of when a slave. Three out of the ten years since I left you, I spent as a common laborer on the wharves of New Bedford, Massachusetts. It was there I earned my first free dollar. It was mine. I could spend it as I pleased. I could buy hams or herring with it, without asking any odds of any body. That was a precious dollar to me. You remember when I used to make seven or eight, or even nine dollars a week in Baltimore, you would take every cent of it from me every Saturday night, saying that I belonged to you, and my earnings also. I never liked this conduct on your part—to say the best, I thought it a little mean. I would not have served you so. But let that pass. I was a little awkward about counting money in New England fashion when I first landed in New Bedford. I like to have betrayed myself several times. I caught myself saying phip, for fourpence; and at one time a man actually charged me with being a runaway, whereupon I was silly enough to become one by running away from him, for I was greatly afraid he might adopt measures to give me again into slavery, a condition I then dreaded more than death.

I soon, however, learned to count money, as well as to make it, and got on swimmingly. I married soon after leaving you: in fact, I was engaged to be married before I left you; and instead of finding my companion a burden; she was truly a helpmeet. She went to live at service and I to work on the wharf, and though we toiled hard the first winter, we never lived more happily. After remaining in New Bedford for three years, I met with Wm. Lloyd Garrison, a person of whom you have *possibly* heard, as he is pretty generally known among slave-holders. He put it into my head that I might make myself serviceable to the cause of the slave by devoting a portion of my time to telling my own sorrows, and those of other slaves which had come under my observation. This was the commencement of a higher state of existence than any to which I had ever aspired. I was thrown into society the most pure, enlightened and benevolent that the country affords. Among these I have never forgotten you, but have invariably made you the topic of conversation—thus giving you all the notoriety I could do. I need not tell you that the opinion formed of you in these circles, is far from being favorable. They have little respect for your honesty, and less for your religion.

But I was going on to relate something of my interesting experience. I had not long enjoyed the excellent society to which I have referred, before the light of its excellence exerted a beneficial influence on my mind and heart. Much of my early dislike of white persons was removed, and their manners, habits and customs, so entirely unlike what I had been used to in the kitchen-quarters on the plantations of the South, fairly charmed me, and gave me a strong disrelish for the coarse and degrading customs of my former condition. I therefore made an effort so to improve my mind and deportment as to be somewhat fitted to the station to which I seemed almost providentially called. The transition from degradation to respectability was indeed great, and to get from one to the other without carrying some marks of one's former condition, is truly a difficult matter. I would not have you think that I am now entirely clear of all plantation peculiarities, but my friends here, while they entertain the strongest dislike to them, regard me with that charity to which my past life somewhat entitles me, so that my condition in this respect is exceedingly pleasant. So far as my domestic affairs are concerned, I can boast of as comfortable a dwelling as your own. I have an industrious and neat companion, and four dear children—the oldest a girl of nine years and three fine boys, the oldest eight, the next six, and the youngest four years old. The three oldest are now going regularly to school—two can read and write, and the other can spell with tolerable correctness words of two syllables: Dear fellows! they are all in comfortable beds, and are sound asleep, perfectly secure under my own roof. There are no slaveholders here to rend my heart by snatching them from my arms, or blast a mother's dearest hopes by tearing them from her bosom. These dear children are ours—not to work up into rice, sugar and tobacco, but to watch over, regard, and protect, and to rear them up in the nurture and admonition of the gospel—to train them up in the paths of wisdom and virtue, and, as far as we can to make them useful to the world and to themselves. Oh! sir, a slave-holder never appears to me so completely an agent of hell, as when I think of and look upon my dear children. It is then that my feelings rise above my control. I meant to have said more with respect to my own prosperity and happiness, but thoughts and feelings which this recital has quickened unfit me to proceed further in that direction. The grim horrors of slavery rise in all their ghastly terror before me, the wails of millions pierce my heart, and chill my blood. I remember the chain, the gag, the bloody whip, the death-like gloom overshadowing the broken spirit of the fettered bondman, the appalling liability of his being torn away from wife and children, and sold like a beast in the market. Say not that this is a picture of fancy. You well know that I wear stripes on my back inflicted by your direction; and that you, while we were brothers in the same church, caused this right hand, with which I am now penning this letter, to be closely tied to my left, and my person dragged at the pistol's mouth, fifteen miles, from the Bay side to Easton to be sold like a beast in the market, for the alleged crime of intending to escape from your possession. All this and more you remember, and know to be perfectly true, not only of yourself, but of nearly all of the slaveholders around you.

At this moment, you are probably the guilty holder of at least three of my own dear sisters, and my only brother in bondage. These you regard as your property. They are recorded on your ledger, or perhaps have been sold to human flesh mongers, with a view to filling your own ever-hungry purse. Sir, I desire to know how and where these dear sisters are. Have you sold them? or are they still in your possession? What has become of them? are they living or dead? And my dear old grandmother, whom you turned out like an old horse, to die in the woods—is she still alive? Write and let me know all about them. If my grandmother be still alive, she is of no service to you, for by this time she must be nearly eighty years old—too old to be cared for by one to whom she has ceased to be of service, send her to me at Rochester, or bring her to Philadelphia, and it shall be the crowning happiness of my life to take care of her in her old age. Oh! she was to me a mother, and a father, so far as hard toil for my comfort could make her such. Send me my grandmother! that I may watch over and take care of her in her old age. And my sisters, let me know all about them. I would write to them, and learn all I want to know of them, without disturbing you in any way, but that, through your unrighteous conduct, they have been entirely deprived of the power to read and write. You have kept them in utter ignorance, and have therefore robbed them of the sweet enjoyments of writing or receiving letters from absent friends and relatives. Your wickedness and cruelty committed in this respect on your fellow-creatures, are greater than all the stripes you have laid upon my back, or theirs. It is an outrage upon the soul—a war upon the immortal spirit, and one for which you must give account at the bar of our common Father and Creator. . . .

I will now bring this letter to a close, you shall hear from me again unless you let me hear from you. I intend to make use of you as a weapon with which to assail the system of slavery—as a means of concentrating public attention on the system, and deepening their horror of trafficking in the souls and bodies of men. I shall make use of you as a means of exposing the character of the American church and clergy—and as a means of bringing this guilty nation with yourself to repentance. In doing this I entertain no malice towards you personally. There is no roof under which you would be more safe than mine, and there is nothing in my house which you might need for your comfort, which I would not readily grant. Indeed, I should esteem it a privilege, to set you an example as to how mankind ought to treat each other.

I am your fellow man, but not your slave,

FREDERICK DOUGLASS.

A WORN PATH

Eudora Welty (1909-   )

It was December—a bright frozen day in the early morning. Far out in the country there was an old Negro woman with her head tied in a red rag, coming along a path through the pinewoods. Her name was Phoenix Jackson. She was very old and small and she walked slowly in the dark pine shadows, moving a little from side to side in her steps, with the balanced heaviness and lightness of a pendulum in a grandfather clock. She carried a thin, small cane made from an umbrella, and with this she kept tapping the frozen earth in front of her. This made a grave and persistent noise in the still air, that seemed meditative like the chirping of a solitary little bird.

She wore a dark striped dress reaching down to her shoe tops, and an equally long apron of bleached sugar sacks, with a full pocket: all neat and tidy, but every time she took a step she might have fallen over her shoe-laces, which dragged from her unlaced shoes. She looked straight ahead. Her eyes were blue with age. Her skin had a pattern all its own of numberless branching wrinkles and as though a whole little tree stood in the middle of her forehead, but a golden color ran underneath, and the two knobs of her cheeks were illumined by a yellow burning under the dark. Under the red rag her hair came down on her neck in the frailest of ringlets, still black, and with an odor like copper.

Now and then there was a quivering in the thicket. Old Phoenix said, "Out of my way, all you foxes, owls, beetles, jack rabbits, coons and wild animals! . . . Keep out from under these feet, little bobwhites. . . . Keep the big wild hogs out of my path. Don't let none of those come running my direction. I got a long way." Under her small black-freckled hand her cane, limber as a buggy whip, would switch at the brush as if to rouse up any hiding things.

On she went. The woods were deep and still. The sun made the pine needles almost too bright to look at, up where the wind rocked. The cones dropped as light as feathers. Down in the hollow was the morning dove—it was not too late for him.

The path ran up a hill. "Seem like there is chains about my feet, time I get this far," she said, in the voice of argument old people keep to use with themselves. "Something always take a hold of me on this hill—pleads I should stay."

After she got to the top she turned and gave a full, severe look behind her where she had come. "Up through pines," she said at length. "Now down through oaks."

Her eyes opened their widest, and she started down gently. But before she got to the bottom of the hill a bush caught her dress.

Her fingers were busy and intent, but her skirts were full and long, so that before she could pull them free in one place they were caught in another. It was not possible to allow the dress to tear. "I in the thorny bush," she said. "Thorns, you doing your appointed work. Never want to let folks pass, no sir. Old eyes thought you was a pretty little *green* bush."

Finally, trembling all over, she stood free, and after a moment dared to stoop for her cane.

"Sun so high!" she cried, leaning back and looking, while the thick tears went over her eyes. "The time getting all gone here."

At the foot of this hill was a place where a log was laid across the creek.

"Now comes the trial," said Phoenix.

Putting her right foot out, she mounted the log and shut her eyes. Lifting her skirt, leveling her cane fiercely before her, like a festival figure in some parade, she began to march across. Then she opened her eyes and she was safe on the other side.

"I wasn't as old as I thought," she said.

But she sat down to rest. She spread her skirts on the bank around her and folded her hands over her knees. Up above her was a tree in a pearly cloud of mistletoe. She did not dare to close her eyes, and when a little boy brought her a plate with a slice of marble-cake on it she spoke to him. "That would be acceptable," she said. But when she went to take it there was just her own hand in the air.

So she left that tree, and had to go through a barbed-wire fence. There she had to creep and crawl, spreading her knees and stretching her fingers like a baby trying to climb the steps. But she talked loudly to herself: she could not let her dress be torn now, so late in the day, and she could not pay for having her arm or her leg sawed off if she got caught fast where she was.

At last she was safe through the fence and risen up out in the clearing. Big dead trees, like black men with one arm, were standing in the purple stalks of the withered cotton field. There sat a buzzard.

"Who you watching?"

In the furrow she made her way along.

"Glad this not the season for bulls," she said, looking sideways, "and the good Lord made his snakes to curl up and sleep in the winter. A pleasure I don't see no two-headed snake coming around that tree, where it come once. It took a while to get by him, back in the summer."

She passed through the old cotton and went into a field of dead corn. It whispered and shook and was taller than her head. "Through the maze now," she said, for there was no path.

Then there was something tall, black, and skinny there, moving before her.

At first she took it for a man. It could have been a man dancing in the field. But she stood still and listened, and it did not make a sound. It was as silent as a ghost.

"Ghost," she said sharply, "who be you the ghost of? For I have heard of nary death close by."

But there was no answer—only the ragged dancing in the wind.

She shut her eyes, reached out her hand, and touched a sleeve. She found a coat and inside that an emptiness, cold as ice.

"You scarecrow," she said. Her face lighted. "I ought to be shut up for good," she said with laughter. "My senses is gone. I too old. I the oldest people I ever know. Dance, old scarecrow," she said, "while I dancing with you."

She kicked her foot over the furrow, and with mouth drawn down, shook her head once or twice in a little strutting way. Some husks blew down and whirled in streamers about her skirts.

Then she went on, parting her way from side to side with the cane, through the whispering field. At last she came to the end, to a wagon track where the silver grass blew between the red ruts. The quail were walking around like pullets, seeming all dainty and unseen.

"Walk pretty," she said. "This the easy place. This the easy going."

She followed the track, swaying through the quiet bare fields, through the little strings of trees silver in their dead leaves, past cabins silver from weather, with the doors and windows boarded shut, all like old women under a spell sitting there. "I walking in their sleep," she said, nodding her head vigorously.

In a ravine she went where a spring was silently flowing through a hollow log. Old Phoenix bent and drank. "Sweet-gum makes the water sweet," she said, and drank more. "Nobody know who made this well, for it was here when I was born."

The track crossed a swampy part where the moss hung as white as lace from every limb. "Sleep on, alligators, and blow your bubbles." Then the track went into the road.

Deep, deep the road went down between the high green-colored banks. Overhead the live-oaks met, and it was as dark as a cave.

A black dog with a lolling tongue came up out of the weeds by the ditch. She was meditating, and not ready, and when he came at her she only hit him a little with her cane. Over she went in the ditch, like a little puff of milkweed.

Down there, her senses drifted away. A dream visited her, and she reached her hand up, but nothing reached down and gave her a pull. So she lay there and presently went to talking. "Old woman," she said to herself, "that black dog come up out of the weeds to stall you off, and now there he sitting on his fine tail, smiling at you."

A white man finally came along and found her—a hunter, a young man, with his dog on a chain.

"Well, Granny!" he laughed. "What are you doing there?"

"Lying on my back like a June-bug waiting to be turned over, mister," she said, reaching up her hand.

He lifted her up, gave her a swing in the air, and set her down. "Anything broken, Granny?"

"No sir, them old dead weeds is springy enough," said Phoenix, when she had got her breath. "I thank you for your trouble."

"Where do you live, Granny?" he asked, while the two dogs were growling at each other.

"Away back yonder, sir, behind the ridge. You can't even see it from here."

"On your way home?"

"No sir, I going to town."

"Why, that's too far! That's as far as I walk when I come out myself, and I get something for my trouble." He patted the stuffed bag he carried, and there hung down a little closed claw. It was one of the bobwhites, with its beak hooked bitterly to show it was dead. "Now you go on home, Granny!"

"I bound to go to town, mister," said Phoenix. "The time come around."

He gave another laugh, filling the whole landscape. "I know you old colored people! Wouldn't miss going to town to see Santa Claus!"

But something held old Phoenix very still. The deep lines in her face went into a fierce and different radiation. Without warning, she had seen with her own eyes a flashing nickel fall out of the man's pocket onto the ground.

"How old are you, Granny?" he was saying.

"There is no telling, mister," she said, "no telling."

Then she gave a little cry and clapped her hands and said, "Git on away from here, dog! Look! Look at that dog!" She laughed as if in admiration. "He ain't scared of nobody. He a big black dog." She whispered, "Sic him!"

"Watch me get rid of that cur," said the man. "Sic him, Pete! Sic him!"

Phoenix heard the dogs fighting, and heard the man running and throwing sticks. She even heard a gunshot. But she was slowly bending forward by that time, further and further forward, the lids stretched down over her eyes, as if she were doing this in her sleep. Her chin was lowered almost to her knees. The yellow palm of her hand came out from the fold of her apron. Her fingers slid down and along the ground under the piece of money with the grace and care they would have in lifting an egg from under a setting hen. Then she slowly straightened up, she stood erect, and the nickel was in her apron pocket. A bird flew by. Her lips moved. "God watching me the whole time. I come to stealing."

The man came back, and his own dog panted about them. "Well, I scared him off that time," he said, and then he laughed and lifted his gun and pointed it at Phoenix.

She stood straight and faced him.

"Doesn't the gun scare you?" he said, still pointing it.

"No, sir, I seen plenty go off closer by, in my day, and for less than what I done," she said, holding utterly still.

He smiled, and shouldered the gun. "Well, Granny," he said, "you must be a hundred years old, and scared of nothing. I'd give you a dime if I had any money with me. But you take my advice and stay home, and nothing will happen to you."

"I bound to go on my way, mister," said Phoenix. She inclined her head in the red rag. Then they went in different directions, but she could hear the gun shooting again and again over the hill.

She walked on. The shadows hung from the oak trees to the road like curtains. Then she smelled wood-smoke, and smelled the river, and she saw a steeple and the cabins on their steep steps. Dozens of little black children whirled around her. There ahead was Natchez shining. Bells were ringing. She walked on.

In the paved city it was Christmas time. There were red and green electric lights strung and crisscrossed everywhere, and all turned on in the daytime. Old Phoenix would have been lost if she had not distrusted her eyesight and depended on her feet to know where to take her.

She paused quietly on the sidewalk where people were passing by. A lady came along in the crowd, carrying an armful of red-, green- and silver-wrapped presents; she gave off perfume like the red roses in hot summer, and Phoenix stopped her.

"Please, missy, will you lace up my shoe?" She held up her foot.

"What do you want, Grandma?"

"See my shoe," said Phoenix. "Do all right for out in the country, but wouldn't look right to go in a big building."

"Stand still then, Grandma," said the lady. She put her packages down on the sidewalk beside her and laced and tied both shoes tightly.

"Can't lace 'em with a cane," said Phoenix. "Thank you, missy. I doesn't mind asking a nice lady to tie up my shoe, when I gets out on the street."

Moving slowly and from side to side, she went into the big building, and into a tower of steps, where she walked up and around and around until her feet knew to stop.

She entered a door, and there she saw nailed up on the wall the document that had been stamped with the gold seal and framed in the gold frame, which matched the dream that was hung up in her head.

"Here I be," she said. There was a fixed and ceremonial stiffness over her body.

"A charity case, I suppose," said an attendant who sat at the desk before her.

But Phoenix only looked above her head. There was sweat on her face, the wrinkles in her skin shone like a bright net.

"Speak up, Grandma," the woman said. "What's your name? We must have your history, you know. Have you been here before? What seems to be the trouble with you?"

Old Phoenix only gave a twitch to her face as if a fly were bothering her.

"Are you deaf?" cried the attendant.

But then the nurse came in.

"Oh, that's just old Aunt Phoenix," she said. "She doesn't come for herself—she has a little grandson. She makes these trips just as regular as clockwork. She lives away back off the Old Natchez Trace." She bent down. "Well, Aunt Phoenix, why don't you just take a seat? We won't keep you standing after your long trip." She pointed.

The old woman sat down, bolt upright in the chair.

"Now, how is the boy?" asked the nurse.

Old Phoenix did not speak.

"I said, how is the boy?"

But Phoenix only waited and stared straight ahead, her face very solemn and withdrawn into rigidity.

"Is his throat any better?" asked the nurse. "Aunt Phoenix, don't you hear me? Is your grandson's throat any better since the last time you came for the medicine?"

With her hands on her knees, the old woman waited, silent, erect and motionless, just as if she were in armor.

"You mustn't take up our time this way, Aunt Phoenix," the nurse said. "Tell us quickly about your grandson, and get it over. He isn't dead, is he?"

At last there came a flicker and then a flame of comprehension across her face, and she spoke.

"My grandson. It was my memory had left me. There I sat and forgot why I made my long trip."

"Forgot?" The nurse frowned. "After you came so far?"

Then Phoenix was like an old woman begging a dignified forgiveness for waking up frightened in the night. "I never did go to school, I was too old at the Surrender," she said in a soft voice. "I'm an old woman without an education. It was my memory fail me. My little grandson, he is just the same, and I forgot it in the coming."

"Throat never heals, does it?" said the nurse, speaking in a loud, sure voice to old Phoenix. By now she had a card with something written on it, a little list. "Yes. Swallowed lye. When was it?—January—two-three years ago—"

Phoenix spoke unasked now. "No, missy, he not dead, he just the same. Every little while his throat begin to close up again, and he not able to swallow. He not get his breath. He not able to help himself. So the time come around, and I go on another trip for the soothing medicine."

"All right. The doctor said as long as you came to get it, you could have it," said the nurse. "But it's an obstinate case."

"My little grandson, he sit up there in the house all wrapped up, waiting by himself," Phoenix went on. "We is the only two left in the world. He suffer and it don't seem to put him back at all. He got a sweet look. He going to last. He wear a little patch quilt and peep out holding his mouth open like a little bird. I remembers so plain now. I not going to forget him again, no, the whole enduring time. I could tell him from all the others in creation."

"All right." The nurse was trying to hush her now. She brought her a bottle of medicine. "Charity," she said, making a check mark in a book.

Old Phoenix held the bottle close to her eyes, and then carefully put it into her pocket.

"I thank you," she said.

"It's Christmas time, Grandma," said the attendant. "Could I give you a few pennies out of my purse?"

"Five pennies is a nickel," said Phoenix stiffly.

"Here's a nickel," said the attendant.

Phoenix rose carefully and held out her hand. She received the nickel and then fished the other nickel out of her pocket and laid it beside the new one. She stared at her palm closely, with her head on one side.

Then she gave a tap with her cane on the floor.

"This is what come to me to do," she said. "I going to the store and buy my child a little windmill they sells, made out of paper. He going to find it hard to believe there such a thing in the world. I'll march myself back where he waiting, holding it straight up in this hand."

She lifted her free hand, gave a little nod, turned around, and walked out of the doctor's office. Then her slow step began on the stairs, going down.

GO DOWN, MOSES

William Faulkner (1897-1962)

1

The face was black, smooth, impenetrable; the eyes had seen too much. The negroid hair had been treated so that it covered the skull like a cap, in a single neat-ridged sweep, with the appearance of having been lacquered, the part trimmed out with a razor, so that the head resembled a bronze head, imperishable and enduring. He wore one of those sports costumes called ensembles in the men's shop advertisements, shirt and trousers matching and cut from the same fawn-colored flannel, and they had cost too much and were draped too much, with too many pleats; and he half lay on the steel cot in the steel cubicle just outside which an armed guard had stood for twenty hours now, smoking cigarettes and answering in a voice which was anything under the sun but a Southern voice or even a Negro voice, the questions of the spectacled young white man sitting with a broad census-taker's portfolio on the steel stool opposite:

"Samuel Worsham Beauchamp. Twenty-six. Born in the country near Jefferson, Mississippi. No family. No——"

"Wait." The census-taker wrote rapidly. "That's not the name you were sen—lived under in Chicago."

The other snapped the ash from the cigarette. "No. It was another guy killed the cop."

"All right. Occupation——

"Getting rich too fast.

—none." The census-taker wrote rapidly. "Parents."

"Sure. Two. I don't remember them. My grandmother raised me."

"What's her name? Is she still living?"

"I don't know. Mollie. Worsham Beauchamp. If she is, she's on Carothers Edmonds' farm seventeen miles from Jefferson, Mississippi. That all?"

The census-taker closed the portfolio and stood up. He was a year or two younger than the other. "If they don't know who you are here, how will they know—how do you expect to get home?"

The other snapped the ash from the cigarette, lying on the steel cot in the fine Hollywood clothes and a pair of shoes better than the census-taker would ever own. "What will that matter to me?" he said.

So the census-taker departed; the guard locked the steel door again. And the other lay on the steel cot smoking until after a while they came and slit the expensive-trousers and shaved the expensive coiffure and led him out of the cell.

2

On that same hot, bright July morning the same hot bright wind which shook the mulberry leaves just outside Gavin Stevens' window blew into the office too, contriving a semblance of coolness from what was merely motion. It fluttered among the county-attorney business on the desk and blew in the wild shock of prematurely white hair of the man who sat behind it—a thin, intelligent, unstable face, a rumpled linen suit from whose lapel a Phi Beta Kappa key dangled on a watch chain—Gavin Stevens, Phi Beta Kappa, Harvard, Ph.D, Heidelberg, whose office was his hobby, although it made his living for him, and whose serious vocation was a twenty-two-year-old unfinished translation of the Old Testament back into classic Greek. Only his caller seemed impervious to it, though by appearance she should have owned in that breeze no more of weight and solidity than the intact ash of a scrap of burned paper—a little old Negro woman with a shrunken, incredibly old face beneath a white headcloth and a black straw hat which would have fitted a child.

"Beauchamp?" Stevens said. "You live on Mrs. Carothers Edmonds' place."

"I done left," she said. "I come to find my boy." Then, sitting on the hard chair opposite him and without moving, she began to chant. "Roth Edmonds sold my Benjamin. Sold him in Egypt. Pharaoh got him——"

"Wait," Stevens said. "Wait, Aunty." Because memory, recollection, was about to mesh and click. "If you don't know where your grandson is, how do you know he's in trouble? Do you mean that Mr. Edmonds has refused to help you find him?"

"It was Roth Edmonds sold him," she said. "Sold him in Egypt. I don't know whar he is. I just knows Pharaoh got him. And you the Law. I wants to find my boy."

"All right," Stevens said. "I'll try to find him. If you're not going back home, where will you stay in town? It may take some time, if you don't know where he went and you haven't heard from him in five years."

"I be staying with Hamp Worsham. He my brother."

"All right," Stevens said. He was not surprised. He had known Hamp Worsham all his life, though he had never seen the old Negress before. But even if he had, he still would not have been surprised. They were like that. You could know two of them for years, they might even have worked for you for years, bearing different names. Then suddenly you learn by pure chance that they are brothers or sisters.

He sat in the hot motion which was not breeze and listened to her toiling slowly down the steep outside stairs, remembering the grandson. The papers of that business had passed across his desk before going to the District Attorney five or six years ago—Butch Beauchamp, as the youth had been known during the single year he had spent in and out of the city jail: the old Negress' daughter's child, orphaned of his mother at birth and deserted by his father, whom the grandmother had taken and raised, or tried to. Because at nineteen he had quit the country and come to town and spent a year in and out of jail for gambling and fighting, to come at last under serious indictment for breaking and entering a store.

Caught red-handed, whereupon he had struck with a piece of iron pipe at the officer who surprised him and then lay on the ground where the officer had felled him with a pistol-butt, cursing through his broken mouth, his teeth fixed into something like furious laughter through the blood. Then two nights later he broke out of jail and was seen no more—a youth not yet twenty-one, with something in him from the father who begot and deserted him and who was now in the State Penitentiary for manslaughter—some seed not only violent but dangerous and bad.

And that's who I am to find, save, Stevens thought. Because he did not for one moment doubt the old Negress' instinct. If she had also been able to divine where the boy was and what his trouble was, he would not have been surprised, and it was only later that he thought to be surprised at how quickly he did find where the boy was and what was wrong.

His first thought was to telephone Carothers Edmonds, on whose farm the old Negress' husband had been a tenant for years. But then, according to her, Edmonds had already refused to have anything to do with it. Then he sat perfectly still while the hot wind blew in his wild white mane. Now he comprehended what the old Negress had meant. He remembered now that it was Edmonds who had actually sent the boy to Jefferson in the first place: he had caught the boy breaking into his commissary store and had ordered him off the place and had forbidden him ever to return. *And not the sheriff, the police*, he thought. *Something broader, quicker in scope*. . . . He rose and took his old fine worn panama and descended the outside stairs and crossed the empty square in the hot suspension of noon's beginning, to the office of the county newspaper. The editor was in—an older man but with hair less white than Stevens', in a black string tie and an old-fashioned boiled shirt and tremendously fat.

"An old nigger woman named Mollie Beauchamp," Stevens said. "She and her husband live on the Edmonds place. It's her grandson. You remember him—Butch Beauchamp, about five or six years ago, who spent a year in town, mostly in jail, until they finally caught him breaking into Rouncewell's store one night? Well, he's in worse trouble than that now. I don't doubt her at all. I just hope, for her sake as well as that of the great public whom I represent, that his present trouble is very bad and maybe final too—"

"Wait," the editor said. He didn't even need to leave his desk. He took the press association flimsy from its spike and handed it to Stevens. It was datelined from Joliet, Illinois, this morning:

Mississippi Negro, on eve of execution for murder of Chicago policeman, exposes alias by completing census questionnaire. Samuel Worsham Beauchamp——

Five minutes later Stevens was crossing again the empty square in which noon's hot suspension was that much nearer. He had thought that he was going home to his boarding house for the noon meal, but he found that he was not. '*Besides, I didn't lock my office door,*' he thought. Only, how under the sun she could have got to town from those seventeen miles. She may even have walked. "So it seems I didn't mean what I said I hoped," he said aloud, mounting the outside stairs again, out of the hazy and now windless sunglare, and entered his office. He stopped. Then he said,

"Good morning, Miss Worsham."

She was quite old too—thin, erect, with a neat, old-time piling of white hair beneath a faded hat of thirty years ago, in rusty black, with a frayed umbrella faded now until it was green instead of black. He had known her too all his life. She lived alone in the decaying house her father had left her, where she gave lessons in china-painting and, with the help of Hamp Worsham, descendant of one of her father's slaves, and his wife, raised chickens and vegetables for market.

"I came about Mollie," she said. "Mollie Beauchamp. She said that you——"

He told her while she watched him, erect on the hard chair where the old Negress had sat, the rusty umbrella leaning against her knee. On her lap, beneath her folded hands, lay an old-fashioned beaded reticule° almost as big as a suitcase. "He is to be executed tonight."

"Can nothing be done? Mollie's and Hamp's parents belonged to my grandfather. Mollie and I were born in the same month. We grew up together as sisters would."

"I telephoned," Stevens said. "I talked to the Warden at Joliet, and to the District Attorney in Chicago. He had a fair trial, a good lawyer—of that sort. He had money. He was in a business called numbers, that people like him make money in." She watched him, erect and motionless. "He is a murderer, Miss Worsham. He shot that policeman in the back. A bad son of a bad father. He admitted, confessed it afterward."

"I know," she said. Then he realized that she was not looking at him, not seeing him at least. "It's terrible."

"So is murder terrible," Stevens said. "It's better this way." Then she was looking at him again.

"I wasn't thinking of him. I was thinking of Mollie. She mustn't know."

°*reticule:* a large, drawstring bag

"Yes," Stevens said. "I have already talked with Mr. Wilmoth at the paper. He has agreed not to print anything. I will telephone the Memphis paper, but it's probably too late for that. . . . If we could just persuade her to go on back home this afternoon, before the Memphis paper . . . Out there, where the only white person she ever sees is Mr. Edmonds and I will telephone him; and even if the other darkies should hear about it, I'm sure they wouldn't. And then maybe in about two or three months I could go out there and tell her he is dead and buried somewhere in the North. . . ." This time she was watching him with such an expression that he ceased talking; she sat there, erect on the hard chair, watching him until he had ceased.

"She will want to take him back home with her," she said.

"Him?" Stevens said. "The body?" She watched him. The expression was neither shocked nor disapproving. It merely embodied some old, timeless, female affinity for blood and grief. Stevens thought: *She has walked to town in this heat. Unless Hamp brought her in the buggy he peddles eggs and vegetables from.*

"He is the only child of her oldest daughter, her own dead first child. He must come home."

"He must come home," Stevens said as quietly. "I'll attend to it at once. I'll telephone at once."

"You are kind." For the first time she stirred, moved. He watched her hands draw the reticule toward her, clasping it. "I will defray the expenses. Can you give me some idea——?"

He looked her straight in the face. He told the lie without batting an eye, quickly and easily. "Ten or twelve dollars will cover it. They will furnish a box and there will be only the transportation."

"A box?" Again she was looking at him with that expression curious and detached, as though he were a child. "He is her grandson, Mr. Stevens. When she took him to raise, she gave him my father's name—Samuel Worsham. Not just a box, Mr. Stevens. I understand that can be done by paying so much a month."

"Not just a box," Stevens said. He said it in exactly the same tone in which he had said He must come home. "Mr. Edmonds will want to help, I know. And I understand that old Luke Beauchamp has some money in the bank. And if you will permit me——"

"That will not be necessary," she said. He watched her open the reticule; he watched her count onto the desk twenty-five dollars in frayed bills and coins ranging down to nickels and dimes and pennies. "That will take care of the immediate expenses. I will tell her—You are sure there is no hope?"

"I am sure. He will die tonight."

"I will tell her this afternoon that he is dead then."

"Would you like for me to tell her?"

"I will tell her," she said.

"Would you like for me to come out and see her, then, talk to her?"

"It would be kind of you." Then she was gone, erect, her feet crisp and light, almost brisk, on the stairs, ceasing. He telephoned again, to the Illinois warden, then to an undertaker in Joliet. Then once more he crossed the hot, empty square. He had only to wait a short while for the editor to return from dinner.

"We're bringing him home," he said. "Miss Worsham and you and me and some others. It will cost——"

"Wait," the editor said. "What others?"

"I don't know yet. It will cost about two hundred. I'm not counting the telephones; I'll take care of them myself. I'll get something out of Carothers Edmonds the first time I catch him; I don't know how much, but something. And maybe fifty around the square. But the rest of it is you and me, because she insisted on leaving twenty-five with me, which is just twice what I tried to persuade her it would cost and just exactly four times what she can afford to pay——"

"Wait," the editor said. "Wait."

"And he will come in on Number Four the day after tomorrow and we will meet it, Miss Worsham and his grandmother, the old nigger, in my car and you and me in yours. Miss Worsham and the old woman will take him back home, back where he was born. Or where the old woman raised him. Or where she tried to. And the hearse out there will be fifteen more, not counting the flowers——"

"Flowers?" the editor cried.

"Flowers," Stevens said. "Call the whole thing two hundred and twenty-five. And it will probably be mostly you and me. All right?"

"No it aint all right," the editor said. "But it don't look like I can help myself. By Jupiter," he said, "even if I could help myself, the novelty will be almost worth it. It will be the first time in my life I ever paid money for copy I had already promised before hand I wont print."

"Have already promised before hand you will not print," Stevens said. And during the remainder of that hot and now windless afternoon, while officials from the city hall, and justices of the peace and bailiffs come fifteen and twenty miles from the ends of the county, mounted the stairs to the empty office and called his name and cooled their heels a while and then went away and returned and sat again, fuming, Stevens passed from store to store and office to office about the square—merchant and clerk, proprietor and employee, doctor dentist lawyer and barber—with his set and rapid speech: "It's to bring a dead nigger home. It's for Miss Worsham. Never mind about a paper to sign: just give me a dollar. Or a half a dollar then. Or a quarter then."

And that night after supper he walked through the breathless and star-filled darkness to Miss Worsham's house on the edge of town and knocked on the paintless front door. Hamp Worsham admitted him—an old man, belly-bloated from the vegetables on which he and his wife and Miss Worsham all three mostly lived, with blurred old eyes and a fringe of white hair about the head and face of a Roman general.

"She expecting you," he said. "She say to kindly step up to the chamber."

"Is that where Aunt Mollie is?" Stevens said.

"We all dar," Worsham said.

So Stevens crossed the lamplit hall (he knew that the entire house was still lighted with oil lamps and there was no running water in it) and preceded the Negro up the clean, paintless stairs beside the faded wallpaper, and followed the old Negro along the hall and into the clean, spare bedroom with its unmistakable faint odor of old maidens. They were all there, as Worsham had said—his wife, a tremendous light-colored woman in a bright turban leaning in the door, Miss Worsham erect again on a hard straight chair, the old Negress sitting in the only rocking chair beside the hearth on which even tonight a few ashes smoldered faintly.

She held a reed-stemmed clay pipe but she was not smoking it, the ash dead and white in the stained bowl; and actually looking at her for the first time, Stevens thought: *Good Lord, she's not as big as a ten-year-old child.* Then he sat too, so that the four of them—himself, Miss Worsham, the old Negress and her brother—made a circle about the brick hearth on which the ancient symbol of human coherence and solidarity smoldered.

"He'll be home the day after tomorrow, Aunt Mollie," he said. The old Negress didn't even look at him; she never had looked at him.

"He dead," she said. "Pharaoh got him."

"Oh yes, Lord," Worsham said. "Pharaoh got him."

"Done sold my Benjamin," the old Negress said. "Sold him in Egypt." She began to sway faintly back and forth in the chair.

"Oh yes, Lord," Worsham said.

"Hush," Miss Worsham said. "Hush, Hamp."

"I telephoned Mr. Edmonds," Stevens said. "He will have everything ready when you get there."

"Roth Edmonds sold him," the old Negress said. She swayed back and forth in the chair. "Sold my Benjamin."

"Hush," Miss Worsham said. "Hush, Mollie. Hush now."

"No," Stevens said. "No he didn't, Aunt Mollie. It wasn't Mr. Edmonds. Mr. Edmonds didn't—" *But she can't hear me,* he thought. She was not even looking at him. She never had looked at him.

"Sold my Benjamin," she said. "Sold him in Egypt."

"Sold him in Egypt," Worsham said.

"Roth Edmonds sold my Benjamin."

"Sold him to Pharaoh."

"Sold him to Pharaoh and now he dead."

"I'd better go," Stevens said. He rose quickly. Miss Worsham rose too, but he did not wait for her to precede him. He went down the hall fast, almost running, he did not even know whether she was following him or not. *Soon I will be outside*, he thought. *Then there will be air, space, breath.* Then he could hear her behind him—the crisp, light, brisk yet unhurried feet as he had heard them descending the stairs from his office, and beyond them the voices:

"Sold my Benjamin. Sold him in Egypt."

"Sold him in Egypt. Oh yes, Lord."

He descended the stairs, almost running. It was not far now; now he could smell and feel it: the breathing and simple dark, and now he could manner himself to pause and wait, turning at the door, watching Miss Worsham as she followed him to the door—the high, white, erect, old-time head approaching through the old-time lamplight. Now he could hear the third voice, which would be that of Hamp's wife—a true constant soprano which ran without words beneath the strophe and antistrophe of the brother and sister:

"Sold him in Egypt and now he dead."

"Oh yes, Lord. Sold him in Egypt."

"Sold him in Egypt."

"And now he dead."

"Sold him to Pharaoh."

"And now he dead."

"I'm sorry," Stevens said. "I ask you to forgive me. I should have known. I shouldn't have come."

"It's all right," Miss Worsham said. "It's our grief."

And on the next bright hot day but one the hearse and the two cars were waiting when the southbound train came in. There were more than a dozen cars, but it was not until the train came in that Stevens and the editor began to notice the number of people, Negroes and whites both. Then, with the idle white men and youths and small boys and probably half a hundred Negroes, men and women too, watching quietly, the Negro undertaker's men lifted the gray-and-silver casket from the train and carried it to the hearse and snatched the wreaths and floral symbols of man's ultimate and inevitable end briskly out and slid the casket in and flung the flowers back and clapped-to the door.

Then, with Miss Worsham and the old Negress in Stevens' car with the driver he had hired and himself and the editor in the editor's, they followed the hearse as it swung into the long hill up from the station, going fast in a whining lower gear until it reached the crest, going pretty fast still but with an unctuous, an almost bishoplike purr until it slowed into the square, crossing it, circling the Confederate monument and the courthouse while the merchants and clerks and barbers and professional men who had given Stevens the dollars and half-dollars and quarters and the ones who had not, watched quietly from doors and upstairs windows, swinging then into the street which at the edge of town would become the country road leading to the destination seventeen miles away, already picking up speed again and followed still by the two cars contaning the four people—the high-headed erect white woman, the old Negress, the designated paladin of justice and truth and right, the Heidelberg Ph.D.—in formal component complement to the Negro murderer's catafalque: the slain wolf.

When they reached the edge of town the hearse was going quite fast. Now they flashed past the metal sign which said Jefferson. Corporate Limit. and the pavement vanished, slanting away into another long hill, becoming gravel. Stevens reached over and cut the switch, so that the editor's car coasted, slowing as he began to brake it, the hearse and the other car drawing rapidly away now as thought in flight, the light and unrained summer dust spurting from beneath the fleeing wheels; soon they were gone. The editor turned his car clumsily, grinding the gears, sawing and filling until it was back in the road facing town again. Then he sat for a moment, his foot on the clutch.

"Do you know what she asked me this morning, back there at the station?" he said.

"Probably not," Stevens said.

"She said, 'Is you gonter put hit in de paper?' "

"What?"

"That's what I said," the editor said. "And she said it again: 'Is you gonter put hit in de paper? I wants hit all in de paper. All of hit.' And I wanted to say, 'If I should happen to know how he really died, do you want that in too?' And by Jupiter, if I had and if she had known what we know even, I believe she would have said yes. But I didn't say it. I just said, 'Why, you couldn't read it, Aunty.' And she said, 'Miss Belle will show me whar to look and I can look at hit. You put hit in de paper. All of hit.' "

"Oh," Stevens said. *Yes*, he thought. *It doesn't matter to her now. Since it had to be and she couldn't stop it, and now that it's all over and done and finished, she doesn't care how he died. She just wanted him home, but she wanted him to come home right. She wanted that casket and those flowers and the hearse and she wanted to ride through town behind it in a car.* "Come on," he said. "Let's get back to town. I haven't seen my desk in two days."

BLACK IS MY FAVORITE COLOR

Bernard Malamud (1914-   )

Charity Sweetness sits in the toilet eating her two hard-boiled eggs while I'm having my ham sandwich and coffee in the kitchen. That's how it goes only don't get the idea of ghettoes. If there's a ghetto I'm the one that's in it. She's my cleaning woman from Father Divine and comes in once a week to my small three-room apartment on my day off from the liquor store. "Peace," she says to me, "Father reached on down and took me right up in Heaven." She's a small person with a flat body, frizzy hair, and a quiet face that the light shines out of, and Mama had such eyes before she died. The first time Charity Sweetness came in to clean, a little more than a year and a half, I made the mistake to ask her to sit down at the kitchen table with me and eat her lunch. I was still feeling not so hot after Ornita left but I'm the kind of a man—Nat Lime, forty-four, a bachelor with a daily growing bald spot on the back of my head, and I could lose frankly fifteen pounds—who enjoys company so long as he has it. So she cooked up her two hardboiled eggs and sat down and took a small bite out of one of them. But after a minute she stopped chewing and she got up and carried the eggs in a cup in the bathroom, and since then she eats there. I said to her more than once, "Okay, Charity Sweetness, so have it your way, eat the eggs in the kitchen by yourself and I'll eat when you're done," but she smiles absentminded, and eats in the toilet. It's my fate with colored people.

Although black is still my favorite color you wouldn't know it from my luck except in short quantities even though I do all right in the liquor store business in Harlem, on Eighth Avenue between 110th and 111th. I speak with respect. A large part of my life I've had dealings with Negro people, most on a business basis but sometimes for friendly reasons with genuine feeling on both sides. I'm drawn to them. At this time of my life I should have one or two good colored friends but the fault isn't necessarily mine. If they knew what was in my heart towards them, but how can you tell that to anybody nowadays? I've tried more than once but the language of the heart either is a dead language or else nobody understands it the way you speak it. Very few. What I'm saying is, personally for me there's only one human color and that's the color of blood. I like a black person if not because he's black, then because I'm white. It comes to the same thing. If I wasn't white my first choice would be black. I'm satisfied to be white because I have no other choice. Anyway, I got an eye for color. I appreciate. Who wants everybody to be the same? Maybe it's like some kind of a talent. Nat Lime might be a liquor dealer in Harlem, but once in the jun-

---

gle in New Guinea in the Second War, I got the idea when I shot at a running Jap and missed him, that I had some kind of a talent, though maybe it's the kind where you have a marvelous idea now and then but in the end what do they come to? After all, it's a strange world.

Where Charity Sweetness eats her eggs makes me think about Buster Wilson when we were both boys in the Williamsburg section of Brooklyn. There was this long block of run-down dirty frame houses in the middle of a not-so-hot white neighborhood full of pushcarts. The Negro houses looked to me like they had been born and died there, dead not long after the beginning of the world. I lived on the next street. My father was a cutter with arthritis in both hands, big red knuckles and swollen fingers so he didn't cut, and my mother was the one who went to work. She sold paper bags from a second-hand pushcart in Ellery Street. We didn't starve but nobody ate chicken unless we were sick or the chicken was. This was my first acquaintance with a lot of black people and I used to poke around on their poor block. I think I thought, brother, if there can be like this, what can't there be? I mean I caught an early idea what life was about. Anyway I met Buster Wilson there. He used to play marbles by himself. I sat on the curb across the street, watching him shoot one marble lefty and the other one righty. The hand that won picked up the marbles. It wasn't so much of a game but he didn't ask me to come over. My idea was to be friendly, only he never encouraged, he discouraged. Why did I pick him out for a friend? Maybe because I had no others then, we were new in the neighborhood, from Manhattan. Also I liked his type. Buster did everything alone. He was a skinny kid and his brothers' clothes hung on him like worn-out potato sacks. He was a beanpole boy, about twelve, and I was then ten. His arms and legs were burnt out matchsticks. He always wore a brown wool sweater, one arm half unraveled, the other went down to the wrist. His long and narrow head had a white part cut straight in the short woolly hair, maybe with a ruler there, by his father, a barber but too drunk to stay a barber. In those days though I had little myself I was old enough to know who was better off, and the whole block of colored houses made me feel bad in the daylight. But I went there as much as I could because the street was full of life. In the night it looked different, it's hard to tell a cripple in the dark. Sometimes I was afraid to walk by the houses when they were dark and quiet. I was afraid there were people looking at me that I couldn't see. I liked it better when they had parties at night and everybody had a good time. The musicians played their banjos and saxophones and the houses shook with the music and laughing. The young girls, with their pretty dresses and ribbons in their hair, caught me in my throat when I saw them through the windows.

But with the parties came drinking and fights. Sundays were bad days after the Saturday night parties. I remember once that Buster's father, also long and loose, always wearing a dirty gray Homburg hat, chased another black man in the street with a half-inch chisel. The other one, maybe five feet high, lost his shoe and when they wrestled on the ground he was already bleeding through his suit, a thick red blood smearing the sidewalk. I was frightened by the blood and wanted to pour it back in the man who was bleeding from the chisel. On another time Buster's father was playing in a crap game with two big bouncy red dice, in the back of an alley between two middle houses. Then about six men started fist-fighting there, and they ran out of the alley and hit each other in the street. The neighbors, including children, came out and watched, everybody afraid but nobody moving to do anything. I saw the same thing near my store in Harlem, years later, a big crowd watching two men in the street, their breaths hanging in the air on a winter night, murdering each other with switch knives, but nobody moved to call a cop. I didn't either. Anyway, I was just a young kid but I still remember how the cops drove up in a police paddy wagon and broke up the fight by hitting everybody they could hit with big nightsticks. This was in the days before LaGuardia. Most of the fighters were knocked out cold, only one or two got away. Buster's father started to run back in his house but a cop ran after him and cracked him on his Homburg hat with a club, right on the front porch. Then the Negro men were lifted up by the cops, one at the arms and the other at the feet, and they heaved them in the paddy wagon. Buster's father hit the back of the wagon and fell, with his nose spouting very red blood, on top of three other men. I personally couldn't stand it, I was scared of the human race so I ran home, but I remember Buster watching without any expression in his eyes. I stole an extra fifteen cents from my mother's pocketbook and I ran back and asked Buster if he wanted to go to the movies. I would pay. He said yes. This was the first time he talked to me.

So we went more than once to the movies. But we never got to be friends. Maybe because it was a one-way proposition—from me to him. Which includes my invitations to go with me, my (poor mother's) movie money, Hershey chocolate bars, watermelon slices, even my best Nick Carter and Merriwell books that I spent hours picking up in the junk shops, and that he never gave me back. Once he let me go in his house to get a match so we could smoke some butts we found, but it smelled so heavy, so impossible, I died till I got out of there. What I saw in the way of furniture I won't mention—the best was falling apart in pieces. Maybe we went to the movies all together five or six matinees that spring and in the summertime, but when the shows were over he usually walked home by himself.

"Why don't you wait for me, Buster?" I said. "We're both going in the same direction."

But he was walking ahead and didn't hear me. Anyway he didn't answer.

One day when I wasn't expecting it he hit me in the teeth. I felt like crying but not because of the pain. I spit blood and said, "What did you hit me for? What did I do to you?"

"Because you a Jew bastard. Take your Jew movies and your Jew candy and shove them up your Jew ass."

And he ran away.

I thought to myself how was I to know he didn't like the movies. When I was a man I thought, you can't force it.

Years later, in the prime of my life, I met Mrs. Ornita Harris. She was standing by herself under an open umbrella at the bus stop, crosstown 110th, and I picked up her green glove that she had dropped on the wet sidewalk. It was in the end of November. Before I could ask her was it hers, she grabbed the glove out of my hand, closed her umbrella, and stepped in the bus. I got on right after her.

I was annoyed so I said, "If you'll pardon me, Miss, there's no law that you have to say thanks, but at least don't make a criminal out of me."

"Well, I'm sorry," she said, "but I don't like white men trying to do me favors."

I tipped my hat and that was that. In ten minutes I got off the bus but she was already gone.

Who expected to see her again but I did. She came into my store about a week later for a bottle of scotch.

"I would offer you a discount," I told her, "but I know you don't like a certain kind of a favor and I'm not looking for a slap in the face."

Then she recognized me and got a little embarrassed.

"I'm sorry I misunderstood you that day."

"So mistakes happen."

The result was she took the discount. I gave her a dollar off.

She used to come in about every two weeks for a fifth of Haig and Haig. Sometimes I waited on her, sometimes my helpers, Jimmy or Mason, also colored, but I said to give the discount. They both looked at me but I had nothing to be ashamed. In the spring when she came in we used to talk once in a while. She was a slim woman, dark but not the most dark, about thirty years I would say, also well built, with a combination nice legs and a good-size bosom that I like. Her face was pretty, with big eyes and high cheek bones, but lips a little thick and nose a little broad. Sometimes she didn't feel like talking, she paid for the bottle, less discount, and walked out. Her eyes were tired and she didn't look to me like a happy woman.

I found out her husband was once a window cleaner on the big buildings, but one day his safety belt broke and he fell fifteen stories. After the funeral she got a job as a manicurist in a Times Square barber shop. I told her I was a bachelor and lived with my mother in a small three-room apartment on West Eighty-third near Broadway. My mother had cancer, and Ornita said she was very sorry.

One night in July we went out together. How that happened I'm still not so sure. I guess I asked her and she didn't say no. Where do you go out with a Negro woman? We went to the Village. We had a good dinner and walked in Washington Square Park. It was a hot night. Nobody was surprised when they saw us, nobody looked at us like we were against the law. If they looked maybe they saw my new lightweight suit that I bought yesterday and my shiny bald spot when we walked under a lamp, also how pretty she was for a man of my type. We went in a movie on West Eighth Street. I didn't want to go in but she said she had heard about the picture. We went in like strangers and we came out like strangers. I wondered what was in her mind and I thought to myself, whatever is in there it's not a certain white man that I know. All night long we went together like we were chained. After the movie she wouldn't let me take her back to Harlem. When I put her in a taxi she asked me, "Why did we bother?"

For the steak, I wanted to say. Instead I said, "You're worth the bother."

"Thanks anyway."

Kiddo, I thought to myself after the taxi left, you just found out what's what, now the best thing is forget her.

It's easy to say. In August we went out the second time. That was the night she wore a purple dress and I thought to myself, my God, what colors. Who paints that picture paints a masterpiece. Everybody looked at us but I had pleasure. That night when she took off her dress it was in a furnished room I had the sense to rent a few days before. With my sick mother, I couldn't ask her to come to my apartment, and she didn't want me to go home with her where she lived with her brother's family on West 115th near Lenox Avenue. Under her purple dress she wore a black slip, and when she took that off she had white underwear. When she took off the white underwear she was black again. But I know where the next white was, if you want to call it white. And that was the night I think I fell in love with her, the first time in my life though I have liked one or two nice girls I used to go with when I was a boy. It was a serious proposition. I'm the kind of a man when I think of love I'm thinking of marriage. I guess that's why I am a bachelor.

That same week I had a holdup in my place, two big men—both black—with revolvers. One got excited when I rang open the cash register so he could take the money and he hit me over the ear with his gun. I stayed in the hospital a couple of weeks. Otherwise I was insured. Ornita came to see me. She sat on a chair without talking much. Finally I saw she was uncomfortable so I suggested she ought to go home.

"I'm sorry it happened," she said.

"Don't talk like it's your fault."

When I got out of the hospital my mother was dead. She was a wonderful person. My father died when I was thirteen and all by herself she kept the family alive and together. I sat shive° for a week and remembered how she sold paper bags on her pushcart. I remembered her life and what she tried to teach me. Nathan, she said, if you ever forget you are a Jew a goy will remind you. Mama, I said, rest in peace on this subject. But if I do something you don't like remember, on earth it's harder than where you are. Then when my week of mourning was finished, one night I said, "Ornita, let's get married. We're both honest people and if you love me like I love you it won't be such a bad time. If you don't like New York I'll sell out here and we'll move someplace else. Maybe to San Francisco where nobody knows us. I was there for a week in the Second War and I saw white and colored living together."

"Nat," she answered me, "I like you but I'd be afraid. My husband woulda killed me."

"Your husband is dead."

"Not in my memory."

"In that case I'll wait."

"Do you know what it'd be like—I mean the life we could expect?"

"Ornita," I said. "I'm the kind of a man, if he picks his own way of life he's satisfied."

"What about children? Were you looking forward to half-Jewish polka dots?"

"I was looking forward to children."

"I can't," she said.

Can't is can't. I saw she was afraid and the best thing was not to push. Sometimes when we met she was so nervous that whatever we did she couldn't enjoy it. At the same time I still thought I had a chance. We were together more and more. I got rid of my furnished room and she came to my apartment—I gave away Mama's bed and bought a new one. She stayed with me all day on Sundays. When she wasn't so nervous she was affectionate, and if I know what love is, I had it. We went out a couple of times a week, the same way—usually I met her in Times Square and sent her home in a taxi, but I talked more about marriage and she talked less against it. One night she told me she was still trying to convince herself but she was almost convinced. I took an inventory of my liquor stock so I could put the store up for sale.

Ornita knew what I was doing. One day she quit her job, the next she took it back. She also went away a week to visit her sister in Philadelphia for a little rest. She came back tired but said maybe. Maybe is maybe so I'll wait. The way she said it it was closer to yes. That was the winter two years ago. When she was in Philadelphia I called up a friend of mine from the Army, now a CPA, and told him I would appreciate an invitation for an evening. He knew why. His wife said yes right away. When Ornita

---

°*shive:* or *shiva*, Yiddish term referring to a period of mourning, usually seven days

came back we went there. The wife made a fine dinner. It wasn't a bad time and they told us to come again. Ornita had a few drinks. She looked relaxed, wonderful. Later, because of a twenty-four hour taxi strike I had to take her home on the subway. When we got to the 116th Street station she told me to stay on the train, and she would walk the couple of blocks to her house. I didn't like a woman walking alone on the streets at that time of the night. She said she never had any trouble but I insisted nothing doing. I said I would walk to her stoop with her and when she went upstairs I would go back to the subway.

On the way there, on 115th in the middle of the block before Lenox, we were stopped by three men—maybe they were boys. One had a black hat with a half-inch brim, one a green cloth hat, and the third wore a black leather cap. The green hat was wearing a short coat and the other two had long ones. It was under a street light but the leather cap snapped a six-inch switchblade open in the light.

"What you doin' with this white son of a bitch?" he said to Ornita.

"I'm minding my own business," she answered him, "and I wish you would too."

"Boys," I said, "we're all brothers. I'm a reliable merchant in the neighborhood. This young lady is my dear friend. We don't want any trouble. Please let us pass."

"You talk like a Jew landlord," said the green hat. "Fifty a week for a single room."

"No charge fo' the rats," said the half-inch brim.

"Believe me, I'm no landlord. My store is 'Nathan's Liquors' between Hundred Tenth and Eleventh. I also have two colored clerks, Mason and Jimmy, and they will tell you I pay good wages as well as I give discounts to certain customers."

"Shut your mouth, Jewboy," said the leather cap, and he moved the knife back and forth in front of my coat button. "No more black pussy for you."

"Speak with respect about this lady, please."

I got slapped on my mouth.

"That ain't no lady," said the long face in the half-inch brim, "that's black pussy. She deserve to have evvy bit of her hair shave off. How you like to have evvy bit of your hair shave off, black pussy?"

"Please leave me and this gentleman alone or I'm gonna scream long and loud. That's my house three doors down."

They slapped her. I never heard such a scream. Like her husband was falling fifteen stories.

I hit the one that slapped her and the next I knew I was laying in the gutter with a pain in my head. I thought, goodbye, Nat, they'll stab me for sure, but all they did was take my wallet and run in three different directions.

Ornita walked back with me to the subway and she wouldn't let me go home with her again.

"Just get home safely."

She looked terrible. Her face was gray and I still remembered her scream. It was a terrible winter night, very cold February, and it took me an hour and ten minutes to get home. I felt bad for leaving her but what could I do?

We had a date downtown the next night but she didn't show up, the first time.

In the morning I called her in her place of business.

"For God's sake, Ornita, if we got married and moved away we wouldn't have that kind of trouble that we had. We wouldn't come in that neighborhood any more."

"Yes, we would. I have family there and don't want to move anyplace else. The truth of it is I can't marry you, Nat. I got troubles enough of my own."

"I coulda sworn you love me."

"Maybe I do but I can't marry you."

"For God's sake, why?"

"I got enough trouble of my own."

I went that night in a cab to her brother's house to see her. He was a quiet man with a thin mustache. "She gone," he said, "left for a long visit to some close relatives in the South. She said to tell you she appreciate your intentions but didn't think it will work out."

"Thank you kindly," I said.

Don't ask me how I got home.

Once on Eighth Avenue, a couple of blocks from my store, I saw a blind man with a white cane tapping on the sidewalk. I figured we were going in the same direction so I took his arm.

"I can tell you're white," he said.

A heavy colored woman with a full shopping bag rushed after us.

"Never mind," she said, "I know where he live."

She pushed me with her shoulder and I hurt my leg on the fire hydrant.

That's how it is. I give my heart and they kick me in my teeth.

"Charity Sweetness—you hear me?—come out of that goddamn toilet!"

° ° °

Daybreak

In this final section seven black writers, most of them contemporary, attempt to give voice to the black experience. Here, no longer in shadow, unmasked and not stereotyped, are black characters offering images of what it means to be truly human.

Gwendolyn Brooks has published a novel and five volumes of poetry. She was born in 1917 and lives in Chicago. Doughtry Long is a young poet whose work has been published by Broadside Press. Samuel Allen (also Paul Vesey in pseudonym) ia a lawyer and teacher whose poetry has appeared in a number of anthologies. The selection by William Melvin Kelley is Part I of his second novel, *A Drop of Patience*. Alice Walker has published two novels, two volumes of poetry, and a collection of short stories. Waring Cuney's poem, "No Images," received first prize in the *Opportunity* poetry contest in 1926. It was published in *The Negro Caravan*, a collection of works by black writers edited by Sterling Brown and published in 1941. Both "Me and the Mule" and "Daybreak in Alabama" reflect Langston Hughes's belief that the best way to learn the truth about the experience of black people is to let them speak, and to listen to them.

THE BEAN EATERS

Gwendolyn Brooks (1917-   )

They eat beans mostly, this old yellow pair.
Dinner is a casual affair.
Plain chipware on a plain and creaking wood,
Tin flatware.

Two who are Mostly Good.
Two who have lived their day,
But keep on putting on their clothes
And putting things away.

And remembering . . .
Remembering, with twinklings and twinges,
As they lean over the beans in their rented back room that is full of beads and receipts and dolls and cloths, tobacco crumbs, vase and fringes.

ONE TIME HENRY DREAMED THE NUMBER

Doughtry Long (1942-   )

one time henry dreamed the number
but we didn't play it,
and do you know, that thing came out straight
3-67?
    yes it did!
we was both sick
for a whole week,
        could'a sure used
            the money then too,
that was back in hoover's time
when folks was scufflin
to make ends meet.
i knock on wood though
        we've lived through it all.
last night after we ate
the last of the meat loaf and greens
and was watching television
henry asked me if i remembered that,
i told him yes,
        we laughed
            then went to bed
and kept each other warm.

A MOMENT PLEASE

Samuel Allen (1917-   )

When I gaze at the sun
    I walked to the subway booth
    for change for a dime.
and know that this great earth
    Two adolescent girls stood there
    alive with eagerness to know
is but a fragment from it thrown
    all in their new found world
    there was for them to know

---

in heat and flame a billion years ago,
    they looked at me and brightly asked
    "Are you Arabian?"
that then this world was lifeless
    I smiled and cautiously
    —for one grows cautious—
    shook my head.
as, a billion hence,
    "Egyptian?"
it shall again be,
    Again I smiled and shook my head
    and walked away.
what moment is it that I am betrayed,
    I've gone but seven paces now
oppressed, cast down,
    and from behind comes swift the sneer
or warm with love or triumph?
    "Or Nigger?"

    A moment, please
What is it that to fury I am roused?
    for still it takes a moment
What meaning for me
    and now
in this homeless clan
    I'll turn
the dupe of space
    and smile
the toy of time?
    and nod my head.

From A DROP OF PATIENCE

William Melvin Kelley (1937-   )

The house was too quiet. His little sister should have been running, screeching in the hallway; behind the house his brother should have been batting stones with a stick; his mother should have been singing. At least there should have been the short, heavy hiss of her broom. Instead the house was so still that the dripping of the kitchen pump was as loud as rocks dropping into a pond.

The house had never before been this quiet—and during the past few days it had been more noisy than ever before. His father had been carrying heavy things out of the house, returning with a lighter step, his load left somewhere behind him. Several times his mother had cried. Earlier this morning he had thought they had all been tiptoeing around him, whispering, then leaving the house and going away. He thought perhaps his mother had kissed him. But he was not certain. He could not always tell if he was awake or dreaming.

But he was sure he was awake now. He felt awake. He lay on his back, his hands moving over the bare mattress, his fingers squeezing the small cotton balls his mother had told him held the bed together. Once he had crawled under the bed, into a dust-filled space, and gripped the cold springs in his hands. He could not understand how such soft cotton balls could hold the bed together.

Finally he sat up, swung his feet onto the splintered wooden floor and bent from the waist, searching for his coveralls. Finding them, the downside damp from the night, he pulled them on and stood up. Perhaps they were on the porch.

He felt his way quickly down the hall. The wall was chipped and scarred in several places, his favorite scar shaped like a hand missing one finger. Under the plaster was a frame of wood.

The tiny wire squares in the screen door were hot. Pushing against the door, he made the spring pop and whine. On the porch his face and his chest, bare except for the bib and straps of his coveralls, began very quickly to blaze. It was late in the morning; the heat was coming from high up. No one was breathing on the porch.

He stood in the heat for a long while, waiting for someone to come for him. He could not go with his friends (who seemed to be playing in the cool woods behind his house); he did not want to be away when his parents returned. Finally, feeling his way to the edge of the porch with his bare feet, he sat down, dangling his legs over the edge. Tall, tough grass grew near the porch and tickled his swinging feet.

Someone came when the heat was on top of his head. He had just put his hand to his hair and found the tiny curls and beads burning when, in the road running past the porch, pebbles began to spray. A man was walking fast. He recognized the footsteps, which stopped at the head of the path. "Papa?"

"Come on, Luddy. Come on, son." His father approached him, dragging his heavy shoes. Ludlow smelled dust in the air. Then his father's hand lifted his own and Ludlow hopped to his feet. His father led him to the road. They went to the right. The dirt on the road was so powdery and dry it felt like hot water. Ludlow complained and his father lifted him up, his arm under Ludlow's thighs like a seat. Ludlow put his arm around his father's neck. Whiskers picked his fingertips. He wondered where he was being carried, whether or not his brother, sister, and mother would meet him there. The ground under his father's feet turned hard; Ludlow felt the shock all the way through his father's body. They were on pavement now. A car chugged by, blowing warm air against his face. They were on a highway, but it must be different from the one to which his brother had always led him; he and his father had turned the opposite way.

His father was marching now, his steps regular and heavy. Ludlow bounced on his arm. Small stones crunched beneath his father's feet. Cars came toward them, bubbling, and blew past.

They turned off the highway. Not far away, birds whistled and clattered in the trees. There was pavement again, and steps. His father leaned against a heavy door and carried him out of the heat. Ludlow's bare arms grew cold. Away, in a long, echoing space, children were talking.

His father put him down, but held his hand. The smooth stone floor sent a shiver through him. A chair skidded and squeaked, and footsteps went away, limping. A moment later, the limping footsteps returned, accompanied by another set.

Ludlow smelled cigar smoke. "This him?"

"Yes, Warden. This him. Luddy. Ludlow Washington, sir." His father squeezed his hand.

"Looks older'n five." The cigar smoke jammed into Ludlow's nose.

"He five, sir." His father was frightened, the first time ever. "Honest to God."

"Don't matter." He paused. "You can write your name, can't you?"

His father let go his hand. "Yes, sir."

"Well, then tell him to sit down. My assistant'll look after him. We got papers to sign." The Warden turned away. "Watch him." The cigar smoke faded with his father's footsteps. The Warden's assistant limped toward him, clutched his arm and snatched him forward. "Sit there and don't make no squawk." Ludlow was spun around and pushed back onto a wooden seat. Running his hands over it, he discovered it was a bench, with arms at either end.

"What you doing there?" The assistant was now some distance away. "I told you not to move!"

Ludlow sat rigid, his palms flat against the bench. After a few moments the assistant's chair scraped and the man's step disappeared behind the far-off sound of the children. Ludlow remained rooted. It could be a trick, the kind his brother sometimes played when he told Ludlow to wait for him because he was going away for a moment. Ludlow would follow his brother's steps away until he was certain his brother was gone. Then he would move and his brother would yell, close again, having sneaked back. They would laugh at his brother's trick. But Ludlow knew the Warden's assistant was not playing.

He sat quietly, trying to decide where he might be and why he and his father had come. Something in the air of the place stung the inside of his nose. Though it was summer outside, inside it was cool and damp. It must be a big place because of the echo that surrounded everyone's words. Far away, the children still talked. He knew he had never been there before. He wanted to leave.

A bit frightened now, he attempted to make himself feel better by sucking his thumb and humming a song his mother had taught him.

"Who that humming?" The voice was hoarse and wet-sounding, like his brother trying to whisper through a mouthful of water. Before he could answer, two hands skittered over his face, the fingers poking in and out of his nose, eye sockets, and mouth, then around to his ears and the sides of his head. They brushed over his hair, then paused. "I don't know you." The watery voice was bewildered. "What you doing here?"

"I don't know." Ludlow too was bewildered. Never before had he met anyone who did the same thing he would have done had he encountered a strange object or person.

"You don't know? Well, I guess I do. You got any money?"

"No."

"What's your name?" The hands moved to his shoulders and down his sides.

"Ludlow Washington."

The hands were searching his pockets now. "How old?"

He hesitated. "Five."

"I'm six." The hands left him. "You'll be on my floor, the third. You remember voices good?" Ludlow nodded. "You remember mines because I'm claiming you for my slave. I'm your master."

"What?" He did not understand what the boy was talking about.

The boy's hand touched his nose, slid across his face, grasped and twisted his ear so it burned. "I said I'm your master."

"Master?" Tears tickled Ludlow's cheeks, but he tried not to make the sounds of crying.

"I'm your master. That mean I own you and when someone ask you something, you tell them to ask me because I'm your master, and I do your answering. That's everybody excepting the Warden and Mister Gimpy. All the boys here."

Ludlow was certain he would soon be leaving, but he decided he would play along with the boy. "Do you—"

The boy slapped him across the face. "When you talking to me call me Master."

Ludlow sighed. "Master, you got a master too?"

The boy twisted his ear before he answered. "Stupid slave! Of course I does. We all got masters. You got a master as long as you live." His hand left Ludlow's ear. "I'll talk to you upstairs. Remember I'm your master."

"What you doing there?" The Warden's assistant yelled at them from a great echoing distance. When his shout faded, his limping footsteps were running toward them.

"Wasn't doing nothing, sir. Just making friends with the new boy." The boy was very polite now.

"Just get away from him."

"Yes, sir. I just leaving, sir. Good-bye, Ludlow. Nice to meet you." The boy's step was soft and quick.

"Didn't I tell you to sit still?" The assistant's voice was over him now. "After them papers is signed, I'll teach you to listen better." Not even his father had ever sounded as angry. He wondered what would happen after the papers were signed.

The assistant backed away. It was quiet now and Ludlow listened for the children. Their voices were shrill. He began to feel lonely. His stomach was upset. He wished his father would return soon and take him into the heat, outside to the call of birds, to the smell of hot tar and grass.

The Warden's voice was coming toward him. "Remember you give up your right to complain. You signed him over to us and we'll teach him to earn his way. But this ain't no nursery; it's a school."

"I don't cause no trouble, sir. I'm just grateful you took him." His father was happier now.

Ludlow did not know whether or not to stand up. He remained in his place. The two men stood over him. His father's voice was higher up, farther away from his ears than the Warden's. "I'll tell him if you want me to."

"Surely, go on. It'll save us the trouble."

The bench sagged as his father sat beside him. "Luddy, I got to tell you something." There was a long silence. Ludlow reached out and found his father's arm; the man was sweating. "You ain't the same like most kids . . . you special . . . yeah, that's it, you special. And I got to leave you here to learn special things. . . ."

He did not really know what else his father said to him. He turned up toward his father's voice, realizing that the boy and the Warden's assistant had known all along. He was staying. He even knew he was staying for a long time. He did not know where he was or how far he had come, and could not get home alone. He began to cry.

Then his father was standing, his hand on Ludlow's head, making his brittle hair sizzle. "Good luck, Luddy." The hand was gone.

The Warden and his cigar were near again. "We can handle it now." The assistant's chair strained and in a few seconds, he had grabbed Ludlow's arms. Ludlow struggled to get free, but could not.

"You better get out now." The Warden was angry.

"Yes, sir." His father's voice came at him. "Good luck, Luddy." Heavy shoes echoed away, meeting the sigh of an opening, closing door.

Ludlow started to kick his bare feet at the assistant and received a burning, ringing slap on his ear.

"Third floor," the Warden shouted.

Recovering from the slap, Ludlow began to scream for his father.

"And for Christ sake, get him quiet!"

Ludlow was lifted into the air, still kicking and yelling. He was carried across the stone floor, above the clicking of the assistant's limping step, was put down, and, without warning, was slapped across the face more times than he could count. He stopped crying and began to moan. "Is that better now, you little bastard?"

The Warden's assistant grabbed him by the wrist and pulled him up three flights of wooden stairs. When they reached the final landing, Ludlow's hand was numb. A doorknob rattled and he was pushed over a doorsill into a room filled with children. The assistant was behind him, holding his neck tightly. "Hey!" The voices stopped. "This is Ludlow Washington." His voice went to the right. "You! Four-Eyes! You're to see his bed gets aired if he pisses in it. If it ain't aired, you sleep in it."

"Yes, sir." Ludlow did not recognize the voice.

The assistant let him go and slammed the door. Ludlow stood very still, waiting for the voices to start again. A great many scraping steps circled in on him, whispering. Then they began to paw him. Their hands moved over every part of him, especially his face and head.

"His ears is like bowls."

"He surely got a big head!"

"Must be a ugly little bastard."

"Wait a minute. Let me have a touch." All hands dropped away except one. "That's him. I found him first, downstairs. I told you." It was Ludlow's master. He was almost happy to recognize even his watery voice. "Ludlow Washington?"

"Yes."

"Yes, master." His master twisted his ear. He was about to cry, but decided not to bother. He realized it would do no good, and only nodded.

"Ludlow Washington, you my slave. The rest of you boys hear that? This my slave. Right, slave?" His master's breath was on his face. "Say it."

Ludlow shuddered. "I'm your slave."

Just so he would never forget, his master twisted Ludlow's ear one last time.

FOR MY SISTER MOLLY WHO IN THE FIFTIES

Alice Walker (1944-)

Once made a fairy rooster from
Mashed potatoes
Whose eyes I forget
But green onions were his tail
And his two legs were carrot sticks
A tomato slice his crown.
Who came home on vacation
When the sun was hot
and cooked
and cleaned
And minded least of all
The children's questions
A million or more
Pouring in on her
Who had been to school
And knew (and told us too) that certain
Words were no longer good
And taught me not to say us for we
No matter what "Sonny said" up the
road.

FOR MY SISTER MOLLY WHO IN THE FIFTIES
Knew Hamlet well and read into the night
And coached me in my songs of Africa
A continent I never knew
But learned to love
Because "they" she said could carry
A tune
And spoke in accents never heard
In Eatonton.
Who read from *Prose and Poetry*
And loved to read "Sam McGee from Tennessee"
On nights the fire was burning low
And Christmas wrapped in angel hair
And I for one prayed for snow.

WHO IN THE FIFTIES
Knew all the written things that made
Us laugh and stories by
The hour   Waking up the story buds
Like fruit. Who walked among the flowers
And brought them inside the house
And smelled as good as they
And looked as bright.
Who made dresses, braided
Hair. Moved chairs about
Hung things from walls
Ordered baths
Frowned on wasp bites
And seemed to know the endings
Of all the tales
I had forgot.

WHO OFF INTO THE UNIVERSITY
Went exploring   To London and
To Rotterdam

Prague and to Liberia
Bringing back the news to us
Who knew none of it
But followed
crops and weather
funerals and
Methodist Homecoming;
easter speeches,
groaning church.

WHO FOUND ANOTHER WORLD
Another life   With gentlefolk
Far less trusting
And moved and moved and changed
Her name
And sounded precise
When she spoke   And frowned away
Our sloppishness.

WHO SAW US SILENT
Cursed with fear   A love burning
Inexpressible

And sent me money not for me
But for "College."
Who saw me grow through letters
The words misspelled   But not
The longing   Stretching
Growth
The tied and twisting
Tongue
Feet no longer bare
Skin no longer burnt against
The cotton.

WHO BECAME SOMEONE OVERHEAD
A light   A thousand watts
Bright and also blinding
And saw my brothers cloddish
And me destined to be
Wayward
My mother remote   My father
A wearisome farmer
With heartbreaking
Nails.

FOR MY SISTER MOLLY WHO IN THE FIFTIES
Found much
Unbearable
Who walked where few had
Understood   And sensed our
Groping after light
And saw some extinguished
And no doubt mourned.

FOR MY SISTER MOLLY WHO IN THE FIFTIES
Left us.

BURIAL

Alice Walker

I

They have fenced in the dirt road
that once led to Wards Chapel
A.M.E. church,
and cows graze
among the stones that
mark my family's graves.
The massive oak is gone
from out the church yard,
but the giant space is left
unfilled;
despite the two-lane blacktop
that slides across
the old, unalterable
roots.

II

Today I bring my own child here;
to this place where my father's
grandmother rests undisturbed
beneath the Georgia sun,
above her the neatstepping hooves
of cattle.
Here the graves soon grow back into the land.
Have been known to sink. To drop open without
warning. To cover themselves with wild ivy,
blackberries. Bittersweet and sage.
No one knows why. No one asks.
When Burning Off Day comes, as it does
some years,
the graves are haphazardly cleared and snakes
hacked to death and burned sizzling
in the brush. . . . The odor of smoke, oak
leaves, honeysuckle.
Forgetful of geographic resolutions as birds,
the farflung young fly South to bury
the old dead.

III

The old women move quietly up
and touch Sis Rachel's face.
"Tell Jesus I'm coming," they say.
"Tell Him I ain't goin' to *be*
long."

My grandfather turns his creaking head
away from the lavender box.
He does not cry. But looks afraid.
For years he called her "Woman";
shortened over the decades to
"'Oman."
On the cut stone for "'Oman's" grave
he did not notice
they had misspelled her name.

(The stone reads *Racher Walker*—not "Rachel"—
Loving Wife, Devoted Mother.)

IV

As a young woman, who had known her? Tripping
eagerly, "loving wife," to my grandfather's
bed. Not pretty, but serviceable. A hard
worker, with rough, moist hands. Her own two
babies dead before she came.
Came to seven children.
To aprons and sweat.
Came to quiltmaking.
Came to canning and vegetable gardens
big as fields.
Came to fields to plow.
Cotton to chop.
Potatoes to dig.
Came to multiple measles, chickenpox,
and croup.
Came to water from springs.
Came to leaning houses one story high.
Came to rivalries. Saturday night battles.
Came to straightened hair, Noxzema, and
feet washing at the Hardshell Baptist church.

Came to zinnias around the woodpile.
Came to grandchildren not of her blood
whom she taught to dip snuff without
sneezing.

Came to death blank, forgetful of it all.

When he called her "'Oman" she no longer
listened. Or heard, or knew, or felt.

V

It is not until I see my first grade teacher
review her body that I cry.
Not for the dead, but for the gray in my
first grade teacher's hair. For memories
of before I was born, when teacher and
grandmother loved each other; and later
above the ducks made of soap and the orange-
legged chicks Miss Reynolds drew over
my own small hand
on paper with wide blue lines.

VI

Not for the dead, but for memories. None of
them sad. But seen from the angle of her
death.

NO IMAGES

Waring Cuney (1906-   )

She does not know
Her beauty,
She thinks her brown body
Has no glory.

If she could dance
Under palm trees
And see her image in the river
She would know.

From *Black Poetry for All Americans*, ed. Leon Weisman and Elfreda Wright. By permission of Globe Book Company.

But there are no palm trees
On the street,
And dishwater gives back no images.

ME AND THE MULE

Langston Hughes (1902-1967)

My old mule,
He's got a grin on his face.
He's been a mule so long
He's forgot about his race.

I'm like that old mule—
Black—and don't give a damn!
You got to take me
Like I am.

DAYBREAK IN ALABAMA

Langston Hughes

When I get to be a composer
I'm gonna write me some music about
Daybreak in Alabama
And I'm gonna put the purtiest songs in it
Rising out of the ground like a swamp mist
And falling out of heaven like soft dew.
I'm gonna put some tall tall trees in it
And the scent of pine needles
And the smell of red clay after rain
And long red necks

And poppy colored faces
And big brown arms
And the field daisy eyes
Of black and white black white black people

And I'm gonna put white hands
And black hands and brown and yellow hands
And red clay earth hands in it
Touching everybody with kind fingers
And touching each other natural as dew
In that dawn of music when I
Get to be a composer
And write about daybreak
In Alabama.

° ° °

OTHER SUGGESTED WORKS

Gwendolyn Brooks, *A Street In Bronzeville.*
Sterling Brown, ed., *The Negro Caravan.*
William Faulkner, *Intruder In the Dust, The Sound and the Fury.*
John Hope Franklin, *From Slavery To Freedom.*
William Melvin Kelley, *A Different Drummer.*
Jean Toomer, *Cane.*
Alice Walker, *In Love and Trouble.*
Margaret Walker, *October Journey.*
Eudora Welty, *Powerhouse.*
Richard Wright, *Native Son.*

QUESTIONS

1a. In "Hidden Name and Complex Fate" Ralph Ellison insists that the personal experience of the writer must become secondary to his art, that the particular facts of injustice are "somewhat beside the point." Explain. Do you agree with Ellison's view of art? Why or why not? How does Ellison differentiate between his identity as a black man and his identity as a writer?

b. Does art have any relationship to experience, in Ellison's view? How are they related? How might a work of art serve the black community? The society in general?

c. What are the functions of a name, according to Ellison? Why does he say that "Our names being the gifts of others, must be made our own"? Explain. What is meant by "unity of self and name"? Does the solution offered by some religious groups (Muslims, Father Divine, etc.) achieve this unity? Why or why not?

d. The reference to T. S. Eliot possibly refers to the first poem in *Old Possum's Book of Practical Cats.* Eliot asserts that every cat must have three names, one for daily use, one for dignity, and one that the cat names himself. Compare this to the preacher's exhortation. What are the "harsh realities, ambiguities, hypocrisies of human history"? "Names are not qualities; nor are words, in this particular sense, actions." Explain.

e. What does Ellison see as the main concern of the American novel? What special circumstances lead American writers to this concern? What does the biracial nature of the society contribute, or require?

2. What image does Claude McKay offer of the position of black people? Who are the mad and hungry dogs? How would McKay describe the relationship between blacks and whites in this society? How might he modify his stand if he were writing today? What does the poem advocate?

3. In ancient times, after a farmer had planted his field and reaped the harvest, poorer people were allowed to pick up what was left over (to glean). The metaphor of the harvest appears frequently in the Bible, particularly in the New Testament where Jesus uses it to illustrate problems of justice. How does Bontemps use this metaphor in "A Black Man Talks of Reaping"? What does "feed on bitter fruit" mean? Give examples of black experience in America which fit this image.

4. Compare Cullen's poem to that of Bontemps. Is there any difference in tone? Explain. What does he mean by "the night . . . is no less lovely being dark"? What is being awaited?

5*a.* What visions of rural life does Jean Toomer create? How would the poem be different if it began "Tall reapers . . ."? What is being "awaited" here, if anything?

b. Compare his use of the metaphor of reaping to those of Arna Bontemps and Countee Cullen. Which reapers would you want to imitate? Why?

6. How would you characterize the black people in these selections? Are they exemplary images, people one might want to emulate? Why or why not? How do they differ from black people encountered in previous sections?

7*a.* What is the "other world" to which DuBois refers? How do people from this world approach him? Why do they pose their questions in an oblique way? Do you think he is exaggerating these encounters?

b. What does he mean by "the shadow"? What is the "Vast Veil"? How does he respond to the existence of this veil?

c. What does DuBois mean by the "twoness of the American black"? What problems does this present for black people? Is it possible for a person to be both Negro and American? Explain.

d. Sketch the history of black people in America from emancipation to the 20th century as DuBois describes it.

e. In what ways does DuBois use the shadow and the mask images?

8a. What does Douglass mean by differentiating between rights that are conventional and those that are personal and essential? Give examples of each.

b. Do you find similarities between Douglass's description of himself as a slave and his escape to freedom and Melville's description of Babo and his attempt to free himself? How are they alike? Different?

c. Describe Douglass's achievements after emancipation. What are his strengths as you see them?

9a. In what ways does Welty's description of Phoenix Jackson fit the stereotypical clichés of old black women? What does the young white man think about her when he finds her in the ditch? Is his opinion correct? Why does Phoenix Jackson ask the white "lady" to lace up her shoe? What does the nurse mean when she says, "But it's an obstinate case"? How does Phoenix Jackson obtain the two nickels? Why does she want them?

b. What is charity? How does the author raise that question? Whom do you admire most in the story? Why?

10a. Describe the grandson, Samuel-Benjamin, in "Go Down, Moses." Why does Faulkner use the words "impenetrable" and "imperishable and enduring" to describe him? Why did the grandson leave the plantation?

b. How well do blacks and whites know each other in the story? Give examples of relationships between black and white people that illustrate understanding or misunderstanding?

c. Why does Miss Worsham want to pay for Mollie's grandson's funeral? Why do Stevens and the editor pay for it? Why does Stevens apologize to Miss Worsham for coming? What does she mean when she says, "It's our grief"?

d. Why did Aunt Mollie want to bring her grandson home? What does her question about putting "all of hit" in the newspaper tell you? Does the explanation for the grandson's behavior, that he is a bad seed, help you understand or accept him?

e. Compare Gavin Stevens to the sheriff in "Pantaloon in Black." Which of them has a better understanding of events? of the nature of the black community? of human motivation? Explain.

f. What is the significance of the title?

11a. List some of the statements Nat Lime makes about his feelings for black people. Do you believe him? Why or why not? What does he mean by "genuine feeling on both sides"? by "if they knew what was in my heart towards them . . ."? by "there's only one human color and that's the color of blood"?

b. What does the friendship with Buster Wilson tell you about Nat Lime? Compare their economic positions. What is similar about their fathers' occupations? Why did Nat go to the black neighborhood at all? What made that neighborhood different at night? What were Buster's feelings about Nat? Why wouldn't he wait for Nat to walk home after the movies? What did Nat learn from Buster?

c. How does Nat meet Ornita? What makes their friendship happen? How does Nat describe her? What are his feelings on their first date? What does his description of that evening tell you about his self image? How does the evening end? Why does Ornita hesitate to marry Nat? Why won't she let him take her home? Do you think Nat understands this? Why does Ornita finally refuse him?

d. What does the incident with the blind man tell you about Nat? about relationships between blacks and whites? What is Nat's "fate with colored people"?

12. What are some of the characteristics of the black people you find in this section? How real do they seem to you? Would you describe them as more or less able than characters in previous sections to reveal themselves? In what ways do they embody exemplary images?

13. What is the significance of the title, "The Bean Eaters"? Why does the poet say that, "Dinner is a casual affair"? Why does she capitalize "Mostly Good"? What does the poet think about old age? How does the couple feel about each other?

14. Who is speaking in "One Time Henry Dreamed the Number"? What is "the number"? How long ago did the event occur? How does the speaker feel about this memory? In what ways have their lives changed since that time? Compare this couple to the pair in "The Bean Eaters." What feelings do they have for each other?

15. Why does the poet offer two voices in "A Moment Please"? Read each voice separately. How does that change the poem? Why does one grow cautious? Who grows cautious? What do you think the girls mean by their questions? Are these the same questions to which DuBois refers in "The Souls of Black Folk"? (How does it feel to be a problem?) Restate the message of the voice in italics. Why does it still require "A moment, please"? to do what?

16a. How do you learn that Ludlow is blind? What special characteristics does his blindness cause in him?

b. What sort of place is Ludlow taken to by his father? Why does the father put him there? How does he feel about leaving his son there? Describe the relationship between father and son.

c. Discuss, "You got a master as long as you live." What parallels do you find between Ludlow's situation and the situation of black people in general? What irony do you find in his blindness?

17. Who is speaking in "For My Sister Molly . . ." What memories are described? What particular concerns are suggested about raising black children? What is the "bright and also blinding" light? Do you recognize Molly as an older sibling? What sympathy do you have for this older sister? Explain how she "walked where few had understood."

18. What does the first stanza of "Burial" describe? Why has the poet gone to this churchyard? What does she mean by "Forgetful of geographic resolutions as birds. . . ."? Describe the funeral. Whose funeral is it? What is noteworthy about the grandmother's life? Why does the poet cry for memories that are not sad?

19. What does the phrase "black is beautiful" mean? Why does she "not know her beauty"? What images are necessary in order for one to know oneself? What is meant by dancing "Naked, under palm trees"? How might returning to Africa help her to see herself?

20. Explain what Hughes means by "You got to take me like I am."

21. Why is the poem called "Daybreak in Alabama"?

22. Describe the black people that you find in this section? Do they seem real? Why or why not? How much do you know about them? How does Langston Hughes's promise to write about "Daybreak in Alabama" describe the efforts of other writers in this section? Put in your own terms what light you think the black writers represented here are shedding on black experiences.